THE ESSENTIAL
FILMS OF
INGRID BERGMAN

THE ESSENTIAL FILMS OF INGRID BERGMAN

Constantine Santas
James M. Wilson

ROWMAN & LITTLEFIELD
Lanham • Boulder • New York • London

Published by Rowman & Littlefield
An imprint of The Rowman & Littlefield Publishing Group, Inc.
4501 Forbes Boulevard, Suite 200, Lanham, Maryland 20706
www.rowman.com

Unit A, Whitacre Mews, 26-34 Stannary Street, London SE11 4AB

British Library Cataloguing in Publication Information Available

Library of Congress Cataloging-in-Publication Data

Names: Santas, Constantine, author. | Wilson, James M., 1959– author.
Title: The essential films of Ingrid Bergman / Constantine Santas, James M. Wilson.
Description: Lanham : Rowman & Littlefield, [2018] | Includes bibliographical references and index.
Identifiers: LCCN 2018004349 (print) | LCCN 2018004698 (ebook) | ISBN 9781538101407 (electronic) | ISBN 9781442212145 (cloth : alk. paper)
Subjects: LCSH: Bergman, Ingrid, 1915–1982—Criticism and interpretation.
Classification: LCC PN2778.B43 (ebook) | LCC PN2778.B43 S36 2018 (print) | DDC 791.4302/8092—dc23
LC record available at https://lccn.loc.gov/2018004349

Printed in the United States of America

To Tamara—JMW

To my children: Christiana, Xenophon, Aristotle—CS

CONTENTS

ACKNOWLEDGMENTS

I would like to acknowledge significant contributions to this work by Professor Emeritus Gerasimos Santas of the University of California at Irvine, who practically read the entire book chapter by chapter as it was being written, offering valuable advice on both form and content. My thanks also go to Joe Dmohowski, librarian of Whittier College, who kept sending me books relevant to this work and for encouraging me throughout the process of writing the book. Also, I wish to thank Harikleia Sirmans of Valdosta Public Library for compiling the index. Thank you to Eugenia Charoni, PhD, assistant professor of Romance languages, director of the Foreign Language Program and Language Lab at Flagler College. And, finally, to Stephen Ryan for his guidance in crafting of *The Essential Films of Ingrid Bergman*. Dr. James M. Wilson wishes to express his thanks to his research intern Colleen McPhee.

A BIOGRAPHICAL NOTE

Ingrid Bergman was born in Stockholm, Sweden, on August 29, 1915, and died in 1982, at the age of sixty-seven. Her father was Justus Samuel Bergman and her mother, Frieda (née Adler) Bergman, was of German extraction, so Ingrid was of mixed Swedish and German blood. From her father, an art dealer and photographer, she inherited her artistic disposition, and from her mother, the Germanic qualities of discipline and order. Frieda Bergman died in 1918 at the age of thirty-three when Ingrid was not yet three years old. She was left to the care of her aunt, Ellen Bergman, an austere Lutheran who took her to church and instilled in her a sense of religious awe. But Ingrid, a vivacious child, learned how to mimic and pose for her father, who constantly photographed her in stills and in motion, implanting in her the desire at an early age to act.

In 1922, at the age of seven, Ingrid entered the Lyceum of Girls, a school located near her residence, where she studied a wide variety of subjects from German to arithmetic, drawing, singing, biology, physical education (Sweden set the example throughout Europe for what was then called "Swedish gymnastics"), and cooking—for which Ingrid showed no taste. In 1929, when Ingrid was thirteen, Justus Bergman died, leaving his daughter to the care of various relatives for as long as she was underage.

After a period of bereavement and depression, Ingrid recovered, and she won high grades in most of her subjects, enough to gain a scholarship in 1933 at the prestigious Royal Dramatic Theatre School, established in 1787 by King Gustav III, where she was supposed to graduate in three years. There she was known for her poetry recitations and acting roles in school productions, and that helped her gain contacts with the Swedish producers by taking small roles as extras in several films. She left the Royal Dramatic School after a year and took a part in her first Swedish film, *Munkbrogreven* (*The Count of the Monk's Bridge*) in 1934, at the age of nineteen. In the next five years, she acted in eleven Swedish films, some of which were quite notable, such as *Intermezzo* and *En Kvinnas Ansikte* (*A Woman's Face*), both remade in Hollywood.

In 1936, Ingrid married Petter Lindstrom, a dentist and medical student, and two years later, Ingrid had a daughter, Pia, so when she came to Hollywood in 1939, she was already a married woman and a mother. Her career took a sudden turn when *Intermezzo* (1936) became an international hit, and Ingrid Bergman soon received a call from producer David O. Selznick. The producer had an uncanny sense of spotting foreign prospects, most recently hiring Vivien Leigh to play southern belle Scarlett O'Hara for *Gone with the Wind*.

Bergman's freshness and lack of affectation were the qualities first noticed by Selznick. Though the actress lacked the exotic demeanor of the likes of Greta Garbo and Marlene Dietrich, Bergman's simplicity of manner and lack of mannerisms endeared her to American audiences.

At first Bergman struggled with the demands of correct enunciation in English, and despite her efforts, her distinct Swedish accent (elongated vowels, emphatic consonants [Emma is heard as "Eemma" in *A Woman's Face*]) remained to the end of her life. Despite this, American audiences accepted her vaguely European qualities and easily identified her as one of them—as, for instance, in *The Bells of St. Mary's*, where she had identified herself as of Swedish origin, and yet nobody seemed to mind it.

Indeed, Bergman surpassed all expectations, and in the next half dozen years of Selznick's contract, she became queen of beauty, grace, and talent—all thanks to her devotion, hard work, and belief in her art. Justus Bergman's daughter soon proved that she had inherited her father's creative talents and her mother's dedication to the values of discipline and hard work.

Above all, Bergman was a meticulous workaholic, totally dedicated to her art wherever it took her—screen, stage, television, or other professional matters. She came to the set fully prepared, knowing her lines and establishing a good rapport with the other actors. She insisted on taking more acting training, even after her best successes in film, and she benefited by working with top actors and directors, learning from and giving advice to

A youthful Bergman from the film *A Woman's Face* (1938). *Svensk Filmindustri / Photofest* © *Svensk Filmindustri*

those around her. Notable actors she worked with included Humphrey Bogart, Cary Grant, Charles Boyer, Gary Cooper, Spencer Tracy, Gregory Peck, Yul Brynner, Helen Hayes, Yves Montand, and George Sanders. Directors included Michael Curtiz, George Cukor, Leo McCarey, Alfred Hitchcock, Victor Fleming, Roberto Rossellini, Anatole Litvak, Anthony Asquith, and Ingmar Bergman. She disliked idleness and hated the breaks between films, when she was forced to remain home away from the set.

Film critics and historians often discussed Bergman's vulnerability in her screen roles, such as Ivy Peterson in *Dr. Jekyll and Mr. Hyde*, Paula Alquist in *Gaslight*, and Alicia Huberman in *Notorious*, to name just a few. The vulnerability of her characters was a result of either exterior menace or of a personal flaw, as in her embodiment of Joan Madou in *Arch of Triumph*, where she appears reckless in the choice of lovers.

Nearly all her major films, and some of the minor ones, show her as a woman running through the gamut of emotions, sometimes in a matter of seconds, her face, and especially her eyes averted when danger is imminent. A shake of the head is also usual, accompanied by her hand covering

Bing Crosby and Bergman celebrating their Oscar wins in 1945 for *Going My Way* and *Gaslight*, respectively. *Photofest*

part of her face. In *Dr. Jekyll and Mr. Hyde*, she retreats with horror, her hand touching her forehead when the monstrous Hyde comes near her with his diabolical grin. *Casablanca* shows her as a troubled woman struggling to repress her emotion for a man she still loves and whose love brings her to the brink of infidelity to her husband, whom she also loves. *Gaslight*, which earned her the first of three Oscars, shows a wide range of emotions throughout the movie. Her radiant face before she is married to Gregory Anton (Charles Boyer) becomes tense, if not hysterical, as he tells her that he is missing his watch during a performance in a concert. In *Notorious*, the moment she realizes she is being poisoned, her eyes show the horror of recognition. Her facial movements often reveal more than her dialogue does.

According to historian Donald Spoto, Bergman's close-ups are particularly impressive, as the camera loved her face from every angle, revealing her emphatic features: arched and strong eyebrows, sparkling eyes—blue in color—penciled lips, and sculpted chin. Roger Ebert, in his commentary of *Casablanca*, argued that the camera favored the left side of her face, as in the scene where she pleads with Sam to play "As Time Goes By." Yet, in the earlier scene as Corinna Mura strums her guitar singing her exotic song, Bergman's face is photographed against the light, her profile silhouetted, revealing a perfect face shadowed in symmetry.

Ingrid Bergman's life in Hollywood was far from smooth, as Selznick often loaned her out to other studios for a considerable profit or in exchange for other stars. After a meteoric rise in Hollywood, and nearly a decade making such movies as *Casablanca*, *Gaslight*, *Spellbound*, *The Bells of St. Mary's*, *Notorious*, and several others, her life and career took an unexpected detour.

In the late 1940s the actress went to Italy to a make a movie, *Stromboli*, with the Italian neorealist director Roberto Rossellini. After the two engaged in an affair, Bergman divorced Petter Lindstrom to marry Rossellini. The resulting scandal shattered her wholesome image, stunned her American fans, and torpedoed her Hollywood career. Bergman was even renounced by a US senator on the Senate floor.

But the actress would recover. After about eight years in Italy, making several films with Rossellini, Bergman reconnected with Hollywood, making *Anastasia* (1956), filmed in London, which netted her a second Oscar and brought on reconciliation with her American fans. Her marriage to Rossellini was annulled, and she married Lars Schmidt, a Swedish play producer and impresario who did a great deal to further her career in Europe.

Bergman had four children: Pia—with Petter Lindstrom—and Renato Roberto (Robertino), Isabella, and Isotta Ingrid (Isabella and Isotta being

Bergman on the set of *The Inn of the Sixth Happiness* with her children, Roberto (left) and twin daughters Isotta and Isabella (far right). *Photofest*

twins) with Rossellini. She was an affectionate and caring mother, but her career and separation from her first two husbands kept her away from her children for considerable stretches of time. In the 1960s, her life was apportioned between filmmaking and a significant stage career, which flourished largely in Europe and in England. Most of her films of the following decade were made in Europe and in London, and she won another Oscar in a supporting role for her performance as a middle-aged, religion-obsessed spinster in the popular hit *Murder on the Orient Express* (1974).

Ingrid's last feature, *Autumn Sonata* (1978), was with her namesake, Ingmar Bergman, the great Swedish director, a film that brought her a seventh Oscar nomination. Bergman had also success as a TV actress in the latter part of her life and received a posthumous Emmy for her role as Golda Meir, the Israeli prime minister, in the TV miniseries *A Woman Called Golda* (1982). She died of breast cancer two months after this show was completed. She was exactly sixty-seven years old, as she died on her birthday, August 29, 1982. She was surrounded by her friends, and, even as frail as she was, she had a party that day and passed away during the night.

The world mourned, as Bergman was universally known and admired for her achievements, in life and in art.

Ingrid Bergman was in the public eye for several decades, from the 1930s to the late 1970s and early 1980s, and during this time she rose to be one of Hollywood's top women superstars (AFI, the American Film Institute, ranks her fourth in its list of the thirty greatest women stars of Hollywood). During the course of her career, she won numerous awards, including a Tony Award for Best Actress (*Joan of Lorraine* in 1947), four Golden Globe Awards (for *Gaslight*, *The Bells of St. Mary's*, *Anastasia*, and *A Woman Called Golda*), and two Emmy Awards (her first for the episode "The Turn of the Screw" on the anthology series *Startime*), and three Academy Awards, two for Best Actress (*Gaslight* and *Anastasia*) and one for Best Supporting Actress (*Murder on the Orient Express*).

Ingrid Bergman is best remembered by audiences for many film roles: Ilsa Lund in *Casablanca*, Alicia Huberman in *Notorious*, Saint Joan in *Joan of Arc*, Anna Koreff in *Anastasia*. She was an actor in the fullest sense of the word, creating numerous characters on the stage, in film and television. She reprised roles from the works of Ernest Hemingway, Maxwell Anderson, Henry James, Henrik Ibsen, Somerset Maugham, and George Bernard Shaw. And at an advanced age and while mortally ill, she undertook to

Bergman and her daughter Isabella in 1973. *Photofest*

re-create the life of one of the greatest women of the twentieth century, Golda Meir. Ingrid Bergman's life goes beyond acting, as she raised money for many causes, one being the orphanage of Gladys Aylward, the missionary she had played in film. She was a humanist and a philanthropist, and a good mother to boot, devoted to her children despite disruptions due to her always heavy schedule. Above all, she was a great artist, and so she will remain in the chronicles of cinematic art.

KEY

In this volume, the authors offer an assessment of each of Ingrid Bergman's classics and other significant films, covering the spectrum of nearly five decades of filmmaking, indeed her entire career as one of the greatest female stars in the history of cinema. Every film, listed chronologically, will be examined in and of itself, offering an introductory paragraph stating why this film is an essential; that is, a film of classic stature rather than a mere vehicle for Bergman. For every entry, a plot synopsis will be given, with important film highlights, appraisals from critics, biographers, and commentators from a variety of sources, including online materials.

Entries will be prefaced by number, title, studio or production company, and a key with ratings will be given to help the reader decide to select a title, out of sequence or as he or she chooses. Five stars (★★★★★) indicate a classic, and not only a Bergman film but one that has stood the test of time and is still celebrated (*Casablanca*, *Notorious*, *Anastasia*). Four stars (★★★★) indicate a great or near-great film that has the essential qualities of Ingrid Bergman and is still attractive to audiences (*Spellbound*, *Murder on the Orient Express*, *Autumn Sonata*). Three stars (★★★) indicate a good film, especially one that has a good Bergman performance in it (*The Bells of St. Mary's*, *Arch of Triumph*, *Indiscreet*). Two stars (★★) indicate an average or below-average film, and one star (★) a dud, or poor film, not considered an essential. These classifications are not meant to inhibit the reader's judgment but to help him or her to choose a film one may never have seen or wishes to revisit. For the convenience of the reader, each chapter has sections, indicating generally to topics discussed in each one—plot, themes and motives, conclusion—although this format sometimes has variations. Specs will include director, producer, cast and crew, release date, duration, and DVD/Blu-ray availability.

❶

A WOMAN'S FACE
[SWEDISH TITLE:
EN KVINNAS ANSIKTE]

(1938)

★ ★ ★

Director: Gustaf Molander
Screenplay: Gösta Stevens, based on a play by Francis de Croisset
Producer: A. B. Svensk Filmindustri. *Cinematographer:* Åke Dahlqvist. *Music*
    Score: Eric Bengtson
Cast: Ingrid Berman (Anna Holm / Anna Paulsson), Tore Svennberg (Magnus
    Barring), Anders Henrikson (Dr. Wegert), Karin Kavli (Mrs. Vera
    Wegert), Georg Rydeberg (Torsten Barring), Erik "Bullen" Berglund
    (Nyman), Sigurd Wallén (Miller), Magnus Kesster (Handsome
    Herman), Gunnar Sjöberg (Harald Berg)
Studio: A. B. Svensk Filmindustri
Released: October 31, 1938
Specs: 101 minutes; black and white
Availability: DVD (Kino Lorber Films)

A Woman's Face (*En Kvinnas Ansikte*) is Ingrid Berman's eighth film made
in Sweden, where she had already successfully established a career as an
actress since 1934, at the age of nineteen. She made a few more movies in
Sweden, among them *Intermezzo* (1936), the Swedish version, before signing a contract with David O. Selznick, who brought her to America and kept
her in Hollywood for the better part of the next decade. *A Woman's Face* is
the fifth film of hers directed by Gustaf Molander, who had been both her
director and mentor (she made one more film with Molander, *Only One*

Night, 1939), and with whom she retained a close friendship until later in her life. The inclusion of the only Swedish movie here serves to show some of the excellent acting Bergman did under the direction of Molander, her maturity as a serious artist at that point, and, most importantly, that this is the only time in her entire career that she played a villain. Bergman had to convince Swedish filmmakers to give her the part, and they did so, despite their fears her audience wouldn't accept it. The filmmakers of *A Woman's Face* did what American filmmakers in her Hollywood and later career apparently wouldn't do—they scarred Bergman's face in her role as Anna Holm.[1] The film had different release dates at various European capitals and went ahead to win a "Special Recommendation" at the Venice Film Festival in 1938. It was remade by MGM, starring Joan Crawford, in 1941, but this was no match for the Swedish Bergman film, which became a classic.

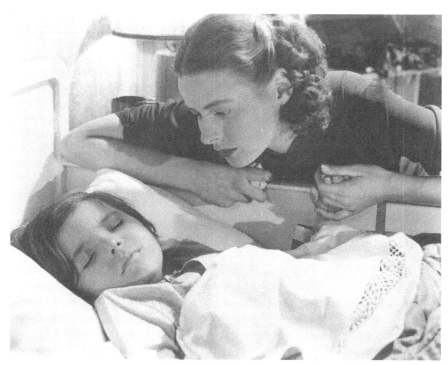

Anna Holm (Bergman) realizes the enormity of her plan to murder the child in her charge, Lars-Erik (Göran Bernhard). *Svensk Filmindustri / Photofest © Svensk Filmindustri*

PLOT

In *A Woman's Face*, Ingrid Bergman plays a unique character, Anna Holm, who runs an extortion ring that steals sensitive materials related to illicit romances and then blackmails the owners, threatening to expose them if they do not pay. Her group consists of small-time crooks who earn up to 5,000 krona per job, with Holm running the operations and finances. Of the four men, three are at the "office": Nyman (Erik "Bullen" Berglund), the Count (Gösta Cederlund), and Miller (Sigurd Wallén), who keeps accounts. A waiter, Handsome Herman (Magnus Kesster), searches the coats of people who look like lovers and steals compromising letters, which are then used for blackmail. The first victim is a woman, Mrs. Wegert (Karin Kavli), who meets her lover at a restaurant to determine how to offset a threat of blackmail, as three letters she had sent him had been taken from his pocket. She defends her adultery by calling it a "modern affair." Vera Wegert negotiates with Nyman in the crook's nest, and he promises to meet her later the same night to exchange the letters for 5,000 krona. Anna does not like the deal and raises the sum to 10,000. A visitor shows up, brought in by the Count, Torsten Bowman, who is in need of a governess to do some business for him. Shrewdly, Holm forces him to reveal his real name, Torsten Barring, the scion of a large fortune of the Barring manufacturing tycoons, but whose direct inheritance will go to a young boy, Lars-Erik, whose parents died soon after he was born. Torsten says Holm could be suitable as the governess if not for her face. Holm forces a deal with Torsten for 75,000 krona, plus 25 percent of the fortune. He agrees reluctantly, and Holm promises to find a woman "with no scruples."

A bit later we see Anna Holm, a hat covering the left side of her face, visiting Vera Wegert in her house to pick up the cash. Anna is harsh and presses for 10,000 krona. Vera gives her some jewelry as partial payment, but the sudden return of her husband interrupts the meeting. Trying to escape, Anna overturns a table and is caught, her foot broken. Dr. Allan Wegert finds his wife's jewelry in her purse, but kindheartedly takes care of her broken foot. While in the room, Holm finds photos of Wegert's work and realizes he is a brilliant reconstructive surgeon. Dr. Wegert had been a plastic surgeon at the Somme during the war and reconstructed the faces of many soldiers and restored their looks. He believes Anna's face could be restored and invites her to stay at the hospital. Next we see Anna in a wheelchair, her bandages about to be removed from her face. It is a tense moment, as Vera is also in the room. She wonders what Anna will do, but Anna hands her the letters, still in her bag, before she is carted inside. We see her entire face later when she is on the train on her way to Forsa where she will serve as a governess to six-year-old Lars-Erik Barring. At the train station, her beauty fully restored, she poses as Anna Paulsson to Torsten Barring, who has secured her a new job as Lars-Erik's governess. Torsten recognizes her from her habit of covering the left side of her face with her hand. Her assignment is to become a part of the family so she can murder the young child so Torsten can inherit the estate.

As soon as she meets the engaging child Lars-Erik and his genial grand-father, the consul Magnus Barring (Tore Svennberg), Anna realizes the enormity of the crime she has agreed to commit. The surprised consul asks why she is so serious, especially since she has already made such a good im-pression—she is young, attractive, and has the look of a person committed to duty. Lars-Erik is also puzzled at her odd behavior when she tells him bitterly that she never had any toys when she was young. The boy says, "You weren't a good girl, then." She promises to care for him by spoiling him, and he kisses her three times. She bursts into tears when she retreats to her bedroom, realizing she has been locked into a terrible moral dilemma.

The tension rises when Torsten suggests how she could go about her "job," gaining the child's, and everyone else's, trust, then an "accident" could happen during the daily sled rides into the country. She is reminded of the idea when the smitten Harald Berg (Gunnar Sjöberg) takes her to a local sightseeing spot overlooking a dramatic and dangerous waterfall, noiseless in the winter as much of the water is locked in ice. It is a perilous location, as Torsten says, dangerous if a careless child were to lean over a wooden fence. Anna is momentarily cheered as Harald makes his feelings for her clear. A crushing irony, since she is now both ashamed and guilty knowing she has no right to expect any good luck. There is just a glimmer of smile on her face at the knowledge that she is admired by a man of merit. The beauty of both sides of her face, and apparently now her interior life, seems to show that she has followed the doctor's admonition to improve herself.

During the night of celebrations on the consul's birthday, the family holds a traditional sleigh ride before dinner, and Anna is terrified when she learns that Torsten will be driving Lars-Erik's sleigh, while she will be seated next to Harald, an arrangement the consul thinks is advantageous as he has urged Harald to propose to her. In the ensuing chase, as Torsten's sleigh begins to speed, Anna reveals the awful truth of her situation and the strength of her new conscience by yelling over the noise of the running horses to Harald that they need to save the child. Torsten will kill him, do-ing the job she was hired to do.

This sequence is equal to any cinematic thriller, a chase in pitch-dark night with only torches lighting the action. Torsten's horse is out of control, while Harald whips his, the terrified Anna by his side. Bringing his sleigh even to Torsten's, Harald grabs Lars-Erik and hands him to Anna, he falls, and Torsten's sleigh vanishes into the night.

We learn what happened indirectly. Nyman and the Count sit in their apartment, when their housekeeper rushes in, bringing them news along with their dinner. She breathlessly tells them that there was an accident—Torsten was killed and Harald severely injured. Startled, realizing their danger, they ask her for the first train out of town. It leaves in half an hour, she says, astonished they haven't finished their dinner. That's the last we hear from them.

The story has actually two endings. One, breaking with her past, is Anna's decision to leave Harald. She meets him at the hospital after she had written him a letter revealing everything. He had read it ten times, he says, and still can't believe it. She convinces him to stay at Forsa with the family he works for and loves. She says a simple good-bye and closes the door behind her. A shot shows Harald's distressed face, his head leaning against a pillow, as if a vision of happiness had vanished.

The other ending is Anna's decision to leave her country altogether and begin a new life. She tells Dr. Wegert that he is the only man who knows her entire story and she has nowhere to go. Incidentally, he tells her, he has had a letter from a cousin in China who is married to an American. They have lost their governess and wonder if he knows a Swedish governess that would like to go to Peking. Anna weighs the idea briefly and says yes, she would like to take the job. Next they are shown together on a ship. Dr. Wegert tells her that everything in the past must be forgotten at this moment, and the future begins now. Dr. Wegert sees past Holm's emotional and physical scars to what she is capable of. Conveniently, he is single now that his wife has left him. Modern life offers new paths for living, but happiness must be earned.

THEMES

One of the themes of the story is that Holm is greedy, but the film is not about money itself but the desire for retaliation and an unformed desire for happiness. She doesn't have a plan as to how money would make her happy. So, it is appropriate that Anna's main source of income takes advantage of "youth and beauty." She says, "I want to be rich. I want it now. I can't enjoy life like others can." She even believes that other women should pay her for their beauty: "Wasn't she beautiful? She should pay for it." Other people's love and modern affairs mean cash to Holm.

Another theme of the film is the post–World War I "modern" life with all the new opportunities and dangers that new life brings. Wegert's residence is simple but elegant—modern as shown in the settings in the movie—clean, simple, elegant, just as Anna's office is simple and clean with just a map of the area behind the desk. When her gang plans to meet Torsten for the first time, one says, "It will be a modern affair. Small but nice. Simple but elegant." The emphasis on mirrors throughout the film is a reflection of how shallow modern life can be. It isn't until Anna visits Harald in the hospital that she walks past a mirror without even realizing it is there.

At first, Bergman's Holm is an ugly, ruthless, greedy but intelligent character, and the left side of her face is symbolic of this. The other side, the young Holm's face, suggests her yearning for happiness, goodness, and a better life. Although she says she wants money to be happy, in her heart she knows that a new face can make her happy. Holm sees an opportunity to change her face in the middle of negotiating a blackmailing scheme with a married woman who wants to keep compromising letters away from her husband. She cunningly makes surgery part of the deal without revealing the blackmail to him. This is a crucial moment signaling the beginning of Anna's rehabilitation, a conscience-awakening moment.

Anna seems to have no scruples about killing the man who is in the way of Torsten's inheritance. However, when she finds out that "Lars-Erik—dictator of Forsa—future king of Forsa and heir to the Barring fortune" is only six years old, she quavers because she lost her parents at an early age like Lars. Later she realizes that "he has everything" and she had nothing as a child, which helps her rationalize her motivation. Consul Barring, Lars-Erik's grandfather, tells her, "I think children should be children while they can. The seriousness of life comes soon enough." Anna knows the seriousness of life from personal experience. "I'll do my best, Consul Barring." She smiles to herself knowing her solution to this statement is quite different from his. When faced with the child in his bedroom, her shoulders slope forward, hands clasped, head down like a vulture, but her resistance to him cracks when she leans down to kiss his forehead and he pulls her down face-to-face. When he kisses her on the face, she is amazed, startled. She leaves his room. Shadows like a cage surround her. What is she to do now? And more importantly, she asks herself: *Who am I now?*

WHY IS IT CALLED A WOMAN'S FACE?

The "scar" was created by Bergman and her husband, dentist Petter Aron Lindstrom, by using a brace that pushed her left cheek down and opened up her eye socket. Bergman thought she looked like Frankenstein.[2] Realistic scarring is important because Holm is bad because of her ugly face; she is embarrassed by it and wants to get back at the world because of it. The left part of her face is a ghastly scar, and it looks as if the scar tissue has hardened and contracted, pulling the skin away from the bottom of her left eye so that it baldly stands out from the face and is a horror to look at. She wears a tilted hat to cover it or stays in the shadows, and when she faces her colleagues, she tries to hide the scar by covering it with her hand. She runs the operation brutally, crushing their objections with cruelty and derision. A bitter woman, she is scarred for life, and her criminal activities are revenge on society for her life of pain and embarrassment caused by her scars. Although the title suggests that it refers to only one woman's face, the suggestion remains that the film is about all women and how society treats women. Anna Holm is a villain, therefore, she deserves an ugly face, the audience assumes. After all, it is a reflection of who she is inside. It is quickly revealed that her cruelty is a consequence of the treatment society gives her, and every mirror she sees reminds her of why she has been cruelly rejected by the world around her. She retaliates by breaking every mirror she finds.

As in the film *M* (Fritz Lang, 1931), the villain is introduced by shadow first; then the back is shown, then the face. Anna's part in her schemes must be from behind the scenes; she is brought in after the fish has been hooked. Torsten suggests that her lack of morals is perfect for removing the obstacle to his inheritance, but that "you'd been suitable yourself if not for . . . ," suggesting her face. She replies, disingenuously, "I'm not as dangerous as I look." Once her surgery is completed, she does not tell anyone about it. Torsten realizes who she is when she moves to cover her face with her hand. Her gang doesn't know she went to the Barring house as the governess. She apparently did not want them to see her new face, suggesting that she would lose power if she had. Would she lose face?

Perhaps she takes the doctor's advice seriously once she leaves his office, that she changes her behavior to match her new, beautiful outside. However, it is not long before her beauty becomes a problem. When Torsten first meets "Miss Paulsson," he asks, "Can a governess look like you?" It seems she will never be qualified for the position because of either her beauty or her ugliness. Even the elderly consul desires her. When he tells her that he likes her, the housekeeper sets a tall vase of flowers between them to keep them separated. Once Anna leaves the room, the consul tells Emma, the servant, that he thinks Miss Paulsson is pretty. Emma launches into a discussion of her long service to him and his family. That night, the consul reminds Lars-Erik to "count the windowpanes and wish for something nice before you fall asleep," but the next morning when Lars asks his grandfather, who is seated next to Miss Paulsson, about his dreams, he says despondently that they will not come true.

CONCLUSION

The film is not without flaws. In the second half of the movie, the filmmakers fell for shallow beauty, as the camera's sharpness in the first half of the film is unforgiving when focused on her scars. After surgery, when Holm becomes beautiful, the cinematographer chose to use a soft focus on close-ups, as it was common practice for film beauties. However, the soft focus hides Anna's new character rather than her facial "flaws"; therefore, Bergman's acting is also affected by the change in focus, as her beauty is restored beyond belief. The film also used expert photographic tricks to become, generally speaking, a compelling viewing experience. The sequence of taking off the bandages is a scene possible only in cinema. Through deft camera work, the healed part of the face is not shown to the viewer. The tension is the same for the audience as for Anna Holm. Did the surgery work? It's not revealed in the doctor's face. "Rather good," Dr. Wegert finally says. She looks at a mirror and sees it, but the mirror hides the left side of her face. This incident will become the focus of the story and Anna's main conflict. Before she leaves the hospital, Dr. Wegert tells Anna that while he could fix her face, it is up to her to rehabilitate her inner self. Cinema art here, even with some flaws, shows *A Woman's Face* as a well-told story of a woman's transformation from a greedy, vicious person when not only her face but her inner world changes.

2

INTERMEZZO: A LOVE STORY

(1939)

★ ★ ★

Director: Gregory Ratoff
Screenplay: George O'Neil, based on a story by Gösta Stevens and Gustaf
    Molander
Producer: David O. Selznick. *Cinematographer:* Gregg Toland and Harry
    Stradling Sr. (uncredited). *Music Score:* Robert Russell Bennett and Max
    Steiner (uncredited)
Cast: Leslie Howard (Holger Brandt), Ingrid Bergman (Anita Hoffman), Edna
    Best (Margit Brandt), John Halliday (Thomas Stenborg), Cecil Kellaway
    (Charles Moler), Ann E. Todd (Ann Marie), Marie Flynn (Marianne)
Studio: David O. Selznick Productions; MGM
Released: September 22, 1939
Specs: 68 minutes; black and white
Availability: Blu-ray (Kino Classics)

As early as 1934, Bergman, then a promising young stage actress, expressed
a strong desire to broaden her horizons and try making movies, telling Olof
Molander, director of the Royal Dramatic Theatre, that she would like to
take a "short cut" and "do a couple of movie parts and get a little reputation, and then come back to the school to continue [her] education."[1] Olof
was the brother of director Gustaf Molander, who directed Bergman on
two films (*The Family Swedenhielms*, 1935, and *On the Sunny Side*, 1936),

before he had the opportunity to work with her again in the original *Intermezzo* (1936), which he wrote and directed. Molander directed three more films with her in Sweden (*Dollar*, *A Woman's Face*, and *Only One Night*), and when she came to America, he was listed as a coauthor of the American *Intermezzo* in 1939. Her Swedish career was not over as she returned to Sweden to make one more film, *Night in June* (1940), before she came to Hollywood to stay for good.

Intermezzo: A Love Story proved a turning point in Bergman's career to a mutual advantage for both Ingrid Bergman and David O. Selznick. As an established young actress from Sweden, she entered the constellation of Hollywood stars, some of whom, like her, had come from Scandinavia or Germany during the preceding decade: Greta Garbo, Hedy Lamarr, and Marlene Dietrich, among several others. Another European import who was to overshadow all the others for a while was Vivien Leigh, who took America by storm as the famous Scarlett O'Hara in *Gone with the Wind*, being made during the same year and released in December of 1939. Leigh had been brought to Hollywood by Selznick, a Hollywood mogul, who had his own production studios and a keen eye for European actors and directors (Alfred Hitchcock had signed up with him about that time), as many cinema personalities came to Hollywood fleeing the menace of Hitler and the Nazis.

The *Los Angeles Daily News* reported that, based on the fact that Bergman had already amassed credits for ten movies in five years in Sweden, producers in Hollywood ought to form a pool to bring her out to this country, "if only to keep her out of Swedish pictures which are getting altogether too good."[2] When one of Selznick's production managers saw the original *Intermezzo,* he opined that this was just "sort of a romantic soap opera type," but that he and others were impressed with Ingrid Bergman and told Selznick "that we all thought she was great, sensational, let's get her by all means."[3] Selznick agreed, and in 1938, after the completion of *A Woman's Face*, he hired Bergman for $2,500 weekly, twice what he paid Vivien Leigh for *Gone with the Wind*. While she made many accommodations to adjust from Swedish to American studios, one she had not anticipated was that she had taken English lessons while in Sweden to prepare herself for a broader future. Once in the United States she realized that she had learned a British accent in the process.[4] When Ingrid arrived in Hollywood in the spring of 1939, Selznick took her under his wing, introducing her to Hollywood high society to help her learn the culture. Bergman proved a quick study and improved her English under the tutelage of Ruth Roberts, a dialogue coach in the Selznick establishment, making a lifelong friend and advisor in

Two guilty lovers, Anita Hoffman (Bergman) and Holger Brandt (Howard), ponder their future.
United Artists / Photofest © United Artists

the process. But when Selznick asked her to change her name and appearance—fix her teeth, trim her eyebrows, and change her hairstyle—Bergman put up a staunch resistance, saying to him boldly that if he didn't like her as she was—simple, honest, and natural—she would take the first train back to New York and thence to Sweden. Selznick gave in, with nods of admiration for Bergman's honesty.[5] Bergman's famous "natural look" was established in Sweden but remained a strong asset in her Hollywood career.

PLOT

The film opens with Holger Brandt (Leslie Howard), violin virtuoso, playing to a large, adoring New York City audience, including many women in the front row. Solo over, fans rush to the stage yelling, "Encore." His accompanist and good friend and former teacher, Thomas Stenborg (John Halliday), will not be touring in the future, which causes their manager and impresario Charles Moler, played by the always refreshing Cecil Kellaway, to cry backstage. Back home in Stockholm, his daughter Ann Marie (Ann

E. Todd, not to be confused with the English actress Ann Todd) plays a recording of "Intermezzo," a piece he wrote, that she and her mother played
every evening when he was on tour. Holger is seen working with his young
daughter on her piano lesson as son Eric slips out to play football. Holger
plays dissonant chords in his violin, revealing his unhappiness being home
and not surrounded by adoring fans. Ann Marie stops her ears, as she believes this to be a mistake. Obviously bored, Brandt expresses a new desire
to retire and travel with his wife, as "it was in the beginning." But Margit
(Edna Best) considers the idea a flight of fancy, a midlife crisis, and urges
her husband to abandon it. She says spring only comes once in one's life.
He's not pleased with her answer.

Ann Marie invites her piano instructor Anita Hoffman (Bergman) to her
birthday party. After cake, while Ann Marie plays the piano, the assembled
group of Brandt's friends urge Anita Hoffman to play. She modestly accepts
and starts playing Edvard Grieg's Concerto for Piano in A Minor; Holger is
startled, springs to his feet, and accompanies Anita with his violin.

Although most of the shots in this scene are from the side of the piano,
the camera settles on Bergman's fingering of the piano from behind the
piano, suggesting her mastery of the instrument and being Holger's equal.
As Bergman was a good pianist, her fingers capture the correct notes for the
camera, while the film's soundtrack is recorded by a professional musician.

Later Brandt invites Hoffman to tour with him. At a restaurant they sit
on one side of the table together. "Young people are making the world to
suit themselves," he says. She reveals that she is one of his fans, saving her
money to hear him play. In a faux pas that subtly reminds him of their age
difference, she says, "Here I am talking to you as to an old friend. Well, a
friend anyway." Outside along the river, he kisses her and they watch the
ice breaking up. It is spring again for Holger, symbolic of melting repres-
sions of a middle-aged man.

The next day she is worried and confused. She tells Stenborg she is thinking of going away. He knows she is running away from Brandt and says,
"Perhaps it's best for both of you. Courage, my friend." Before she leaves,
she tells Margit Brandt that she's leaving. Margit suspects the truth. Margit is dressed somberly in black, her hair pulled back. Hoffman's youthful
hair is curlier, longer, while her clothes are light colored. Hoffman's face
is half-hidden in shadow. "I'm sure you're doing what's right," Mrs. Brandt
says. Before Anita leaves the city she meets Brandt at a restaurant. She is
uncomfortable inside, so they walk along the street to the window of a business. Through the reflection of a window, she tells him she is leaving and
not to turn around until she is gone. Brandt returns home to talk to Margit.

It's obvious to her that he plans to become Hoffman's lover, and he tells her so in the privacy of their bedroom.

Determined to keep her near him, Brandt stops Hoffman at her train and says he doesn't have a home any longer. Her surprise is quickly quelled, and they tour together. They play a concert in Cannes, which Ann Marie listens to on the radio. She knows the concert isn't over until her father plays "Intermezzo" for his fourth encore. Margit turns off her daughter's radio, but turns on the radio in another room, leans on a cabinet, and cries.

When they stop in Italy for an idyllic interlude, Anita gradually realizes that he misses his family, especially his young daughter Ann Marie, when he makes friends with a young girl, Marianne (Marie Flynn), Ann Marie's age. Conscience stricken, Anita decides to leave Holger. Thomas Stenborg arrives, bringing a request from Ann Marie for a camera and divorce papers from Margit. Brandt's unwilling to sign, saying, "Do you think it's as easy as that, Thomas—to cut out the best part of one's life, tear up the last roots?" Pointing out the obvious, Stenborg says, "I thought you had done that long ago." At Stenborg's last concern, Holger calls him his friend and teacher. It seems the roles have not changed.

Alone, Stenborg and Anita discuss the relationship. "I'm divinely happy," Anita says, smiling. It cracks, then disappears. Stenborg delivers the film's moral: "I wonder if anyone has built happiness on the unhappiness of others." She retreats into the shadows, wanting to be less real. She makes a decision: "I'm—I would say I have been an intermezzo in his life. You gave me a good word once, 'Courage.'" On the train, her face is in the corner, dark, clouded by fog. She leaves him a letter, as in *Casablanca* when Ilsa Lund leaves Paris and leaves a letter for Rick to read. Alone, Brandt signs the divorce papers.

A year goes by; it is spring again when Brandt purchases a camera for his daughter and returns to Stockholm. He drives out to Ann Marie's school alone. When he arrives, she sees him, calls out to him, runs across the road, and is hit by a passing car. He picks her up and takes her home, calling for a doctor as she hangs limply from his arms. "Intermezzo" is playing on the record player when Ann Marie wakes for a moment and hears the music. "He's come. He's here." As he waits for news from the doctor, Eric (Douglas Scott) arrives and chastises him: "Why did you come back at all? We don't need you anymore." Holger is in complete shadow when he objects weakly: "We're none of us gods. We're all human. Tragically human. Even if you don't need me anymore. It's I who need you." The doctor reports, "Your little girl will recover." Holger picks up his hat and coat and attempts to leave, in spite of what he said to Eric. Margit stops him from leaving and says, "Welcome home." His wife loves him as a mature person would, without adoration. Brandt's shame, causing so much pain for his own self-ishness, leads him to settle down and his wife to accept him back.

THEMES

Intermezzo: A Love Story is a conventional romance where a straying, middle-aged husband falls in love with a younger woman in a fit of passion. Friend and teacher to both, Stenborg is ambivalent about this extra-marital affair, possibly because he sees how it benefits each person, and refuses to stop it although it hurts Brandt's family and Hoffman's future. He eventually asks the central question of the film, although he knows the answer: "I wonder if anyone has built happiness on the unhappiness of others." The "intermezzo," a movement coming between the major sections of an extended musical work, works as metaphor for love, which the movie suggests may only come intensely once in a person's life, but a second time seems to cheat fate. Causing hurt, as Hoffman says, "How can that cause happiness?"

The film parallels some of Bergman's own conflict with her personal and her professional life. Bergman left her theater education early to go into films. Hoffman leaves her studies with Stenborg to tour with Brandt. As with Bergman's pursuit of an artistic dream by moving to work in Hollywood, her character is a woman desiring to expand her artistic powers and willing to work hard to achieve it. Hoffman teaches young children while she studies her art. She is also youthful and is easily caught up in the excitement of the moment, which often causes her to do the opposite of her plans. The theme of the pianist as artist and the pain that being an artist can cause is also significant in Bergman's film *Autumn Sonata*, directed by Ingmar Bergman.

Selznick knew very well that *Intermezzo* was a lightweight movie, but he went ahead with the project for the sake of Ingrid Bergman, whom he wanted to showcase to American audiences and sign to a long-term contract, knowing she had the potential to become a top star in Hollywood. He was at that time busy with *Gone with the Wind*, which had started at the beginning of 1939 and was not ready for release until the end of the year, and preparations for *Rebecca*—two big projects. *Intermezzo* was squeezed in in the summer of 1939, and was released on September 22, whereas *Gone with the Wind* was not released until the fifteenth of December, so American audiences saw Bergman on the screen before Vivien Leigh.

Doing double duty, running from one production set to another, Selznick felt relieved to assign some of the production duties to Leslie Howard, who of course was also playing the violinist and lover of Bergman, Holger Brandt. Until this point, Howard had produced some short subject films, but in *Intermezzo,* Selznick gave him a coproducer credit. Making use of his new status, and after seeing Bergman's various screen tests, Howard was convinced that "from every point of view, hair and appearance, the one marked 'no makeup' is the best. . . . Without makeup she looks much more natural and much more attractive and much less Hollywood."[6] Of course, it was Selznick who took control over the way Bergman was photographed in this film, calling it "effect lighting." That meant that Bergman was photographed "with a high-angle shot of the left side of her face, usually with a great deal of high contrast that puts part of her face in shadow and gives her eyes her signature dewy look."[7] Photographing Bergman, especially by Gregg Toland, who two years later photographed *Citizen Kane,* became a prime concern of Selznick's and accounts for the "fresh" and "natural" look that she became famous for. Although she had appeared in nearly a dozen films in Europe, Howard and Selznick got credit for "introducing" Ingrid Bergman to the movies.

CONCLUSION

As Anita Hoffman in the 1936 Swedish *Intermezzo,* directed by Gustaf Molander, Bergman had played an identical character with Gösta Ekman, a middle-aged Swedish actor, who embodied Holger Brandt, the violinist, and whose libido is aroused by a young girl half his age. In that movie Bergman looks younger, more innocent and susceptible to the advances of a man in midlife crisis, who appears to be more of a seducer than lover. The Swedish *Intermezzo,* at ninety-three minutes—about twenty-five minutes longer than the American—contained scenes of natural beauty, spring melting snow, images that suggest awakening of desires and loosening of morals for the sake of sensual love. In the American *Intermezzo,* Leslie Howard looks more dashing and younger than Ekman (Howard died two years after the movie was finished at the age of forty-seven, his plane from Portugal to England having being shot down by Germans over the Bay of Biscay), and plays his character with more subtlety. His Holger Brandt is in control of his art but not his emotions. He is a man who adores adoration, is facing midlife, and is driven by desire, but he is often feckless, letting others make decisions for him.

Like *A Woman's Face*, the film explores the dropping of Victorian values and the desire to reveal the truth about marriage that love and affection ebb and flow over the course of a real marriage. Bergman's character, however, is unchanged from her previous appearance, as she manages to balance the age difference within the limits of an acceptable love affair between an older man and a younger girl. Their love affair is the result of mutual passion and spontaneity, as both fall in love against their will, ignoring any sense of propriety. But there is still a seducer in Howard's Holger, as he stops her from leaving on the train to run away from dangerous passion, and she, weakening, stays with him. This reveals Holger's rapacious nature, his insensitivity toward his wife and children, and his blindness toward a young talented lover, pressuring her to abandon her promising future to follow him. Holger is somewhat redeemed by his feelings toward Marianne, the young girl he befriends. He too realizes the intermezzo is over but does not have the willpower to break it off. It remains for Anita to take the decisive step and go away. As she has done throughout the film, Bergman conveys a range of emotions, her grief, guilt, and passion, with flawless simplicity with a depth of an accomplished artist. In a way, it was Bergman's dossier of Swedish movies that she had compiled during her five-year career (1934–1939) there, not just her first Swedish *Intermezzo* or a whim of Selznick's, that brought Ingrid Bergman to Hollywood.

❸

DR. JEKYLL AND MR. HYDE

(1941)

★ ★ ★

Director: Victor Fleming
Screenplay: John Lee Mahin, based on the novella *The Strange Case of Dr. Jekyll and Mr. Hyde* by Robert Louis Stevenson
Producer: Victor Saville. *Cinematographer:* Joseph Ruttenberg. *Music Score:* Franz Waxman
Cast: Spencer Tracy (Dr. Henry Jekyll / Mr. Hyde), Ingrid Bergman (Ivy Peterson), Lana Turner (Beatrix Emery), Donald Crisp (Sir Charles Emery), Ian Hunter (Dr. Lanyon), C. Aubrey Smith (Bishop Manners), Barton MacLane (Sam Higgins), Sara Allgood (Mrs. Higgins)
Studio: MGM
Released: August 12, 1941
Specs: 113 minutes; black and white
Availability: DVD (Warner Bros.)

Dr. Jekyll and Mr. Hyde was the fourth movie of Bergman's in Hollywood after *Intermezzo: A Love Story* (1939), which followed at the footsteps of the Swedish original in 1936. The two US films that followed *Intermezzo*—*Adam Had Four Sons* (1941) and *Rage in Heaven* (1941), rather undistinguished movies—did not carry her career too far. *Jekyll and Hyde* was based on Robert Louis Stevenson's novella, *The Strange Case of Dr. Jekyll and Mr. Hyde*, which had been a best seller in the United States after its publication in

1886. It was first made into a movie in 1931, directed by Rouben Mamoulian, starring Fredric March, who won an Oscar for his efforts. The 1941 version, starring Spencer Tracy as Jekyll/Hyde, proved a bonanza for Ingrid Bergman, who actually campaigned to play the role of Ivy Peterson, the hardworking barmaid who became a victim of Hyde. David O. Selznick stalled, fearing the image of his Swedish import might be sullied by her role as a low-class flirt, but he eventually gave in to pressure by Victor Fleming and Bergman herself. Tracy, who played the benevolent Dr. Jekyll and the vicious Hyde, was so struck by Bergman's commitment to this role that he predicted the movie would be remembered more for Bergman's Ivy than for his fearsome monster.

The Stevenson novella contains only male main characters: first, a Mr. Utterson, who provides the main thread for the narrative. Utterson is a respectable lawyer in whose care Dr. Henry Jekyll's will has been entrusted. He finds it strange that Jekyll's inheritor is a Mr. Edward Hyde, whose reputation of savagery is disturbing to Londoners. Utterson visits Jekyll, but he is unable to extract any information from the secretive doctor, whose frequent disappearances remain a mystery. After the murder of a distinguished Londoner, Sir Danvers Carew, Utterson seeks Hyde and he encounters a small, repulsive person who refuses to tell him anything. Aided by Jekyll's butler, Poole, Utterson breaks into Jekyll's laboratory, and there he finds Hyde dead. He and Poole discover two letters, one from Dr. Lanyon and the other from Jekyll himself. Dr. Lanyon, a middle-aged doctor and friend of Jekyll (both are middle-aged in the novella) writes about his last communication from Jekyll, who implores him to find and bring to him a set of phials (vials) that contain certain drugs. Lanyon complies, but it is too late to save Hyde. His letter reveals his gradual discovery of the radical steps his friend had taken to become Hyde. The other letter, from Jekyll, occupying the last chapter of the book, reveals the mystery of his scientific research to find the other side of the dual nature of man, the result of which is his change into a monster. As Hyde, he had tried desperately to change back into his former self, but failed. He had always counted on the assumption that his metamorphosis would not have been irreversible.

PLOT

The 1931 film version adds two female characters, Ivy Pearson (Miriam Hopkins), the barmaid Hyde lusts after, and Muriel Carew (Rose Hobart), the woman Dr. Jekyll intends to marry. The latter is the daughter of Sir

Ivy Peterson (Bergman) temptingly asks Dr. Jekyll (Tracy) to examine her side. *MGM / Photofest* © *MGM*

Danvers Carew (Halliwell Hobbes), a carryover character from the novella, in which he is murdered by Hyde. In the film, Sir Danvers, a brigadier general, disapproves of Jekyll's ideas and takes his daughter to Bath for a vacation, leaving Jekyll alone and dispirited. Jekyll seeks to relieve his anxiety by taking a potion he has concocted to recover his mood. Soon after, he changes into a short, repulsive being with long canine teeth and hairy hands and skin, a creature much resembling a monkey. Jubilantly, he cries that he is "free," free to behave as he says he felt, paralleling Stevenson's Hyde who says he feels "younger, lighter, happier in body," free "from the bonds of obligation," free "to be more wicked, ten times more wicked."[1] By achieving that, Jekyll, among other motives, seeks to shatter the façade of social respectability during the Victorian era. Director Mamoulian uses visual imagery to express psychological moods: a boiling pot that blows off its top to suggest repression; a fireplace with only flames to express the ghostly image of Hyde; a shot of impatient feet hitting the ground as Jekyll prepares to drink the potion. Erotic imagery is also suggestive of Hyde's hyperactive libido: a set of nude statues in sensual poses in Hyde's amorous nest and a nearly nude Hopkins in bed after her encounter with Jekyll, trying to seduce him. As the Hays Code had not taken full effect in 1931, the filmmakers exploited this license to expose Hyde's lewdness. While Stevenson's Jekyll/Hyde admits he had committed indiscretions, he never mentions specifically that he lusts after women, or a specific woman. A film, however, with a romantic lead like Fredric March, would not have been effective without female counterparts. From that point of view, the film story of *Dr. Jekyll and Mr. Hyde* is the story of the tormentor of two innocent females. Stevenson's Hyde, on the other hand, revels and gloats over evil acts as a form of liberation.

The MGM remake, starring Bergman, follows the story line of the previous film, retaining the two female characters: Ivy Peterson (Pearson in the first film) and Beatrix Emery, each representing the two sides of womanhood that Jekyll yearns for. Lana Turner and Ingrid Bergman are well poised as sexual idols to show Jekyll's dual nature; Turner as the alluring and mannered social butterfly, while Bergman appeals to his raw sexual craving. Bergman's performance is so electric that her image dominates the screen the first moment she is seen. During her first encounter with Tracy's Dr. Jekyll, she mumbles and complains until she raises her eyes and looks at the doctor looking down on her, half-smiling, gentlemanly, genial, and ready to offer help. What plays to her advantage is the use of close-ups. In the earlier film, as the filmmakers often left Hopkins's entire body in the frame rather than closing up on her face, her image remains somewhat remote, rendering her a secondary character. Bergman conquers the screen from the start. The moment she looks up at Tracy's Jekyll, her face, fully under the lights, brightens and fills with potent sexuality, more intense and enticing than Hopkins's full-body scene in which Hopkins is nearly nude. Hobart's Muriel Carew in the earlier film is easily outmatched by Turner's aristocratic bearing and dewy charm. March's rendition of Jekyll/Hyde is powerful but subject to the jerky mannerisms and spasmodic facial expressions of the silent era. March's Jekyll is almost demented from the start. Tracy's image of Jekyll is overeager but capable of normal behavior and genuine empathy. Tracy's Hyde is also a more complex individual, one who dreams of classical beauties, such as Athena and the muses, asking an uncomprehending and frightened Ivy Peterson to read Milton's *Paradise Lost*.

Dr. Henry Jekyll, an ambitious doctor high up in the social ladder in late nineteenth-century London, announces at a dinner that man has two natures, good and evil, and that it is possible to differentiate one from the other through medical research, something that shocks his dinner companions. Among them is his fiancée, Beatrix Emery (Turner, then only twenty-one and a sparkling young beauty), and her old-fashioned and anx-

ious father, Sir Charles Emery (Donald Crisp), who finds such talk alarm-
ing and dangerous. Bishop Manners (C. Aubrey Smith) reprimands Jekyll,
arguing that only God could change the nature of man—for the better. On
the way home, Jekyll and Dr. John Lanyon (Ian Hunter), his friend, save
a young woman from an attacker. Ivy Peterson (Bergman), pretending she
has twisted her ankle, allows herself to be carried to her apartment by a
sympathetic Dr. Jekyll. The attraction on both sides is immediate and passionate. While Jekyll seems reserved and jokes about her supposed injury,
he is entranced by the luscious and vulgar beauty who throws herself at him
with such unreserved craving. When she kisses him, Dr. Lanyon interrupts
and they have to leave, but she still pleads, with tears in her eyes, telling
him she is not "a bad girl." As a gift to the gentlemanly doctor, she gives him
her garter to remember her. Dr. Jekyll feels an irrepressible desire for her,
but he controls himself and soon forgets the incident.

Back in his laboratory, Jekyll mixes his brew, drops in a vial, then a liquid
that foams to the top, and drinks it with both fear and relish. As he checks
his vitals, his pulse is at seventy-two, but before he has time to do anything
else he falls down in a convulsion. His eyebrows thicken, his eyes glare, and
his mouth takes a beastly form as his lips swell and draw back, revealing a
set of menacing teeth that resemble an animal's. By taking an antidote, he
can change back into his normal self, something that enables him to live
with two natures.

Later, at the suggestion of valet Poole, who fears his master has been too
dejected by the absence of his fiancée, he decides to visit the Palace of Frivolities, but he takes the potion and goes there as Hyde, to avoid detection.
As soon as he spots Ivy, the barmaid he had rescued from a street attacker,
singing merrily at the bar, he orders champagne to be served by her. By
causing a commotion, he ensures she is kicked out of that establishment.
He then entices her to a luxury apartment and keeps her there, torturing
and sexually abusing her.

He changes back to Jekyll by taking the antidote, and for a while he continues his plans to marry Beatrix, when unwittingly he reverts to his beastly
nature. In a burst of remorse, he sends 50 pounds to Ivy, and when she
visits Jekyll and tells him about her tormentor, he solemnly promises that
Hyde will not bother her again. His decision is so firm that he even melts
his key to his lab from where he comes and goes as Hyde. But as he treads
toward his fiancée's home whistling merrily the barmaid's song, a sudden
spasm causes him to sit down on a bench; then his features change and in a
few moments he turns into the beastly Hyde. He rushes to Ivy's apartment,
where she sips champagne to celebrate her freedom, and he smothers her

to death as she screams and tries to run away. When the neighbors gather after hearing her screams, he escapes by hitting them with his cane and bounding down the stairs, running into the street, leaping over fences, running with the agility of a fiend. After he attacks Beatrix and kills her father, he seeks the help of his colleague Lanyon. When Hyde goes on a rampage and attempts to stab Lanyon with a knife, the latter shoots at him three times, killing him. As Hyde lies dying, his face gradually regains Jekyll's normal features, as death cleanses the evil side of him.

THEMES

The main theme of *Dr. Jekyll and Mr. Hyde* harkens back to the biblical dilemma of man's curiosity to see what the snake has to offer—knowledge of good and evil and, potentially, power over his creator. It is also a scientific theme—which Jekyll introduces to the guests at dinner—that a doctor/scientist has an obligation to study man's inner world, especially his dual nature. In post-Darwinian England, scientific research had gained force but was also thought provocative and dangerous by established society.

The example that Jekyll offers to the skeptical dinner guests is that of a patient of his, Sam Higgins (Barton MacLane), who was heard shouting during a church service earlier that day. Higgins is taken to the lunatic asylum where he later dies. In that man, Jekyll says, evil has dominated his soul, an idea that outrages dinner guests, especially his future father-in-law, Sir Charles Emery, who advises him to quit his outlandish notions and continue to be the distinguished physician that conforms to current social mores. Jekyll rejects the idea, not wanting, as he says to his friend Dr. Lanyon, to spend his life curing colds and mumps instead of heeding his scientific curiosity to do research for the advance of medicine. On its face, this motive seems sound enough, but soon the viewer discovers that Jekyll's motivation is infected by desire for the lively Ivy Peterson, the cheery and fun-loving barmaid.

As in the biblical story, temptation initiates the drama. Sir Charles, wanting to think over Jekyll's dangerous ideas, takes his daughter Beatrix to the Continent for a vacation lasting weeks. Jekyll, after Poole's suggestion, decides to visit the Palace of Frivolities, and as he prepares to go, he sees the garter that the playful barmaid had given him when he had left her apartment. It is the garter that becomes the stimulus of Jekyll's libido, even before he takes the potion. Up to that moment, his experiment with the concoction he invented had been caused by scientific curiosity. Now it could also be a means of disguise to do what his butler had innocently suggested. The disguise could also be his alibi, as nobody would know that he had visited an establishment disapproved of by proper society. The result is disastrous, as he has, unwittingly, unleashed the demon that resided inside him. As soon as Hyde's eye spots Ivy, carefree and singing, "You should see me dance the polka," he asks the proprietor to let her serve him champagne, and she merrily does so but shrinks back when she sees his glazing eyes staring at her. There begins one of the most bizarre love relationships in screen history. Ingrid Bergman's Ivy Peterson is a buoyant, fresh beauty serving beer to customers behind that bar, babbling out the tunes the bare-legged dancers on the stage are singing. She joins the merriment, seemingly without a care in the world, when a menacing customer asks the manager for champagne served to him by her. She is immediately repulsed by the beastly man's thick eyebrows, glaring eyes, and twisted smile. His voice is a hoarse whisper, more like the growl of a carnivore than the polished speech one hears in Jekyll's social circle. Her common cockney patter (Bergman had been carefully coached to imitate it) mixed well with her distinct Swedish accent, matching her exquisite looks, curved eyebrows, perked-up nose, brilliant eyes, and sensuous mouth. Ivy is an archetypal mixture of a beauty and sensuality attracting the lustful attentions of a beast. But in this particular case, the beast is not just enamored of her. He is bent on cannibalizing her—bringing her down to his level. The more Hyde is conscious of her revulsion and fear of him, the more he torments her, sadistically enjoying her terror. Ivy takes one step, however, that will make her relationship with Hyde even worse. She visits Dr. Jekyll in search of his help, as she remembers his kindness during their initial meeting. He gives her solemn assurances that her beastly tormentor will not bother her again. Jekyll sees now, with his temporarily sane eyes, the devastation Hyde's actions have wrought. As she is going out, she says, "For a moment I thought that maybe . . ." This is the moment of recognition, and it seals her doom.

CONCLUSION

Both films are departures from Stevenson's novella, as both add female counterparts to the Jekyll/Hyde persona, thus expanding the focus of the story from the dangerous experiment with human nature to a tense melodrama where a beast is loose to attack both male and female targets. What makes the second movie more compelling, however, is Bergman's performance. Her Ivy Peterson, the tormented victim of a maniac, turns out to be the dominant character in the movie. (Spencer Tracy's fears that she might steal the show may have turned out to be true.) Literally, this is the Beauty and the Beast syndrome, but whereas in Cocteau's famous movie *Beauty and the Beast* (made only a few years later), the Prince is liberated and humanized by love, Jekyll has crossed the boundaries into evil and is irredeemable. In the process, Lana Turner's character loses the Prince, and Ivy Peterson's "benefactor," the beastly Hyde, dies tragically at the hands of his friend, who has recognized his identity. Dr. Jekyll's experiment has failed, the two natures of man collide, and the evil wins—in a bitter self-destructive struggle. The movie does not offer a catharsis to the reader (just as Stevenson's novella does not), but Bergman, the actress, is lifted as an erotic icon, one that she never quite achieved again.

4

CASABLANCA

(1942)

★ ★ ★ ★ ★

Director: Michael Curtiz
Screenplay: Julius J. Epstein, Philip G. Epstein, and Howard Koch, based on
    the play *Everybody Comes to Rick's* by Murray Burnett and Joan Alison
Producers: Hal B. Wallis and Jack L. Warner. *Cinematographer:* Arthur Edeson.
    Music Score: Max Steiner
Cast: Humphrey Bogart (Rick Blaine), Ingrid Bergman (Isla Lund), Paul
    Henreid (Victor Laszlo), Claude Rains (Captain Louis Renault),
    Conrad Veidt (Major Heinrich Strasser), Peter Lorre (Ugarte), Sydney
    Greenstreet (Signor Ferrari), S. Z. "Cuddles" Sakall (Carl), Madeleine
    LeBeau (Yvonne), Dooley Wilson (Sam), Joy Page (Annina Brandel),
    Marcel Dalio (Emil, the Croupier), Leonid Kinskey (Sascha), John
    Qualen (Berger)
Studio: Warner Bros. / First National
Released: November 26, 1942
Specs: 102 minutes; black and white
Availability: DVD, Blu-ray (Warner Bros.)

Ingrid Bergman was always amused when fans said *Casablanca* was their favorite film, or that it was often listed as one of the greatest films ever made and held in such high regard. *Casablanca*, which premiered in November 1942, was a box office hit, and, at awards season the following year, it received the 1943 Oscar for Best Picture. Based on the play *Everybody*

Comes to Rick's by Murray Burnett and Joan Alison, the film owes its success partly on timing because of strong current issues relevant to audiences then, such as the rising numbers of displaced persons and World War II and America's entrance into it. But as the great classic it has become, *Casablanca* is justly praised for its larger universal themes of sacrifice, duty, and long-lost love.

Although *Casablanca* is mostly seen as Humphrey Bogart's film, it can, by equal measure, be seen as one of Bergman's major achievements, albeit one she reluctantly acknowledged. At the time, the latter part of 1941 and early 1942, Bergman was spending her time in Rochester, New York, where she and her husband and their daughter lived, languishing for work and anxious to hear from David O. Selznick what her next role would be. Ernest Hemingway had campaigned for her to play Maria in *For Whom the Bell Tolls*, and that idea mostly occupied Ingrid's mind. Instead, she got the role of Ilsa Lund in *Casablanca* after intense efforts by Hal B. Wallis, an independent producer at Warner Bros., and Bergman returned to Hollywood with little enthusiasm for the project. She was in awe of Humphrey Bogart, a big Hollywood star at the time, and went repeatedly to see *The Maltese Falcon* to familiarize herself with his style. Although she had already done several movies in America, including *Intermezzo: A Love Story* (1939) and *Dr. Jekyll and Mr. Hyde* (1941), Bergman felt that *Casablanca* would become her grand entrance to American cinema and that her success would hinge on a convincing performance. David O. Selznick, who had a vested interest in Bergman, received $125,000 for her loan-out to Warner Bros., while Bergman only cost him her contractual salary of $35,000.[1] Selznick feared that Sweden's potential alliance with the Axis powers, Germany and Italy, would harm Bergman's image, and he was anxious for her to get to work before that happened. Sweden remained neutral and that factored into the success of *Casablanca*.

Bergman was quite alarmed with the bad state of the production when she arrived in Hollywood in April 1942. There were daily changes in the script, authored by the Epstein brothers (Philip and Julius), Howard Koch, and Casey Robinson (who, used to solo credits, withdrew in the end, thus missing out on the Oscar), and the daily ad hoc manner of shooting. Bergman's character had a lover, Rick Blaine (Humphrey Bogart), and a husband, Victor Laszlo (Paul Henreid), an underground leader, both of whom were in love with her, but no one knew at this point who would win her. Neither she nor anyone around her had a sense that such a chaotic production would wind up being that classic that generations would revere.

PLOT

In a smooth, historical sweep, the opening sequences reveal the drama of the refugee trail out of the European war zones of the Second World War and into Africa. The voice of a narrator intones that crowds of refugees from Europe have chosen an escape route from Marseilles, across the Mediterranean to Oran, Algeria, and from thence the exotic city Casablanca, Morocco, where they hope to obtain exit visas to Lisbon, Portugal, and from there to America. The action of the movie occurs just weeks before Pearl Harbor, late in 1941, before America had entered the Second World War. Casablanca was then part of "unoccupied France," but in essence under the Vichy government of Marshal Pétain, and the Gestapo had already established a foothold there.

In Casablanca, the chaotic and dangerous streets are filled with desperate people scheming ways to leave Morocco. Inside Rick's Café Américain, a casino near the ocean and next to the airport, people from all walks of life gather to make secret deals. The situation in Casablanca is intensified when two German couriers carrying letters of transit, signed by General Charles de Gaulle himself (and therefore "cannot be rescinded"), are murdered on their way there. Mass arrests are made in the streets; one man, whose papers are three weeks out of date, is shot just in front of a large street sign of Marshal Pétain. In his pockets, the police discover a leaflet with the words *"Liberté, Egalité, Fraternité,"* the motto of the French underground.

Quickly, the camera switches to Rick Blaine, the owner of the café, drinking, smoking, and playing chess by himself. Relaxed, but still sharp eyed, Rick is seen signing a check, with his typical "O.K. Rick," short for his name, two lines jotted under it, as if to show the finality of his authority in his small kingdom. While a ranking German is trying to gain access into the gambling room, protesting, "Do you know who I am?" Rick replies, "I do. You're lucky you can spend your money at the bar." While this is going on, a short fellow squeezes himself in. It is Ugarte (Peter Lorre), who claims Rick's attention for a few minutes, trying to impress him. He sells exit visas to poor refugees, thus aiding their cause. "It is so parasitic?" he asks. "I don't mind a parasite," says Rick, "I object to a cut-rate one." But Ugarte has a surprise for Rick. He is in possession of the lost letters of transit, stolen from the murdered couriers. Before he hands them over to Rick to hide, he says, "Because you despise me you are the only one I trust." Rick confesses, "Yes, Ugarte, I am a bit more impressed by you." A few moments later, Rick is seen sliding the letters under the cover of the piano that Sam, his singer and pianist friend, plays.

Meanwhile, in one of the opening scenes, Major Strasser (Conrad Veidt), a swaggering Gestapo officer, is seen arriving at the Casablanca airport, welcomed there by the opportunistic and obsequious Captain Renault (Claude Rains), chief of police in Casablanca. He assures Strasser that the murderer of the couriers will be caught that very evening at Rick's casino. "I expected no less," says Strasser. Indeed, Ugarte is summoned while playing roulette, tries to escape, and is caught while pleading with Rick to help him. Rick refuses, stating his standard phrase: "I stick my neck out for nobody."

In a few moments, while Sam is pounding the keys, singing, a dramatic change occurs when a tall man enters accompanied by a beautiful woman— Victor Laszlo and Ilsa Lund (Henreid and Bergman). While Laszlo tries to find out what happened to Ugarte, Ilsa asks Sam to play "As Time Goes By," a song he used to play when she and Rick were lovers in Paris, some time back. Rick barges in enraged to hear his singer sing a song he was told never to play. It is an electric moment when Rick sees Ilsa looking at him, her eyes full of tears. Renault soon joins the group, and all four sit down. Both Laszlo and Renault are surprised that Rick and Ilsa know each other. Renault especially is taken aback that Rick has broken his habit never to drink with customers.

For Ilsa's part, she ignores their surprise and focuses on Rick. It's clear to her immediately that, in spite of any hostility he has toward her, she has found support for her husband's plans to leave the country. The close-ups of her face reveal the tensions and conflicting emotions she feels. We know she does not say all she is thinking. Her deep emotional maturity keeps her from speaking to Rick about their past and from explaining to Laszlo who Rick is to her; she quickly processes her conflicted emotions for the two men now in her life. It is clear to the audience that Ilsa is the woman who could have knocked Rick out of the orbit of his own life. Charming, beautiful, sophisticated, intelligent, she is a planetary force to be reckoned with. The film's success hinges on Bergman's performance. She must overcome the misery she caused Rick in Paris, which changed him to be a cynic, and then change him back again.

From now on, events move rapidly. Laszlo is questioned by Strasser and asked to reveal a list of resistance leaders in major European capitals in exchange for exit visas. Laszlo refuses, knowing that he and his wife may be held in Casablanca for a long time. Ilsa visits Rick at his apartment at night, but fails to conciliate, as she finds Rick drunk, bitter, and shockingly rude. She and Laszlo try to obtain exit visas from Rick's competition across the street, but Signor Ferrari, owner of the Blue Parrot bar, can only help one of them—Ilsa. They turn him down, and he tells them that Rick may have

Ilsa (Bergman) and Rick (Bogart) listen to guns in the distance as the Germans approach Paris.
Warner Bros. Pictures / Photofest © Warner Bros. Pictures

the letters. Laszlo offers Rick a large amount of money for the visas, and
when he is refused, he asks the reason. Rick gives a clipped answer: "Ask
your wife." Puzzled, Laszlo does, but he already suspects that there is some
secret behind Rick's stubbornness.

Rick drinks alone that night and remembers when he was with Ilsa in
Paris. The flashback reveals the dramatic change between "Richard," as Ilsa
usually calls him in Paris, and "Rick" of Casablanca. Richard is happy, smiling, and lives without concern. Their relationship is a modern affair as they
know little about each other. He knows only that she had her teeth straightened and that the other man in her life is dead. They are at a bar with Sam
playing the piano when an announcement is made that the Germans have
surrounded Paris. They decide to meet at the train station to leave the city.
At the station it is chaos as people attempt to leave the city. Ilsa is not there
and instead leaves him a note. He knocks over the glass after the flashback
is over. This is the halfway point in the film and is Rick's nadir moment. He
has begun drinking again, and the woman who turned his life upside down
in Paris is now in Casablanca doing it again.

In the most dramatic scene in the movie, Ilsa arrives at Rick's apartment
holding a gun and demanding that Rick hand the letters to her. Rick, pointing to his heart, says, "Shoot, you will do me a favor." She breaks down and

confesses she loves him. As the lovers reconcile, Rick devises a plan to get both of them out of Casablanca. Taking the initiative; he promises Renault that he will deliver Victor to him in exchange for a visa for Ilsa and himself. But at the last moment, he holds Renault captive with a gun and takes the group to the airport, where he forces him to put Laszlo's name on the visas, not his own. Renault complies, but he has in the meantime called Strasser, who arrives and furiously phones to the tower to stop the plane from taking off. He attempts to shoot Rick, but Rick is quicker. Strasser falls dead, and when the police arrive, Renault, in a change of heart, tells them to "round up the usual suspects," a phrase that every *Casablanca* lover has memorized.

THEMES

Famous for its universal themes of sacrifice, duty, and lost love, *Casablanca* is also known as a work of cinematic art, which was achieved despite the uncertainties of its production. Though this is an American movie made at the Warner Bros. Studios, it conveyed the impression that the action took place in an exotic land, Casablanca, Morocco, where strangers from various European countries converged, bargaining for a visa to America and to freedom. Aside from Bogart and Dooley Wilson, everybody else in *Casablanca* is or strongly resembles a foreign character. In the 1930s, during Hitler's ascent, many actors, directors, and writers fled Europe aiming to find a job in America—and many did—although some had to adjust to circumstances and take lesser roles, as, for instance, Marcel Dalio, the noted French actor who had excelled in Jean Renoir's *The Grand Illusion* (1937) and *The Rules of the Game* (1939) and who had fled France after the German invasion. In *Casablanca* he plays Emil the Croupier. Dalio fled Paris with his wife, Madeleine LeBeau. LeBeau, who plays Yvonne, Rick's jilted girlfriend, had real tears in her eyes when Laszlo led the chorus at Rick's singing the French national anthem. Their roles were small but important, as indispensable to the whole as were most of the minor characters in *Casablanca*.

Claude Rains, an English actor with long-established credentials in Hollywood, plays a French police officer, conveniently pliable with the Gestapo, amoral, exploitative, and, as he himself says, "blowing with the wind." It is one of the delights in *Casablanca* to see a collaborator turn virtuous on a whim. His foil, Major Strasser, gives credence to the archetypal Nazi villain, the embodiment of evil, hated and feared by all except for his small cadre. He is played by Conrad Veidt, in truth an affable man, in exile because his wife was Jewish.

None of the characters in *Casablanca* is too small to contribute something worthwhile to the whole. Hungarian actor S. Z. "Cuddles" Sakall plays Carl, the sentimental waiter and general supervisor of Rick's, adoringly kissing his boss when he sees him help the Bulgarian girl's husband win enough the money at roulette to obtain an exit visa. Always alert about pickpockets, Carl is later seen getting ready to go to an underground meeting, letting the viewer know that he is also a member of the resistance. Other international bit players, most uncredited, add color and comedic touches in almost every scene.

Casablanca does not allow the viewer to relax for a moment. Transactions, most illegal, flood the place. Characters of infinite variety—from trashy thieves to elegant malefactors—keep the eye of the viewer busy— arrests, fear, and anxiety amid ongoing fun. History has wiped out many movies of the time that were branded patriotic, but *Casablanca* easily outmatches most of them.

One character who seems to link all the characters—a sort of a Greek chorus—is Sam (Dooley Wilson), the singer and entertainer who softens Rick's hard-shelled demeanor, knows his past, and gives him someone he can confide in, as well as trust to protect him. It is Sam who leads the crowd in a rousing rendition of "Knock on Wood." The lyrics suggest that no matter how unhappy one feels, he should "knuckle down and knock on wood"—that hope exists. Sam knows, though few others do, that Rick's cynicism is the result of lost love, a matter of a broken heart. Rick had been an idealist who wanted to change the world, but now he hides his idealism behind a profit motive. Ilsa's sudden appearance at Rick's Café Américain startles and saddens Sam, for he knows his boss's wound is still raw. She coaxes him into singing her favorite song, "As Time Goes By." When Sam pretends he does not remember the song, she hums it to him. Her face glows as she does. He picks up the lines from there, and responds, as if a siren had beckoned to him from afar.

The name "Ilsa" was given to Bergman's character by Michael Curtiz, the Hungarian director of *Casablanca*, who had long established himself in Hollywood. He associated Ilsa to Ilse, the heroine in a poem by Heinrich Heine, "Princess Isle" in *The Harz Journey*. She sings and beckons heartbroken men: "I am Princess Ilse / and dwell in Ilsenstein; / Come with me to my castle, / We will be happy there. . . / You will forget your pain, / O heartsick man!"[2] As historian Aljean Harmetz points out, "Ilsa also had an element of danger about her. Much like the Ilse of the poem, she was part lover, part destroyer, an enchantress whose innocence could both beguile a man and lure him to his destruction."[3] Ilsa, the mysterious and beautiful Norwegian, had lured Rick in Paris, caused him to fall in love with her, and then, without any clue, left him heartbroken in the train station.

When they are reunited in Casablanca, she offers him an excuse, that she did not want him to know she was married to a hunted man in order to protect him. That sounds reasonable enough, but perhaps she had underestimated her own power over him. In an earlier scene, when she had come to his apartment at night and found him drunk, she offered him the worst excuse a woman could offer a rejected man: that in her youth she had met a nobler man, who had sparked in her his lofty ideals. That remains a knotty ethical problem in *Casablanca*. Ilsa does not quite seem aware of the damage she had done to Rick when she visited him at the apartment that first night. When she found him drunk and cynical, instead of showing regret, she offered an explanation. The following morning, when he is "relatively sober" and asks what it is she wanted to tell him, she dismisses his question and blames him for the "hatred" she saw in his eyes. She also tells him she is married, "and was," to Laszlo. Ignoring the past with Rick, she only thinks of how to get the visas for her and her husband.

That changes the movie's ethical configuration—and the plot. Now Rick becomes Laszlo's and Ilsa's target. When Laszlo appeals to him, mentioning Rick's background as a man who had fought for the underdog and that the winning side would have paid him much more, Rick cynically replies that he was never "much of a businessman." When later Ilsa confronts Rick with a pistol, he says, "Shoot me." For Ilsa this becomes the moment of recognition. She realizes how much he really loves her, and how severe was the damage she had done him.

With that, Rick assumes the burden of a solution, as the story is still without an end. He has power over the situation, something that soothes his ego, but he also has the most to lose. If he goes with her, he will have to endure her guilt for leaving her husband behind to certain death.

Rick's final decision shows his moral growth because he sacrifices himself for Ilsa, for her husband, and for Western democracies. Ilsa teaches him this lesson, but she has assistance from Annina Brandel (Joy Page), the woman in the Bulgarian couple whose experience through the film parallels and slightly precedes Ilsa's and Victor's experiences in Casablanca: She asks Rick in the bar, "If someone loved you very much so that your happiness was the only thing that she wanted in the world and she did a bad thing to make certain of it, could you forgive her?" Rick answers with bitterness: "Nobody ever loved me that much."

Ilsa is also trapped by his decision, whatever it is. If she goes with Laszlo, she leaves Rick behind, the man she truly loves and had just said she had no power to leave him for a second time. She faces the alternatives of duty versus love, and, by the same token, of love and sacrifice. She puts up a resistance when Rick mentions the names of Victor Laszlo and Ilsa Lund to be put on the letters, which Renault is filling out, but when Rick explains to her why she must go with her husband, she reluctantly agrees. "Here's looking at you, kid," says Rick with unparalleled grace, and she responds with, "God bless you." The married couple moves toward the plane. True to his word, Rick shoots Strasser after the latter tries to stop the plane from taking off. One way to view the film's ending is that Rick loses everything when Ilsa leaves him in Paris, and then again in Casablanca: He loses the bar, kills a German officer, and, we assume, is forced to live on the run. But once the siren Ilsa flew to Lisbon, Rick became himself again—a fighter for the underdog—and he pulls with him an amoral turncoat who, like him, had become a patriot. The two walk in the fog, into a potential "beautiful friendship."

CONCLUSION

Ingrid Bergman's Ilsa remains the most electrifying part of *Casablanca* over the years. When several decades later Lord John Brabourne, coproducer of *Murder on the Orient Express* (1974), heard that Bergman was to be in the film even in a bit role, he ran to see *Casablanca*. Bergman herself did not seem to care much for the movie, and for years she expressed surprise when people praised her for her role as Ilsa Lund, feeling, as many did, that *Casablanca* was Bogart's movie. Finally she acknowledged that "there was something mystical in it," and that it had "a life of its own." *Casablanca* was a movie of its time; there was a need for it, and it filled that need, she added.[4] At the time she made *Casablanca*, in 1942, her three Oscars, six nominations, and numerous other awards were yet to come. Yet, it can be argued that the longevity of *Casablanca* may be attributed to a great extent to Arthur Edeson's photography, which catches her face in soft focus profiles (during Corinna Mura's Latin song, for instance), in hard light when she pleads with Sam, also at the moment she admiringly looks at Laszlo when he leads the band to sing "La Marseillaise," the French national anthem. Renault, a connoisseur (and exploiter) when it comes to female charm, calls her the most beautiful woman ever to visit Casablanca. The allure of Ilsa is real. Two worthy men are competing for her; she adorns

Rick's as she enters looking like a European princess—Henreid not too bad as a prince at her side—and, as long as she reigns in Rick's heart—she rules the place. Many things happen at Rick's café, but the most important is the love between Ilsa and Rick.

In *Casablanca*, Bergman was the gem and the prize, a beautiful woman courted by two powerful men. One had the grandiosity and the manner of the hero, who could be looked up to with awe, respect, and glorified love. The other was down to earth, practical, commanding in his small world and seemingly indifferent to any cause but this own. But both men were enslaved to this woman. She was the queen yearned after, granting or withdrawing favors to both, determining their fate. Her marriage to the hero Laszlo seemed solid, but Rick's caustic behavior and his berating her for leaving him had its effect. Torn between sentiment and duty, she yields suddenly to her heart's demands, and the configuration of the group changes. Once again, her appeal obliges Rick to become magnanimous, patriotic, and even heroic, as he allows Strasser to shoot first. He is no murderer, as Strasser would be, nor a coward. He accepts his fate, plunging from the security of the casino to fighting underground, while his loved one will fly to freedom with her husband and continue to fight for the right reasons, to free the world from the Nazis. There is sacrifice on both sides. While Laszlo is the beneficiary of Rick's decision, Ilsa is also benefiting from Rick's sacrifice. She is flying to freedom. As for her love? "We will always have Paris," Rick assures her. Not bad, for a memory.

5

FOR WHOM THE BELL TOLLS

(1943)

★ ★ ★

Director: Sam Wood
Screenplay: Dudley Nichols, based on the novel by Ernest Hemingway
Producer: Sam Wood. *Cinematographer:* Ray Rennahan. *Music Score:* Victor
    Young
Cast: Gary Cooper (Robert Jordan), Ingrid Bergman (Maria), Akim Tamiroff
    (Pablo), Katina Paxinou (Pilar), Joseph Calleia (El Sordo), Vladimir
    Sokoloff (Anselmo), Arturo de Cordova (Agustin), Fortunio Bonanova
    (Fernando)
Studio: Paramount Pictures
Released: July 14, 1943 (New York); wide release 1944
Specs: 168 minutes; color
Availability: DVD and Blu-ray (Universal Home Entertainment)

For Whom the Bell Tolls became another turning point in Ingrid Bergman's
career, right after she had triumphed in *Casablanca*. This undertaking allowed her to costar with one of America's most popular actors, Gary Cooper, in a film of epic scope based on the novel by Ernest Hemingway. It
was a project she had long aspired to be in. When the novel was published
in 1940, Hemingway, who had seen Bergman in *Intermezzo: A Love Story*,
immediately thought she would be the ideal actress to play Maria, the

tormented young woman, victim of the cruelties of the Spanish Civil War. Her lover, Cooper, also handpicked by Hemingway, played an American dynamiter committed to aiding the Spanish rebels against the Fascist dictatorship of Generalissimo Francisco Franco. The project took its time to develop. There was the question of a large budget (estimated at $3 million), of location, but most importantly, of the leads and the large cast required for an epic movie. Shooting the film in Spain was out of the question during the war, so Sam Wood and Paramount production manager B. G. DeSylva opted for the rugged terrain of the Blue Canyon of Sierra Nevada in Northern California, which turned out to be a perfect natural setting. The most important problem of casting was obtaining Bergman, then under contract to David O. Selznick, who would not loan her out to Paramount without a nifty profit for himself, which eventually amounted to $150,000, while Bergman was content with her contractual salary of $34,895.[1] Besides, Bergman was still tied up with *Casablanca* until the middle of July 1942 and was unable to arrive at the filming location until early August when the filming had already begun with another actress having taken the role of Maria—a ballerina named Vera Zorina. Sam Wood found some excuse to send Zorina off, and Bergman took her natural place besides Gary Cooper, with whom she soon developed an intense friendship—both on and off the screen.

The cast was bolstered by superior character actors: Akim Tamiroff, a Hollywood stalwart, plays Pablo, a chieftain of the mountain guerilla band; Katina Paxinou, an outstanding Greek stage actress playing Pablo's common-law wife, Pilar; and as Anselmo, Vladimir Sokoloff, an expert in playing colorful non-American characters; plus a host of others who added color and diversity to the epic film. The film went ahead to become a huge popular success, grossing a staggering $7 million in the US alone, and netting nine Oscar nominations—though only one win,[2] for Paxinou for Best Actress in a Supporting Role. The critics were not so favorable, though; they relentlessly attacked the film as overlong, tedious, lacking much action, and lapsing into some serious distortions of the political landscape Hemingway had built in his novel. *For Whom the Bell Tolls* has faded over the years, especially in comparison to its Bergman predecessor *Casablanca*, which maintained its glitter throughout the decades. However, *FWTBT* still deserves attention as an essential vehicle in Bergman's development as a Hollywood personality on the rise, her peerless matchup with Cooper, and Hemingway's brave message of the fight against Fascism, which survives in the film despite the crass commercialism dominating its making.

PLOT

The film starts with two men running away from a big explosion, a train blown up. The two shadowy figures stop when one of them is hit, and then the other fulfills a promise to shoot him if wounded, so he will not be captured alive. The viewer recognizes Cooper as the shooter, and soon we learn that he was the dynamiter of the train. We also learn that his name is Robert Jordan, a tall American, whose presence there is not fully explained until later. Soon he is seen entering a dark room next to a saloon where he meets General Golz (Leo Bulgakov), a Republican; that is, a fighter against the forces of Franco (a Soviet officer in Hemingway's novel) to whom he reports the train blowup and the execution of Kashkin (Feodor Chaliapin), which he calls "murder." The general gives him his new orders, to blow up a bridge at a crucial point near Segovia, where Franco's Nationalist forces are supposed to pass in their march to fight the Republicans, a revolutionary front preparing for a big offensive. He gives him a guide, Anselmo, an elderly man who will take him to a spot on the mountains where a unit of rebels is hiding. When they arrive there, carrying the dynamite on their backs, they meet Pablo, a drunken ruffian who proclaims the territory is his and the rebel band there is under his command. Calmly but decisively, Jordan persists that he has orders and that his mission will be accomplished. A small group gathers around him waiting for a meal, and soon a young girl with close-cropped hair emerges from the cave distributing bread and bowls of soup. When she sees the tall and handsome American, she smiles at him enticingly. He too admires this young beauty (Maria [Bergman]) who looks unspoiled, despite the horrible truths she relates to him later. A few moments later, a stout and imposing woman emerges from the cave and greets Jordan, whom she calls "Inglés." Photographed from below, Pilar looks larger than life, possibly to conform to the image of Hemingway, who describes her as large.

Friendships as well as tensions develop. Pablo is not only drunk and unmannerly, but also treacherous. In a confrontation with Pilar, he backs off when she thunders, "I am in command!" She takes over the group, pledges full support to Jordan's plan; together, with the help of the others, Jordan maps out the course of action. To do so they also have to design an escape route. For that they will need horses, but horses leave tracks if it snows. Someone scoffs at the idea, as this is the middle of May. Still it snows. They seek the services of another chieftain, El Sordo (Joseph Calleia), who must provide horses, as the operation cannot be postponed. He is slightly deaf and sounds erratic, but he offers to cooperate. There are fifteen men in both groups and ten horses, so he suggests stealing some. Meanwhile, Jordan and Maria's friendship becomes passionate love, and at some point Maria tells him how her father and mother were killed by the Nationalists, and she was gang-raped and her hair shorn before she was taken under the wing of Pilar and escaped with her to the mountains.

The plan to blow up the bridge suffers a serious setback when Pablo steals the detonators, and Jordan is forced to resort to a new device: a hand grenade to explode the dynamite. But that would require a far greater risk. He and Anselmo would have to place the hand grenade under the bridge with a wire attached to it to be able to detonate it from a safe distance, moments before the tanks arrive—an extremely dangerous job. Then they would use the horses to get away.

The plan goes awry. An impulsive El Sordo, intent on securing extra horses, attacks a searching party of the enemy, giving away his position. Planes fly over shortly and bomb his location on the mountain peak where he and his companions are hiding. Three explosions announce their demise. Repentant, Pablo comes back to help, but the damage he has done cannot be repaired. Jordan and Anselmo wire the bridge and explode it just before the enemy tanks begin to pass overhead. Anselmo refuses to pull the wire until Jordan is safe. Jordan pulls the wire just in time; the bridge is blown, but Anselmo is buried under the debris. When the remainder of the group retreat, Jordan, riding last, is wounded, both his legs mutilated. He cannot ride a horse, so he urges the others to ride on and escape, while he will stay and hold the enemy for as long as he can. Maria screams as she sees him blown up. The last shot shows Jordan, about to pass out, firing at the camera with a Lewis machine gun. The film ends with a bell tolling.

THEMES AND MOTIVES

Three main themes seem to dominate *For Whom the Bell Tolls*: the price paid to fight for freedom against Nazism; a doomed love affair, as seems typical in Hemingway's major novels; Hemingway's motto of "grace under pressure," which survives in the film.

In 1942, the fight for freedom was very much a subject of the movie kingdom in Hollywood. But most war movies were concentrating on the war going on against the Nazis in Germany and Mussolini's Fascist Italy—the Axis powers, which included imperial Japan in the Pacific front. The Spanish Civil War, which started in 1936, was already behind the times but was considered by many, including Hemingway, who made several trips there as a correspondent as it was going on. The civil strife in Spain was thought by many a prelude to World War II. His novel *For Whom the Bell Tolls*, aside from its historical and folklore value, is a cry for freedom from repression by the so-called Republicans (some confusion occurred among viewers back home as to whose side Jordan was on, as Cooper himself was a staunch Republican) who were supported by the Soviet Union—something the film only hints at. The larger parameters of Hemingway's novel (as of the film, partially) suggest that the Spanish Civil War was the start of the collision of two opposed ideologies—Fascism and Communism—that lasted through the better part of the twentieth century. After all, Jordan took his orders to blow the bridge directly from General Golz, a Soviet operative, as his veiled appearance in a dark room may suggest. The Nationalists were the armed forces of dictator Francisco Franco, who had at his disposal a regular army equipped with armored tanks and an air force. On Franco's ruling side were also some special forces, the Phalangist Party, known for their savagery and responsible for the rape of Maria. (They were not unlike the Fascist Blackshirts of Mussolini and the SS of Hitler's Nazis.) They raided villages and committed atrocities against anyone suspected of siding with the rebels. Maria's father, the mayor of a town, along with his wife, was executed for that reason.

The film, by and large following the tracks of Hemingway's novel, shows that the motivations of the groups fighting were not always the same. The group that Jordan was directed to contact is split, as its leader Pablo, seeing defeat coming ("I am a drunk, but not stupid"), does not want Jordan to carry out his mission to blow up a bridge, an act that was supposed to hinder the Nationalist forces from crossing it while an attack by the Republicans would be under way. Pilar, who is brave and patriotic, commits to the cause, and, by dint of goodwill she supports the efforts of Inglés, a foreigner who came to fight for freedom in her country. Pablo switches sides, twice, seeing that alone he cannot survive. He used to be a brave man and a leader of his tribe, but the futility of the war, as he sees it, makes him cynical. Yet seeing that he would be alone against the group, he rejoins them. Hemingway's approach, and the film's, is carried out not by a united front but relies on the activities of split groups, each looking out for its own survival, however in the end they join forces to fight. The film, following at the steps of the novel, concentrates on these groups. The film shows, in flashbacks, earlier times when Pablo fights alongside Pilar inside a large unit that takes a Nationalist town and torments and executes its leaders by throwing them over a wall to their deaths. Thus, the idea of freedom becomes muddled, at times looking like an internecine war of tribal chiefs rather than a unified force

Robert (Cooper) and Maria (Bergman) before he leaves on a mission. *Paramount Pictures /*
Photofest © Paramount Pictures

resisting tyranny. The only person that remains steady through the film's narrative is the American dynamiter who will carry out his orders because he believes in his cause. His commitment finally prompts the groups to unify and fight, but he is also one who pays the ultimate price.

Love affairs in Hemingway's fictional narratives seem doomed from the start. Jake Barnes in *The Sun Also Rises* is emasculated by a war wound yet does not lose his lust for life. Frederic Henry of *A Farewell to Arms* (filmed with Gary Cooper and Helen Hayes in 1932) is not able to live "happily ever after" with Catherine Barkley, the nurse he fell in love with, as she dies in childbirth. Both Cooper and Bergman were handpicked by Hemingway to play Jordan and Maria, and, as it turns out, the matching worked well on a certain level, as the two were attracted to each other from the first moment. Cooper, already a Hollywood legend by that time, looks like the embodiment of Robert Jordan, tall and handsome. Even Pilar, a middle-aged, rugged warrior woman, seems to have fallen under his spell; her calling him "Inglés," not "Roberto," as Maria does, perhaps indicates that a certain distance should be held, proper to her rank. No other female figure beside those two enters the scene, nor would Jordan expect any, least of all for romance. But when he sees Maria emerging from the cave, this even-tempered, unruffled man breaks his silence, if only with his eyes. Even if he maintains his composure as a leader dedicated to his task at all times, it is evident to everyone around, and especially to Pilar, that he has been smitten by this fresh beauty. For him, as for the audience presumably, Bergman as Maria makes a stunning entrance. For the first time in her career the viewer sees her in color. Her chestnut-colored hair is cropped but nicely curled (by a hairdresser who ran around the hills with her); her cheeks are rosy, the result of the efforts of the makeup department to warm up her natural pallor; and her blue eyes scintillate when she first sees the tall and handsome specimen of another race enter the wilderness where a bunch of rugged cavemen reside.

Visually, Cooper and Bergman look perfectly matched despite their all-too-apparent difference in age. Pilar gives Maria's age as nineteen, and she looks it, though Bergman was twenty-seven at the time. Cooper was forty-one, and he looked every minute of it. In most cases this would have been described as a love affair between a naive teenager and an attractive older man. Maria, who had been gang-raped and kept in captivity by savages, looks fresh and playful like a kitten huddling into her older lover's gargantuan arms. At five feet nine and a half inches, Bergman had been considered too tall to be your everyday Hollywood actress (and caused some concern to Selznick for that), and indeed she dwarfed some of her screen partners—Bogart, Boyer, Brynner, for instance—but Cooper, at six feet three inches, towered over her, and all those around him. This worked to Bergman's advantage. In the heartbreaking scene where Maria describes the killing of her parents and is about to tell of her being dragged to the barbershop where her hair was cropped (and presumably the spot she was raped), Jordan covers her mouth—her entire face actually, with his massive hand. Here he is not a mere lover, but almost a father figure, one talking to a distressed younger family member. This lover–father figure, perhaps more beloved for that reason, is to disappear from her life forever because circumstance demands—a very Hemingwayesque figure dedicated to what must be done. This ambivalent relationship—fresh youth versus mature middle age—enhanced by Bergman's real feelings for Cooper, may have been the cause of the mixed reception of *FWTBT*. Even Bergman admits as much:

> I enjoyed it so much, particularly Gary Cooper. What was wrong was that my happiness showed on the screen. I was far too happy to honestly portray Maria's tragic figure.[3]

If she looked too happy, Cooper as Jordan looked too sober. The young, beautiful female that was clinging on him may have given him pause to think of the pleasures of real life with a young companion (after all in *High Noon*, almost a decade later, Cooper as Will Kane was not held back by creaking age from marrying an almost nubile Grace Kelly). But a real Hemingway hero is usually committed to a nihilistic heroism. Jake Barnes is unmanned forever. Frederic Henry sees doom and gloom as his story evolves toward its last few pages. And Jordan knows what will happen to him after Pilar reads his palm, a totem ritual for the gypsy half-breed, and refuses to tell him what she saw. Jordan is astonishingly unruffled by danger throughout this adventure, although he is extremely vigilant about the dangers he and his companions are exposed to. When a sorry-looking Pablo returns, Jordan tells him he has already an alternate device to blow the bridge. While Pilar curses Pablo, Jordan doesn't shoot him, because, as he tells him, he still needs him. Pablo, a cunning old fox, brought horses that will help the others escape after the bridge is blown. All throughout the three-and-a-half-days' adventure Jordan has not lost his temper once, has faced each setback calmly, and let the group know that he was there to finish the mission assigned to him. He has taught his disparate group to move quietly and efficiently and has infused his sense of purpose to them. Cooper was just about the only actor of his time who could embody a Hemingway hero so completely. He indeed displayed "grace under pressure."

CONCLUSION

When Bergman asked Hemingway whether he had seen the movie, he replied that had indeed—five times. Astonished, she said, "You liked it so much?" Hemingway went to lengths to explain to her that he left the theater five minutes after the movie had started, had to go in again and left again a few minutes later, and it took him five visits to complete his viewing it. "That's how much I liked it," he concluded.[4]

Though praises for her abounded, in general *For Whom the Bell Tolls* had enough bad criticism—"the guts of the original have been decorously disemboweled," declared Herb Sterne of *Screen*[5]—to consign the movie to the ranks of mediocrity, rather than oblivion. Its slow pace and length are two factors that caused audiences, then and later, to keep it out of the ranks of classics, today rewarded by restoration[6] in Blu-ray and the Criterion Collection. *FWTBT* has enough quality and distinctions to keep it afloat, especially for those who continue to value it. Hemingway's gritty tale survives, and most of its players shine in splendor: Cooper, Tamiroff, Paxinou, Sokoloff . . . and Bergman's electrifying looks, even if she declares that her image of Maria was tampered with. Bergman survived even flawed movies, more than once, and she fully deserved her Oscar nomination for Best Actress.

GASLIGHT

(1944)

★ ★ ★ ★ ★

Director: George Cukor
Screenplay: John Van Druten, Walter Reisch, and John Balderston, based on the play *Angel Street* (1938) by Patrick Hamilton
Producer: Arthur Hornblow Jr. *Cinematographer:* Joseph Ruttenberg. *Music Score:* Bronislau Kaper. *Editor:* Ralph E. Winters
Cast: Ingrid Bergman (Paula Alquist/Anton), Charles Boyer (Gregory Anton / alias Sergis Bauer), Joseph Cotten (Brian Cameron), Dame May Whitty (Miss Bessie Thwaites), Emil Rameau (Maestro Guardi), Barbara Everest (Elizabeth Tompkins), Angela Lansbury (Nancy Oliver), Tom Stevenson (P. C. Williams), Heather Thatcher (Lady Mildred Dalroy)
Studio: MGM
Released: May 4, 1944
Specs: 114 minutes; black and white
Availability: DVD (Warner Home Video)

After *Casablanca* made her world famous and *For Whom the Bells Tolls* netted her an Oscar nomination, Bergman was loaned out to Metro-Goldwyn-Meyer by David O. Selznick, who found occasions to profit from his rising Swedish star, still new to American audiences. MGM wanted Bergman to play Paula Alquist, a woman in distress, opposite Charles Boyer's Gregory Anton in *Gaslight*, based on a play that had been a smash hit both in London and on Broadway. George Cukor, who had directed Greta Garbo in *Camille* and Katharine Hepburn in *The Philadelphia Story*, was known as a director who pressed his female protagonists to externalize their inner conflicts at moments of great stress. Cukor's choice of Bergman—Irene Dunne and Hedy Lamarr had been considered—could not have been more fortuitous. Bergman actually campaigned to get the part since Selznick refused to loan her out to MGM because Boyer's name would appear first in billing. Finally, after Bergman protested that she didn't mind who was top billing, Selznick yielded and Bergman delivered one of her greatest individual performances that won her universal popular and critical approval, plus her first Oscar.

Cukor's script was based on Patrick Hamilton's popular play *Gas Light* (1939), performed in London to great success and renamed *Angel Street*, which became a smash hit and had 1,295 performances on Broadway.[1] The play was made into a film, *Gaslight* (1940), featuring Anton Walbrook, a prelude to MGM's Bergman vehicle in 1944, also titled *Gaslight*. Here Bergman had an opportunity to showcase her talents, playing a woman who almost loses her mind under the psychological torments of a malevolent husband. Shot in Hollywood's Culver Studios, subbing for a foggy London in late 1800s, the film puts her at center stage, between a criminal husband who tries to drive her out of her mind and a savior detective on his tracks. The plot is tight and quickly paced. The film was photographed in contrasts of lights and shadows, with dimly lit streets and flickering house gaslights, which become visual clues of the heroine's state of mind. The success of *Gaslight* can be attributed to Bergman's nuanced performance of a woman in the grip of terror, verging on paranoia and near self-destruction, but also to Charles Boyer's masterful rendition of a prototypical villain. *Gaslight*, as most of Bergman's great forties movies, has been outshone in following decades by *Casablanca*, the yardstick that all subsequent Bergman movies are measured. But *Gaslight* is a first-rate thriller, and of all of Bergman's films, it is the only one to focus from start to finish on a single man and woman, narrowing the scope of the story to Boyer and Bergman's step-by-step battle for existence.

PLOT

Gaslight is the story of a tormented woman, Paula Anton (Bergman), whose husband, Gregory Anton (Boyer), is trying to drive her mad in order to have her admitted to an asylum and thus be able to search for jewels owned by

Alice Alquist, Paula's aunt, whom he had murdered ten years earlier. The film begins with Bergman as a young girl leaving her home after her aunt's murder in Thornton Square. After some quick early sketches she is shown as a grown-up woman taking voice lessons in Italy. She decides against a musical career and instead marries her accompanist Gregory Anton. After he insists they move to London, to Thornton Square, apartment 9, where Alice was murdered, Anton begins psychological warfare, trying to convince his wife that she is going mad. But, without knowing it, Paula has a supporter, Brian Cameron (Joseph Cotten) of Scotland Yard, who recognizes her as being related to Alice Alquist and suspects that something is amiss in her household. He discovers that Gregory's actual name is Sergis Bauer, who had murdered the elder Alquist. Now that he had married Paula, he had been searching for Alice's famous jewels in the attic, which he had been visiting every night pretending he was at some office of his to do his work. Cameron visits Paula and reveals to her that Anton has planned to have her admitted in a mental institution so he could be alone in the house and search freely. As Anton enters through the boarded door from the attic, having found the jewels, Cameron, with the help of Constable Williams, captures Anton as he exits the attic and returns to the house.

While the film's focus is on terror and suspense, the secondary characters give it moments of humor and even whimsy. Especially prominent in this regard is Miss Thwaites (Dame May Whitty) who introduces herself to Paula as "Bloodthirsty Bessie," the voracious reader of detective novels. Her reading material on the train includes a man with "six wives in the cellar," to which Bergman delivers with deadpan delivery: "That's a lot." The film even gives Miss Thwaites the final word—"Well!"—which is humorously played. Barbara Everest plays the cook, Elizabeth, whose slight deafness becomes instrumental to Paula's fears as she can't hear the noises in the attic, just above her bedroom, produced by Anton's footsteps when he visits the attic in search of jewels during the night. But in the end, Elizabeth remains loyal and assists Cameron in the crucial final moments. The maid that Gregory Anton hires after moving to London is Nancy, played by Angela Lansbury who was nominated for an Academy Award for Best Supporting Actress. Her performance is often humorous and flirtatious. Anton often brings Nancy into the room to do preposterously meaningless tasks such as stoking the kindling in the fireplace. "What are servants for?" he says absurdly, while Paula shrinks and surrenders. Paula often endures his flirtations with Nancy, when he talks to her about how pretty she is and the number of hearts she has broken. "Pass your secrets onto your mistress to help her with her pallor." Although Nancy seems embarrassed by his overtures, privately she delights in his attention, even singing him a snippet of a song from a popular music hall show. Her actions suggest she would like to replace Paula as the wife, and the unsung lyrics emphasize it:

> Up in a balloon, boys,
> Up in a balloon,
> What a jolly place to go
> And spend your honey moon.[2]

THEMES

From the outset, the viewer becomes conscious of the motives of Gregory Anton to induce Paula, his wife, to lapse into a mental state that ultimately will prove that she is insane. The hasty marriage and his insistence to go to London to live in the place where her aunt had been murdered seem peculiar requests to a puzzled Paula, who, however, gives in, eager to please the man she loves. In London, the pair is seen entering apartment 9, at Thornton Square, where the memory of a ghastly murder of a famous singer is still raw. The house is cheerless, full of covered, dusty furniture. Paula is uncomfortable with her memories, though Anton assures his bride that their happy honeymoon will cheer her up. He opens the windows and tells her not to worry about the old furniture, that he is happy to place these things in the attic as she suggests. Ironically, a woman passes by the house selling lavender, which commonly symbolizes purity, silence, and devotion.

Anton's strategy rests on three tactical approaches: The first is a methodical isolation of Paula from the outside world, so he can control her and prevent others from finding the jewels. Anton is also alarmed by the fact that a man in the neighborhood seems to have recognized Paula during one of their walks and tips his hat to her. She responds by a slight bow of her head, which infuriates Anton. But on the whole his plan seems to work. Determined to leave the house for even a minute, Paula must convince Nancy that she can leave; then she hesitates outside the door, turns back, turns away, but then goes back inside, defeated. Confined in narrow, ghostly quarters, Paula becomes an easy tool, more easily manipulated by her evil husband.

The second tactic is to convince her that she is forgetful and losing things; he gives her a precious broach that "belonged to his mother," putting it in her bag and exhorting her not to lose it. When she realizes it is not in her bag during their visit to the Tower of London, she begins to believe that she

Sergis Bauer (Boyer), caught and tied, listens to a vindictive Paula Anton (Bergman), whom he had planned to drive insane. *MGM / Photofest © MGM*

has actually lost the broach. Later, during Lady Dalroy's (Heather Thatcher) party, he removes his watch from his vest pocket, and, without being seen, he places it in her bag, where he finds it with a sadistic grin of satisfaction.

The third leg of his diabolical plan—something that he puts into practice from the very beginning—is that she "dreams" things, a method that tightens the screws and, indeed, brings her to the brink of madness. The first instance happens just after they have settled into their home and he is playing the piano. Paula finds a letter in a songbook from one Sergis Bauer. He jumps up and screams at her, almost letting her see behind his mask. He puts the letter in his pocket and later insists that the letter is a figment of her imagination.

In each of these methods Anton moves in dizzying quickness between cruelty and feigned tenderness. Like the first piece played at Lady Dalroy's party, Beethoven's *Pathetique* sonata, the film plays like a sonata, which typically has three movements in contrasting forms and keys. Anton swears his love and devotion to her and then, and, moments later, he flaunts his sexual prowess with Nancy in front of her. Then, again, he assures his bride of his love and concern for her.

Anton's aim is, of course, to search for the jewels that her aunt Alice Alquist wore, jewels of mythical value, as they had been given to her by some unnamed royal as a gift for her immense talent. The jewels themselves would not make him rich, as he would be unable to sell them without incriminating himself. When they visit the Tower of London, the film reveals two of his characteristics: his aim to cause her to lose her mind and his love of jewels. While there, she cannot find the cameo he gave her earlier and then surreptitiously removed from her purse. He follows her into a torture chamber filled with equipment used for physical torture to torture her mentally.

For Anton, jewels have "a life of their own," and are so dear to him that he committed murder for them and was ready to commit a woman who had loved him to the madhouse. He does not see himself as cruel, just impatient to gain what he was so close to attaining when he murdered Alquist. His intense, grasping nature is first revealed as Bergman leaves the train car in Italy. Anton's hand, reminiscent of *Nosferatu*, reaches out from the side of the door and grabs her, a clear hint to the careful viewer of what this character has planned for the heroine.

Putting his plan into effect and working methodically and "passionately" to gain the upper hand, unbothered by any guilt or scruples, Anton is able, step by step, to apply more pressure on Paula as the tension in the story rises. As Paula's mind begins to disintegrate, Anton's plan is to have Paula taken away so that he will take full possession of the house, free to search and even enjoy the "graces" of a cheeky young servant he has hired, Nancy. The latter is given instructions "not to bother" her mistress for any reason, unless asked, to keep Paula isolated.

The viewer becomes aware of Anton's plan long before Paula does. The camera captures Anton's reactions, revealing his anxiety that she might guess his game at any moment. For instance, when Paula finds his letter, sent to Alquist two days before she was murdered, he jumps and screams at her. But not to betray his real anxiety, he eases into a smile and expresses his concern that the letter is a sign that she is too worried about the past. He assures her, hypocritically, that he takes steps to protect her. He behaves as a father figure, and the irony, obvious to the viewer, is that he himself causes her to believe that she is mentally ill. The servants, especially Elizabeth, the older maid, do not believe that there is anything wrong with her. Anton becomes paranoid, fearing the nosy old neighbors such as Miss Thwaites, who insists on visiting with her "nephew" who happens to be a suspicious Scotland Yard inspector. When he hears they are downstairs, Anton becomes furious, knowing that just a small detail can ruin his plan, and in a fit of fury he shouts out that he does not want any visitors. To a frightened Paula, who says she would like to see them, he says he didn't know she wanted to see them. "Why didn't you say so?" Of course she did. The viewer is of course on the side of Paula, but also sees Anton's nerves are on edge. Boyer is a master of shaded screen personas, and he can play a villain just as well as a sympathetic character. His Anton is a masterpiece of nuance.

He is himself a victim of his addiction to jewels—"They have a life of their own," he says to Paula at the Tower of London. His behavior would arouse anybody's suspicions, all except Paula's, who fully believes that he goes out at night to work on a new composition. She notices the lowered flame of the gaslight lamps and the noises from the attic, but she believes that she "sees" and "hears" things, supposing that, as her husband tells her, she is ill. In other hands, these scenes would be unbearably melodramatic, but Bergman underplays these mental conditions. She appears fearful and assailed by a paralysis of the will. The film's writers were concerned Bergman's height and size would make the plot less believable, but director George Cukor said, "What's the difference? What if we do have a powerful woman? It will be twice as interesting to see whether she will be able to fight back, whether he will be able to really ruin her, or break her spirit."[3] Paula is not entirely passive, however. After Anton has rudely dismissed the visiting neighbors, she summons up some resolve and dresses to go to Lady Dalroy's party. When the astonished Anton sees her, he says he has already declined the invitation on account of her ill health; she informs him decisively that she will go alone. Immediately he changes his tune and accompanies her to the concert. Cunningly, before they leave, he takes his watch from his vest pocket and slips it into her handbag. When he tells her it is missing during the performance, she breaks down immediately; he apologizes to the hostess and takes her home.

This might be the turning point in the story. Anton has succeeded in convincing his wife that she is ill and crushed her last remnants of resolution. However, it is at this moment that her savior, Brian Cameron, the detective, decides to take action. He has already suspected that something unusual—and mysterious, to use the phrase of his neighbor—is taking place. Anton, too, has noticed during the concert that the man who was sitting behind them has been staring at him. Cameron's intervention comes at the point when Anton has already announced his intention to have two doctors examine Paula, a prelude to his plan to place her in an institution. Cameron enlists the help of Constable Williams, asking him to move his night beat near no. 9 and to attract the attentions of Nancy. Williams brings back the information that Paula is about to go away for a long time. With his help, Cameron tracks Anton's nightly walk (a pretense to his wife that he works at his office) and soon concludes that Anton enters the attic via an empty apartment, no. 5, and enters no. 9 through the roof and searches for the jewels. The climactic scenes unfold quickly. Cameron visits Paula, assured that her husband has left. By this time she is almost insane with fear, but when he produces the white glove of her aunt and she matches it with the one her aunt had cherished, she allows him to produce evidence that her husband was trying to harm her. Soon she finds in Anton's desk the letter signed "Sergis Bauer." Finding this "imaginary" letter causes an intense moment of recognition in Paula as the truth of her husband's malicious plan unravels.

The viewer may notice that *Gaslight* is a film with the basic film noir characteristics. The premise of film noir is that one can fall because of his or her own weaknesses and vulnerabilities. Another characteristic is symbolism, expressed in images of darkness and shadow, requiring careful lighting of each scene essential. Slight movements of the lights and shadows on Paula's face demonstrate her moods, and the gaslight itself, which dims and brightens at critical moments, not only drives her to madness but becomes a visual clue of the heroine's state of mind. Shooting in a typical Victorian home, the filmmakers darken and significantly constrict the space, sometimes claustrophobically, with dark curtains throughout.

Gaslight can also be categorized as film noir, in which atmosphere tends to be gloomy, a villain is lurking behind every corner, and a spiral of evildoing is unfolding. The film is also a bona fide thriller, for the pace and tension increase in every scene. Fully displaying the nuances of a disintegrating mind under the menace of a tyrannical monster, Bergman captivates the viewer, who understands more about the danger she is in, and she delivers a screen performance for the ages.

Most of the film plot is a visual description of this torment. Her outfit for the party, although appropriate to the time period, is more constricted than her previous dresses, and is emblematic of her situation, her physical constraints, and the pressure on her mentally. The dress is stunning, while with a tiny and severely restricted waistline, pearls wrapped like chains across the front, and a long train. Her hair is pulled back, and she wears a tight choker up against her throat. The only part of her outfit that does not suggest constriction are the flowers in her hair. Dressed as she is, psychologically frail, she often moves as if her back does not have the strength to hold her shoulders and head up.

The party scene plays out like a silent film while the pianist plays Chopin. There are significant looks between Cotten and Anton. Anton interrupts

Paula's enjoyment of the pianist with "Paula, my watch is gone" and a significant stare. He presses her further by digging the watch from her purse. She breaks down slowly, although she resists it and finally is led away while she cries into her purse.

After the party, Anton goes out of the house. Paula is left alone. The camera moves to a close-up on a dark lamp in the dining room, tracks to where her shadow from below is on the ceiling, then tracks from the ceiling, backing off to reveal her standing, frozen, looking up at the ceiling. The one lit lamp dims significantly. The film cuts to her face, her eyes looking up. She hears footsteps and then screams. She runs to get Elizabeth, who, being mostly deaf, cannot confirm what is happening. The next night, when Cameron talks himself into the house, the light is bright. He holds the glove, still the little boy admirer. Paula grips the reunited pair of gloves. It is a rare moment of happiness, but then the light dims; she notices but does not comment on the fact. Cameron finally notices the darkness, and she is thrilled that he notices without her having to point it out.

CONCLUSION

The motivator for every character, it seems, is love. As in many of Bergman's films, the motivator is not merely about romantic love, but a transformational love that can change lives. Anton's love is for jewels and is a perversion of a transcendent love; Paula's is for Anton, and it causes her to stay her hand at the end. Cameron's ostensible role is to be a Scotland Yard detective, but he actually rescues her for love—first for his remembered love of Alice Alquist, whom Paula resembles, then protecting her for the same reason, and then for his own affection for her. According to the film's scriptwriter Reisch, in the penultimate scene after Cotten has tied Anton to the chair and left Paula alone with him, Cukor wanted Bergman for a passing moment to be "a goddess of vengeance."[4] Paula regains her balance, begins a romance with Brian, and has Mrs. Thwaites exclaim, "Well!" one final time.

Again, as in many films before and after, a beautiful and rather innocent woman is menaced by a villain but saved by a hero at the end. *Gaslight* succeeds where others do not because it hinges on Bergman's ability to show the psychological torment of the horror of the past lingering on in a house like a gothic novel, and the terror of coming to the conclusion that one may be going insane. But, as Donald Spoto has put it, Ingrid realized that Paula could not be portrayed "as an anemic Gothic-Victorian heroine."

Rather, he says, "Paula . . . would have to infuse the pain of psychological suffering into a woman of established strength who had clear memories of earlier happiness—only then could her plight be more agonizing and her final triumph more resounding."[5] This sums up her fine performance even more than her Oscar win.

7

SPELLBOUND

(1945)

★ ★ ★ ★

Director: Alfred Hitchcock
Screenplay: Ben Hecht; adaptation by Angus MacPhail, based on the novel *The House of Dr. Edwardes* by Francis Beeding (pseudonym of Hilary Saint George Saunders and John Leslie Palmer)
Producer: David O. Selznick. *Music Score:* Miklos Rozsa
Cast: Ingrid Bergman (Dr. Constance Petersen), Gregory Peck (Dr. Anthony Edwardes / John Ballantyne), Leo G. Carroll (Dr. Murchison), Michael Chekhov (Dr. Alexander Brulov), Rhonda Fleming (Mary Carmichael), Norman Lloyd (Garmes), John Emery (Dr. Fleurot)
Studio: David O. Selznick–United Artists
Released: October 31, 1945
Specs: 111 minutes; black and white
Availability: DVD and Blu-ray (MGM)

By 1945, Ingrid Bergman had been directed by Victor Fleming, Michael Curtiz, Sam Wood (twice), and George Cukor and had been paired with Spencer Tracy, Humphrey Bogart, Gary Cooper (twice), and Charles Boyer, some of the screen's top male stars of the era. At that time, she was still under contract to David O. Selznick and so was Alfred Hitchcock, and, as both were available, Selznick arranged to have the two of them work together for the first time. Her collaboration with Hitchcock proved a new and significant step in her career. *Spellbound* was based on a novel by Hilary Saint George Saunders and John Leslie Palmer (both under the pseudonym of Francis Beeding), *The House of Dr. Edwardes*, a story that takes place in a lunatic asylum, replete with psychopaths and other deviant types, a topic highly suited to Hitchcock's tastes. As Freudian psychoanalysis was at its peak at the time, the material at hand offered opportunities for new explorations, and both Hitchcock and Bergman, plus a youthful-looking Gregory Peck (he was younger than Bergman), happily agreed to work together. Ben Hecht was hired to write the scenario for the film, and Hitchcock asked Salvador Dali, the prominent surrealist artist, to design the dream sequences. Bergman was to play a psychoanalyst who takes on the role of a detective to save the man she loves. She had no difficulties accepting Hitchcock as a director and mentor, and their collaboration continued with two more movies: the brilliant *Notorious* (1946) and *Under Capricorn* (1949), the latter made in England and a rare failure for Hitchcock. But director and star became lifelong friends, and it could be argued that their collaboration changed both of their careers. *Spellbound* went on to receive six Oscar nominations: Best Picture; Best Director; Best Supporting Actor;

Constance (Bergman) realizes how dangerously ill John Ballantyne (Peck) is. *United Artists / Photofest © United Artists*

Best Visual Effects; Best Cinematography, Black and White; and winning one, Best Musical Score, by Miklos Rozsa. A favorite of Selznick's, Rozsa, who had scored *Gone with the Wind*, made use of the theremin, an innovating musical instrument that added to the eerie atmosphere of the movie. Bergman did not earn an Oscar nomination, but *Spellbound* expanded her horizons and showcased her ability to respond to challenges beyond the ken of most of her colleagues in the art of cinema.

PLOT

The scene is set at Green Manors in Vermont, a psychiatric hospital, where Dr. Constance Petersen (Bergman) works as a brilliant young psychiatrist amid a group of middle-aged and aging colleagues, one of whom, Dr. Murchison (Leo G. Carroll), is about to retire for health reasons. His replacement is Dr. Anthony Edwardes, who arrives at Green Manors soon after the introductory scenes. Edwardes, embodied by a youthful Gregory Peck, falls in love with his female colleague at first sight, and she falls for him. Edwardes becomes visibly ill when he looks at the tablecloth design of parallel lines, and a few hours later he collapses while performing surgery. Dr. Petersen visits him in his quarters at night and tries to help him by asking him to remember who he is, as she believes he is suffering from amnesia and a guilt complex. When she asks for him in the morning, she hears from the police and Dr. Murchison that he has left the institution during the night. Unbeknownst to them, he has left a letter for her, and, using that, she travels to New York, where she tracks him down at the Empire State Hotel. Together they visit Dr. Alexander (Alex) Brulov (Michael Chekhov), her former teacher and mentor, pretending they are newlyweds. He guesses that Edwardes is ill when he sees him at night descending the stairs with a razor blade in his hand, looking menacing. Brulov insists that the man is irreparably ill and dangerous and that he must be reported to the police. But Constance insists the man can be cured if she and Brulov can unravel the mystery of his past, especially his childhood, and see if some childhood trauma accounted for the loss of his memory and identity. Seeing that she is passionately in love with him, Brulov gives her only a few days to come up with a solution before he reports to the police. Both he and Constance try to help the patient by interpreting the dream he had during the night. Calmly at first, he recollects a series of images—eyes, scissors, playing cards, a masked man, wings, a man slipping from a roof, a man dropping a wheel. But after he has another fit seeing parallel lines left on the snow by a ski, Constance takes him skiing, and as they ski toward a precipice he suddenly recalls the scene where he accidentally killed his young brother, and he is cured of his amnesia. She learns his real name is John Ballantyne, that he had been injured in a plane crash and that he had been treated by Dr. Edwardes at that ski resort. But the police arrest him for the murder of Edwardes, the man he had been incorporating, who was found dead in that location, a bullet in his back. She soon guesses that the real killer is Murchison, and when she confronts him, he pulls a gun on her—the same gun from which the bullet came that killed Dr. Edwardes. As Murchison threatens to kill her, she calmly walks away. He is seen turning the gun on himself, and as she closes the door behind her, we hear a shot, indicating that he killed himself.

THEMES

The film combines several themes: love, amnesia, loss of identity, and a guilt complex; Freudian psychoanalysis is applied by an analyst to uncover a murder and prove the innocence of a wronged man—a theme that runs through the Hitchcock repertory consistently. Love in the film happens on several levels. A psychiatrist (Bergman) tries to help a patient who is also her lover, and, as she believes, an innocent man. The film is a psychodrama, in which a Freudian analysis is applied, but also a whodunit thriller. In the end, it is the love story that gives the story its form and dynamics. Bergman combines the roles of analyst and detective admirably, but it is her love for her patient that motivates her to resolve a case involving an amnesiac and guilt-ridden man.

In *Spellbound*, Ingrid Bergman's character, Constance Petersen, falls in love instantly with the newcomer as she looks at his face, and so does he looking at hers. It is "love at first sight" in its fullest sense (commentator Thomas Schatz compares it to Michael Corleone's instant love for Apollonia in *The Godfather*),[1] something difficult to capture on camera as adeptly as Hitchcock does here. Masterly close-ups leave the audience in no doubt as to the electric moment of this love affair that begins at first sight.

Within hours, Constance also discovers that Edwardes is ill. He has lost his identity; he is an amnesiac, and he is running away from some peril. She is in love, and she is a psychiatrist; she decides to help him to unravel the mystery of his illness and possibly free him from his guilt and recover his true identity. She has to overcome the bias of her older colleagues—and, as it seems, the malice and cunning of the real culprit. As he is hunted by the authorities and escapes in order not to implicate her, her position becomes more precarious when she follows him to his hotel, leaving a trail of suspicion behind. The critical point of the love story comes when they both, now fugitives, arrive at her mentor's, Dr. Alex Brulov's, where the patient becomes dangerous and nearly homicidal. There, the love of Constance for JB (John Ballantyne, the patient's real name) is so deep-rooted that, against her mentor's advice, she decides to go through with her plan to cure him by unlocking his lost memories of childhood. In other words, the psychiatrist/ lover becomes a detective who does not at first seek physical proof—that will come later—but analysis. The patient must reach down and uncover the causes of his troubled state, in this case a childhood trauma: Ballantyne had witnessed the death of his young brother in a sled game during which the young boy had been impaled on the spikes on a fence at their home.

SPELLBOUND BY FREUD

The film is fraught with Freudian terms, such as guilt complex, amnesia, interpretation of dreams, and it was packed with Freudian symbolism. Peter Ackroyd, Hitchcock's biographer, states, "Psychoanalysis was the fashion of the age in the United States" at the time, "for those who could afford it."[2] As both Selznick and Ben Hecht were then undergoing analysis, they supported the Freudian ideas of turning *The House of Dr. Edwardes* into a psychological thriller. Hitchcock was in favor of the project, and he and Hecht visited mental asylums and psychiatric wards to get firsthand information about patient treatment.[3] Selznick's own analyst, May Romm, MD, went over the script to clean up mistakes in the use of correct terms before filming began.[4] Hitchcock was intrigued by the prospect of doing a film on psychoanalysis, but in the end he considered this *his* movie, and so, armed with the panoply of Freudian ideas, he made them work for his ends: to produce a movie about a wronged man who was also ill, yet saved by the woman he loves. Hitchcock knew how to explore tensions by creating anxiety in the audience at every plot twist, and in *Spellbound* this anxiety is not relieved until the last shot of the film.

A guilt complex is the result of an action in childhood that is too painful for the child to bear, causing amnesia and unbearable guilt that haunts the adult, making him ill, even schizophrenic and dangerous. A psychiatrist can try to help the patient recollect the act that caused the guilt. In this case, what incapacitated Ballantyne was the geometric shape of two parallel lines that made him swoon, followed by a spasm of agony or collapse, as it happened while he was about to perform an operation on a patient. The parallel lines continue to haunt him until they are finally explained by Dr. Petersen, who will not rest until the mystery of his ailment is solved. Part of the trouble, she discovers, is Ballantyne's amnesia, which is a means of shielding a horrible act that occurred in the past, in this case the death of the younger brother of John Ballantyne. Consciously, with the help of the analyst, the patient tries to remember, but the truth resists surfacing, prevented by guilt. Amnesia shields the guilt feelings of the patient, who in this case believes that he is the murderer of the real Edwardes.

The dream sequences are meant to reveal an intricate symbolic pattern that the patient and his analyst want to understand. Only a correct interpretation of the dream can reveal the truth, according to the prevailing Freudian theories at the time. Thus the function of the analyst is to find out what the dream symbols represent and where they lead. Once Ballantyne recovers from his nightmarish night, Dr. Brulov and Constance ask him to remember his dream. It is to be noted here that the dream sequences were designed by Salvador Dali, but in the final cut only about five minutes survived of the twenty-minute original sequence. Even so, these Dali images are crucial for the resolution of the psychic anomaly that ailed Ballantyne. He is first shown sitting on a chair, not a couch, so his facial expressions are fully visible to the viewer. Brulov listens, while the bespectacled Constance takes notes. Ballantyne remembers his dream: He is in a gambling house, where the curtains are adorned with large eyes, with emphasis on precision that marks Dali's art. Someone with a pair of scissors is cutting the curtains; a girl wearing a dress cut to ribbons (Rhonda Fleming is playing that part) kisses one of the men; Ballantyne deals cards to a man with a beard, three sevens of hearts, and the bearded man wins a game of twenty-one. A masked man turns over the cards; they are blanks. A man on a slanting roof falls into a chasm. The masked man stands on the roof and tosses down a distorted wheel. The shadow of a huge bird with wings chases him.

Brulov identifies Constance as the flying bird: an angel trying to save her fleeing lover. That triggers a reaction from Ballantyne, who first mutters, "Angel Valley," soon correcting the name to Gabriel Valley, a ski resort. That is where he had gone on a skiing trip with the real Dr. Edwardes, who was helping him to recover from a war wound he received when his plane crashed. Despite his resistance, Constance insists on taking him on a trip to Gabriel Valley where they both ski downhill. The moment they are about to fall into a chasm, he holds her back. His memory returns, as he tells her that when he was a child and playing with his brother, he accidentally had hit him from behind on a roof covered with snow and the young boy fell on a spiked fence and was killed. This traumatic experience had blocked his memory and caused his guilt.

But the two lovers do not have time to celebrate. Police arrive and arrest Ballantyne, charging him for the murder of Dr. Edwardes, as a bullet was found in his back. With her lover now in jail, Constance insists on his innocence but takes Brulov's advice to stop her effort to cure Ballantyne, resigned there is nothing she can do, when unexpected help arrives from the murderer himself. Chatting with Dr. Murchison, as he welcomes her back to her position at the Manors, she hears him say that he knew Dr. Edwardes, though slightly. She stops, muttering, "Knew . . . knew," gradually tracking a path. Murchison had said earlier that he had not personally met the doctor who was coming to succeed him. She goes into his office and confronts Murchison. He told her he had guessed that she had noticed his blunder mentioning he knew Edwardes and that her "young agile mind" would guess the rest. *The symbols in the dream now come back to her.* She explains that he, Murchison, was the man with the stocking hiding his head in the dream. She now tells him that the twenty-one of clubs that Ballantyne had been dealing Edwardes represented Club 21, in New York, where Murchison had met Edwardes and threatened to kill him, knowing that the latter would replace him at Green Manors. There was an argument, which waiters would remember, and also at Gabriel Valley, where Edwardes was going for a ski vacation, where Ballantyne was also there recovering from his war wound. He had seen the ski tracks down the valley where Edwardes was shot to death under a tree. When Murchison asks what the wheel in the dream represents, Constance adds that that was pistol he used to kill Edwardes; the fingerprints were on it. At this point, Murchison pulls the pistol out of his drawer and points it at Constance, saying that she is a brilliant analyst but "a very stupid woman." Ironically, he echoes Dr. Brulov, who had also remarked that a woman cannot be a good analyst if she falls in love—implying that a woman involved in an affair cannot think clearly. Constance proves them both wrong. Not only did she see clearly and had unraveled a complicated psychological mystery and found a murderer, but also she stays cool when Murchison threatens to kill her, telling him that his first murder could have extenuating circumstances, as he could plead mental illness; he would not avoid the electric chair if he committed a second, a deliberate murder. As she walks out of the door, in an astounding point-of-view shot, the gun that Murchison is holding turns 180 degrees, and it is heard firing—the shot splashing in red color across the screen.

CONCLUSION

Despite the Freudian jargon used in the film, which a critic called "sopho-moric,"[5] the plot works, for good reasons. The Salvador Dali sequences, though truncated, were so compelling in clear design and symbolism that they energized the audience's curiosity, adding to the anxiety about a persecuted man's plight. The dream sequences as they appear, with cuts in Ballantyne's recollections so Constance and Brulov could make comments or take notes, seemed too neatly dovetailed to fit the plot twists. Ballantyne's memory seems to have been adjusted by the screenwriter to fit the dream exactly as needed to resolve Constance's questions. Though this neat fitting of the dream sequences to action might defy logic, it works dramatically. This is owed in large part to Bergman's performance. She proves a woman undaunted by the resistance of her mentor Dr. Brulov—not to mention the police persecution—a woman whose brilliance does not desert her nor is her judgment beclouded by the fact that she is in love with a patient—a no-no in Freudian terms (such a relationship is called "countertransference").

An important point that needs to be added here is that most of the hero-ines Bergman had embodied so far were women dominated by men: In *Casablanca*, Ilsa Lund's only options are to choose between Victor Laszlo and Rick Blaine, and in the end the choice is made for her by one of the two men. In *Dr. Jekyll and Mr. Hyde*, Ivy Peterson, a playful barmaid, is the victim of a vicious monster over whom she has no control. And in *Gaslight*, Paula Alquist is nearly driven mad by a scheming con artist who is after her aunt's jewelry. In *Spellbound*, Bergman's Constance Petersen dominates the scene; her lover is not a hero but a man weakened by illness and victimized by a conniver. She takes over the role of doctor, lover, and detective with admirable adeptness that reverses her film image from a woman dominated or tyrannized by men to a woman who leads. As if luck had it, Hitchcock was the master filmmaker whose deft arrangement of the dramatic sequences baited audiences to want to know who the culprit really is, or what happens to the lovers. The multitalented Bergman seemed to be one of the few women of the silver screen at that time that could make this improbability of the plot work. Of course, Gregory Peck had his own charisma to begin with, not to mention the talented group of secondary characters. No nominations came her way, but Bergman came through as the heroine who dominates the screen from start to finish.

8

THE BELLS OF ST. MARY'S

(1945)

★ ★ ★

Director: Leo McCarey
Screenplay: Dudley Nichols, based on a story by Leo McCarey
Producer: Leo McCarey. *Cinematography:* George Barnes. *Music Score:* Robert
    Emmett Dolan
Cast: Bing Crosby (Father Chuck O'Malley), Ingrid Bergman (Sister Mary
    Benedict), Henry Travers (Horace P. Bogardus), Una O'Connor (Mrs.
    Breen)
Studio: RKO Radio
Released: December 6, 1945
Specs: 126 minutes; black and white
Availability: DVD and Blu-ray (Olive Films)

The evening of the Oscars in 1945 was a big night for Leo McCarey, the writer, producer, and director of *Going My Way*. He won an Oscar for Best Director; his star, Bing Crosby, won Best Actor; and his choice for the leading female for the sequel, *The Bells of St. Mary's*, was Ingrid Bergman, who was honored for winning Best Actress for her work in *Gaslight*. When Bergman addressed the audience, she said, "I'm glad I won, because tomorrow morning, I start shooting the sequel to *Going My Way* with Bing Crosby and Leo McCarey, and I was afraid that if I didn't have an Oscar, they wouldn't speak to me."[1]

McCarey's hard work to sign Bergman to the sequel was paying off. David O. Selznick had been against loaning out Bergman for the role of a nun, Sister Benedict, fearing that this role would harm her career. She was a star now, he argued, and he had worked very hard to elevate her to her current status. After the enthusiastic reception of *Gaslight*, he feared that McCarey's movie, a sequel, would be doomed to failure. But McCarey persisted, offering Selznick all he asked in loan money and RKO properties, and Selznick finally gave in. *The Bells of St. Mary's* turned out another big hit, cementing Bergman's career and enchanting audiences with her grace, good cheer, and yes, a bit of comedic bent not expected in movies where piety is the norm. Rumor had it that many mothers in America bemoaned the fact that their daughters expressed the wish to become nuns, Sister Benedict having become their role model.

Bergman had a great enthusiasm for playing the role of a nun. Her instincts as an artist were unfailing, and she thought—and so did McCarey—that she could humanize the usually stilted images of nuns in movies and fictions: angelic figures, praying and holding rosaries for most of their

Father O'Malley (Crosby) informs Sister Benedict (Bergman) that she is not being dismissed but sent away on account of her health. *RKO Radio Pictures, Inc. / Photofest © RKO Radio Pictures, Inc.*

days. By contrast, the film would show Bergman as Sister Benedict as a living person working hard to educate the handful of students at St. Mary's, a financially strained institution, with empathy and affection, caring for students, teaching them schoolwork but also games with fun and laughter.

PLOT

As a sequel to the popular *Going My Way*, *The Bells of St. Mary's* follows the structure of the first: A youthful priest, Father O'Malley, is on a secret mission from the bishop to close a broken-down facility with money problems. The priest is progressive, relaxed, seemingly negligent, believing that attitude somehow wins the day. Once he passes the hostile woman at the gate, he challenges the authority of the facility, and in the meantime he must help a troubled young woman. In *Going My Way*, he must convince Father Fitzgibbon to leave the church he built more than forty-five years ago so he can close it down. In *The Bells of St. Mary's*, he must convince Sister Benedict to sell the church school to a businessman who wants to raze it and use the land for a parking lot. In both films, Father O'Malley fails in his mission but rejuvenates each of his challenges.

Because *Going My Way* and *The Bells of St. Mary's* are the same schematically, the most important update needed in the sequel was for Father O'Malley to have a new, more difficult challenge. Instead of an old priest stuck in old ways as a foil, he faces not the difficult woman the housekeeper predicts but a young, vital nun with a life lived out in the real world, outside the nunnery, not unlike O'Malley himself. Like him, she brings enthusiasm and humor to her work.

Father O'Malley passes by the church and walks to the school. It's clear that the school is run down, worn, and its shrubbery overgrown. He is a jaunty man with a musical rhythm when he walks and wears a straw boater hat and seems out of place at that school and in a clerical cassock. Father O'Malley is sent to close to the school, sell the property to Horace P. Bogardus (Henry Travers)—a wealthy businessman who is building an office building next door—and move the children to another school. From the first moments of the film, it is clear that he is not up to the task.

The housekeeper, Mrs. Breen (Una O'Connor), welcomes Father O'Malley to the school by calling him a "poor man." She says the previous priest, Father Fogarty, was taken, mumbling in his wheelchair, to "Shady Acres." The housekeeper describes Sister Benedict, the mother superior, as a termagant. She blames her for the former priest's early exit and his illness.

Sister Benedict, she says, not only drove out the previous priest but caused him physical and mental harm. The housekeeper is actually afraid for the new priest's health.

In spite of her warnings, O'Malley visits the nuns, and, jaunty man he is, leans nonchalantly against the doorway, not realizing that the annoying alarm is sounding because he's pressing against the button used to call children to class. He is escorted to a meeting room where he stands as each nun enters, each arriving so that he sits and needs to stand again immediately, nun calisthenics. Finally, after all seem to have arrived, they all stand when Sister Benedict enters from behind Father O'Malley, who believes they stand for him. After they've all arrived, he speaks to them, and doesn't realize the reason they laugh at his talk is that a cat is playing with his hat on a shelf behind him.

His first act as the new head of the school is to give the students the day off. Sister Benedict is concerned that it was unplanned. His defense to Sister Benedict was that his school was in the country and "when I was a kid I would live for holidays. . . . We shouldn't get too far from childhood." When the children leave, they play on Bogardus's construction site, previously the playground, which Sister Benedict and the sisters sold to Mr. Bogardus so they could pay for repairs to the building, including the fire escape and roof. They pray that he will donate the new building to them. Sister Benedict says, "If faith could move mountains . . ." to which O'Malley responds, "You figured you could move in." O'Malley speaks to Bogardus, who, as the chair of the city council, threatens that he will have the school torn down if it is not sold to him so he can use the space as a parking lot.

THEMES

The story is enlivened by Sister Benedict's sense of humor, which adds to the comedic bent of crooner Crosby and keeps the action from being tearful and melodramatic. Bergman, known for her serious or even tragic heroines, joins in the tomfoolery with abandon, keeping the tone light until the last part of the story, which turns serious. She is aided by the presence of a few minor characters; one is a little girl who decides to fail in order to stay at the school rather than join her mother and father who are separated and about to be reunited, thanks to the reconciliation efforts of Father O'Malley. The father, by the way, is a musician, who plays the piano, so there is another obligatory song by Crosby, just so the audience is rewarded for waiting to hear their favorite crooner's soothing tune from the obliging and charismatic priest. When the little girl falls behind in her studies, Sister Benedict questions her but receives no answers. Using her method of reading a face by "painting" it, the sister seems to understand and even know all that the child is thinking, but not saying, just by looking at it. Later, she challenges O'Malley's own lack of transparency by saying, "Did anyone ever tell you that you have a dishonest face . . . for a priest?"

Bergman shows she possesses a sense of humor and more than a little of the talent of a comedian. As a child, Benedict played sports with the boys. After a couple of boys fight, Sister Benedict is upset, but O'Malley says, "On the outside it's a man's world." She takes seriously O'Malley's suggestion that she might be taking her womanly influence too far, so she visits a sporting goods store to buy a book on the "manly arts of self-defense." As she reads about boxing, O'Malley reads Latin. In a scene with one of her young students, who always lost boxing matches to a bully, she teaches him to duck and deliver a blow with a right, and, in spite of her excellent footwork, she receives a good punch to the chin that makes her sit down to recover. She exclaims, "I ran right into the payoff." Her student subsequently won a match, and his self-esteem was bolstered.

But Sister Benedict is to exchange more than punches with the recently arrived Father O'Malley, who has more traditional ways of educating than the innovative and fun-loving nun. Crosby plays his role perfectly, showing that he too cares for students, as demonstrated when he manages to reconcile the young female student with her estranged parents. There is a certain friendly antagonism between the lively nun and the sympathizing priest, to the tune of a mild-mannered romance that one could call a platonic relationship, given his attractive nature and her beauty, though her body and head were covered except her sensuous face, still capable of "launching," or tempting, a thousand priests.[2] Being Crosby, he croons of course, and to synchronize, she also sings a Swedish song—all about love, though when she is asked what it is about, she answers that it is about "spring." Here she has a chance to reveal that she is Swedish, thence her endearing Swedish accent fits in naturally.

The Bells of St. Mary's is often considered to be a Christmas film. Over O'Malley's time at the school, they prepare for Christmas. O'Malley teaches the children a Christmas song and playfully shakes the hand of a boy who is no longer singing flat. He's horrified to hear from Benedict that there's no room for Christmas music in a Christmas pageant being put on by first graders. Instead of a traditional song, the children sing "Happy Birthday" to the baby Jesus.

In the gift-giving season, the curmudgeonly Bogardus is persuaded by the sweet-talking nun to donate the building to the school. But Sister Benedict does it accidently, believing that O'Malley had already convinced Bogardus to donate it, and she is effusive in her joy and thanks. Seeing her reaction before he has made the commitment, he relents, and, believing he only has a few months to live, is now convinced that giving is good for his heart. The school is saved from financial failure, and all ends touchingly. There are no miracles, at least none of a supernatural kind, and yet the solution appears miraculous and plenty down to earth.

CONCLUSION

This is a story that cannot have a happy ending, at least not when two attractive stars meet, but it can have a bittersweet one. Sister Benedict is diagnosed with the early stages of tuberculosis and has to be told that, for the sake of her health, she must enter a sanatorium. But since Father O'Malley and the others know she would not go voluntarily, she is told she is being transferred. Sister Benedict, who thinks she is being removed because of incompetence, is truly hurt, but at the very end, when they are about to part, Father O'Malley tells her the truth, and immediately her face beams, because she knows that she is not being dismissed. This is a touching moment, which Bergman plays with distinction. She underplays her considerable gifts, both as an actress and character, and she fits well into the story. Selznick was astonished that the failure he predicted was rewarded by a simple but wholehearted performance by Bergman and all those around her. As for Leo McCarey, he killed two birds with one stone. As the Oscars poured in for his *Going My Way*, audiences, along with Selznick, were assured that a sequel was worth the try.

NOTORIOUS

(1946)

★ ★ ★ ★ ★

Director: Alfred Hitchcock
Screenwriter: Ben Hecht
Producer: Alfred Hitchcock. *Cinematographer:* Ted Tetzlaff. *Music Score:* Roy
    Webb
Cast: Cary Grant (T. R. Devlin), Ingrid Bergman (Alicia Huberman), Claude
    Rains (Alex Sebastian), Leopoldine Konstantin (Madame Sebastian),
    Louis Calhern (Paul Prescott), Alex Minotis (Joseph), Reinhold
    Schunzel (Dr. Anderson), Moroni Olsen (Walter Beardsley), Ivan
    Triesault (Eric Mathis), Wally Brown (Mr. Hopkins), Ricardo Costa
    (Dr. Barbosa)
Studio: RKO Radio Pictures
Released: August 15, 1946
Specs: 101 minutes; black and white
Availability: DVD, Blu-ray (Criterion Collection)

Notorious was Ingrid Bergman's last film with David O. Selznick, ending
her prolific five-year contract with him, which had netted her two Oscar
nominations and one win and catapulted her to fame and superstardom.
When negotiations for *Notorious* started, Bergman's husband, Petter Lindstrom, who was acting as her attorney, resisted the project, feeling that
Selznick had taken advantage of his wife by pocketing large profits from his

loan-outs to her financial detriment. Selznick ignored the complaint and sold the rights to RKO for a neat $800,000, plus 50 percent of the profits. As the movie grossed more than $4 million nationwide (plus larger profits in its international release), there was plenty to go around, with Selznick, as always, picking up the lion's share. The success of *Notorious* was owed in large part (if not entirely) to Alfred Hitchcock, the producer and director of the film, also under contract to Selznick. Hitchcock obtained the services of Ben Hecht, who had worked with him on *Spellbound*, and the scenario of *Notorious* soon took shape. It was based on a short story, "The Song of the Dragon," by John Taintor Foote, published in the *Saturday Evening Post* in 1921, with David O. Selznick having acquired the rights in 1941. The story, which featured federal agents recruiting a beautiful actress to infiltrate a ring of fifth columnists conspiring to destroy military targets throughout the country, appealed to Hitchcock, who used it as the basis for his film. Bergman's costar was Cary Grant, whom Hitchcock preferred over Selznick's choice of Joseph Cotten. Claude Rains was selected as the Nazi leader Bergman was to spy on, using her charms to elicit secrets from a

At the party, a jealous Alex Sebastian (Rains) suspects the goings-on between Alicia (Bergman) and Devlin (Grant). *RKO Radio Pictures, Inc. / Photofest © RKO Radio Pictures, Inc.*

cabal of postwar Nazis who operated in Brazil to construct an atomic bomb. With such attractive superstars, an equally intense love story develops, and, under the masterful guidance of Hitchcock, Bergman delivered one of the most haunting performances as a woman who risked her life to serve her country.

PLOT

Alicia Huberman is seen exiting her father's trial in Miami, Florida, ignoring the numerous photographers crowding around her. She has the reputation of a "party girl," aside from being "notorious" as the daughter of a Nazi who was just found guilty of treason. She is soon seen holding a glass among dancing couples at her apartment, while a figure of a man photographed from behind in shadow follows her movements. As the partying peters out, the man in the shadow stays, as if to try to outdrink his hostess. He follows Alicia, who wants to go for a "picnic," a drive during which she exceeds the speed limit, just to make him "wipe the smile off his face." When a cop stops her, the man produces a license, after which the cop salutes him and lets them go. Alicia is enraged, calling Devlin a "copper," and demands that he leave her at once. In the ensuing struggle between them, Devlin subdues her with a karate chop, it would seem, as this happens out of sight of the viewer. Back at Alicia's apartment, Devlin has prepared a glass with fizzing aspirin for her, as she awakens to see his image above her upside down in a subjective shot familiar in Hitchcock's work. Devlin explains that he has a "job" for her, appealing to her "patriotism" by playing a phonograph recording in which she disapproves of her father's Nazi activities. Alicia goes along with his plan, despite her initial dislike of him.

Together they fly to Rio de Janeiro, Brazil, where she is told that she must penetrate a network of Nazis who have regrouped in that part of the world, hiding under the name of I. G. Aspen Enterprises, which seeks to accumulate uranium and build an atomic bomb. When they arrive in Rio, Devlin's boss, Paul Prescott (Louis Calhern), informs him that one of Alicia's former admirers, Alex Sebastian (Claude Rains), now with the Nazi group, must be approached by Alicia, and she must "land him." Alicia accepts the assignment and becomes friendly with Sebastian, to the great chagrin of Devlin, whose jealously beclouds his judgment of her. Soon Alicia becomes Sebastian's wife and proves an able informer when she and Devlin discover that Sebastian's wine cellar contains numerous bottles full of uranium ore. But Sebastian catches them in the act and soon discovers she is a spy. He and his mother plan the poisoning of Alicia as his only means of not giving the secret of who she is to the Nazis, and soon Alicia is ill and near death. Devlin suspects the truth, arrives at Sebastian's home, and just in time saves Alicia, while Sebastian is left to Nazi retribution.

THEMES

Notorious is rich in themes, which for the sake of brevity can be divided in two categories: (a) the themes related to the love story, and (b) those related to the spy thriller and Hitchcock's techniques and methods.

Generally speaking, Hitchcock did not make films that were entirely romantic. Romance may be an essential part of almost any movie of his— *Suspicion, Spellbound, To Catch a Thief, Rear Window, Vertigo,* among others—but these love stories are embedded in the larger boundaries of the suspense thriller. *Notorious* has a tight plot thanks to Ben Hecht, one of Hollywood's most prolific screenwriters, who wrote several of the Hitchcock films and was always in tune with the master. The story features an alluring protagonist caught in harm's way, fascinating and attention-grabbing villains, and cinematic wizardry, unique to Hitchcock's canon. Romantic love built into a spy thriller is an example of two themes closely entwined, point and counterpoint, like a Bach cantata. Some commentators, including the former host of Turner Classic Movies, Robert Osborne, and Rudy Behlmer, in his Criterion Collection commentary (2001),[1] have described *Notorious* as one of the greatest love stories of all time.

Notorious has also been criticized as an example of blatant exploitation by government agents willing to allow a woman to go into harm's way by using sexual favors. Bergman's biographer, Donald Spoto, comments about female exploitation by government agents:

> It is also astonishing that the movie was produced at all (and that it was such an immediate success), since it contains such a blunt dialogue about government-sponsored prostitution: the sexual blackmail is the idea of American intelligence agents, who are blithely willing to exploit a woman (and even let her die) to serve their own ends. The depiction of the moral murkiness of American officials was unprecedented in Hollywood—especially in 1945, when the allied victory ushered in an era of understandable but ultimate dangerous chauvinism in American life.[2]

The criticism is fair enough, but also "understandable," as Spoto points out, given the postwar conditions after the defeat of Germany, and the fear of Nazis reemerging at some other part of the world trying to build an atomic bomb. Alicia seems to be fully cognizant of that danger, even before she knew what her particular assignment could be. She flies to Rio with Devlin consensually and initially seems happy, staying away from drink and dallying with Devlin. When Devlin hears from his boss, Paul Prescott, that she has to make contact with Alex Sebastian, a prominent Nazi, and use her sexual powers to coax secrets out of him, Alicia mutters, "Mata Hari"—the name of a notorious courtesan who had been executed as a double agent by the French in 1917, accused of spying for the Germans. The idea evoked is that a government would (or even should) exploit the sexual assets of a woman agent to learn war secrets. Thus, as Spoto points out in the above quotation, "government-sponsored prostitution" comes into play.

Devlin tries to avert her mission, weakly telling Prescott that she "wasn't trained for that kind of job," but Prescott scoffs at him, and Alicia agrees to meet Sebastian. She plays coy with him, telling him, "What a brat I was," pretending that she is now ready to accept his advances. She attends a dinner at Sebastian's home, saying little and keeping her eyes and ears open, as she had been instructed by Prescott, and reports to Devlin on a weekly basis. Embittered and jealous, Devlin meets her at the races, but a jealous Sebastian notices her chatting intimately with Devlin during the horse races. Soon after that, she visits Prescott and tells him that Sebastian has asked her to marry him. "Are you prepared to go that far for us?" an amazed Prescott asks. She says she is, and shortly she is married to Sebastian. Devlin only mutters, "It's a useful idea," shocked to the core that she would do that.

Two points emerge from the above description: One is that Alicia was a patriot, and she went to Rio to prove that she could be a different woman, useful to the Allied cause. The second is that she could have refused to marry Sebastian. Even Prescott is surprised at her willingness to go that far; he seems not altogether devoid of feelings, and he could be accommo-dating if she had refused to marry Sebastian, embarking on an adventure that almost cost her life. Part of the above suggests that Alicia went along with the agents' scheme out of true desire to shed the image of notoriety that had been haunting her. She wanted to prove that she was worthy of such a mission. It is also worth mentioning that Bergman's Alicia shows bravery on her own, acts in accordance to what she had accepted to do and behaves as a heroine who takes self-humiliating steps to serve her country. That of course does not excuse Devlin's callousness, caused by his envy of his opponent, "fear of women," as he himself says, and his unwillingness to see her point or commend her for what she is doing. By contrast, Prescott commends her by stating that "the whole thing has been handled with great intelligence." These developments compound the ironies of the plot, as Alicia has to cope with the jealousy of two men, one being a pawn of his mother, the other pushing a woman to do what he himself loathes.

Another theme crucial to the complexity of the plot is Sebastian's domineering mother, Madame Sebastian, played by the distinguished European actress Leopoldine Konstantin (in her only role in America). This is the first of several subsequent Hitchcock movies where the Oedipal complex[3] becomes crucial to the plot. (Others include *Strangers on a Train, Psycho, The Birds, Marnie*.) Claude Rains, a distinguished actor in several movies in Hollywood, plays Alex Sebastian with admirable empathy for his character, almost compelling the viewer to feel sorry for him. He loves Alicia with almost a teenager's passion (he says so himself), courts her arduously, but he is not quite convinced that she loves him, seeing her converse with Devlin frequently. When he decides to propose and hurries to proceed with the marriage immediately, he stumbles upon his mother's stubborn resistance. He asserts himself against his mother and marries Alicia, and then like a penitent boy comes back to his mother to say he has erred and begs for help. There she devises the diabolical scheme to poison Alicia slowly, so nobody will suspect his blunder. "You are protected by the enormity of your stupidity," she says, callously demolishing her son's manhood with one telling blow. Of course, the son becomes the pawn of his mother from that point on. He is trapped by circumstance, love, and his mother's malice. Any sympathy for him is eradicated when we see him feigning indifference while Alicia is drinking her poisoned coffee. He becomes almost tragic when Devlin presses the button of his car, driving away with Alicia and leaving Sebastian to face his murderous colleagues.

Hitchcock's Cinematic Tricks: The MacGuffin at Work

As said earlier, the romance blends smoothly with the thriller, and that might be a fair assessment of the movie's action. Yet, the thriller aspect becomes the dominant part of the story, containing some of Hitchcock's most famous tricks—the MacGuffins, for example, and several scenes of what he has called "pure cinema." Let us explain.

As the plot spins into its complications, it is Hitchcock's techniques and methods that enhance its effectiveness. One of these is the MacGuffin, a term that he invented, much talked about in Hitchcock's critical commentary. Asked what this term meant, Hitchcock told a story: Two men travel on a railway, and one of them has a suitcase on the baggage rack;

asked by the other what this is, he replies that it is a MacGuffin. Puzzled, the other asks, "What is a MacGuffin?" The first man says it is "a device to capture lions in Scotland." "But there are no lions in Scotland," the other man counters. "Then it is not a MacGuffin," the first man replies. With this Pythic utterance Hitchcock implies that an object exists only if it is found in a larger context. The plot in a movie is the larger context. Then an object circulating visually within the plot becomes a signal for meanings, but also a device for advancing the plot.

Here, the most prominent object obtruding upon the viewer's attention fairly early is a bottle. A bottle of champagne is bought by Devlin when he is called to his boss's office, while Alicia has remained behind at the apartment to prepare a meal. He is to celebrate their love union with her, and the wine was intended for that. The bottle, however, is forgotten at Prescott's office when Devlin, agitated by learning that Alicia must become Sebastian's lover, leaves it there. A reaction shot, following Prescott's eyes, shows the bottle on his desk—and the viewer follows his logic—and his suspicion that this may not be an easy, or proper, relationship between agents, for that would endanger their mission.

Later, as Alicia is introduced to Sebastian's colleagues during a first dinner, one of them, Emile Hupka, points to one in a row of bottles on a wine cabinet, in a way that is highly noticeable, and of course Alicia observes the scene and reports it. The other Nazis get nervous fearing he has given away an important secret, and they soon get rid of him. Alicia, however, reports this incident to Devlin, who now knows that he must look for bottles in Sebastian's wine cellar to find out what they contain.

Here another MacGuffin is introduced, for Hitchcock never said that a plot must contain only one. There, the two MacGuffins intermingle and both advance the plot. This second MacGuffin is the key that Alicia must obtain from her husband's chain and pass on to Devlin, who would use it to get to the wine cellar. Alicia asks Sebastian for the keys for the closets near her bedroom, and Sebastian obliges, though this causes a scuffle with his suspicious mother, and Alicia is able to get access to several closets except one. "That is the wine cellar, Madame," says an obliging butler, Joseph (Alex Minotis). "Mr. Sebastian has that one." (The name on the door lock says *UNICA*, "the only one" in Spanish.) In their next meeting, Devlin tells Alicia she must get that key. "Get it, how?" she asks. "Don't you live near him?" Devlin responds with heavy sarcasm. Subsequently, he tells Alicia to ask Sebastian to throw "a large shindig," to introduce his beautiful wife to the Brazilian society. Here is a perfect example of two MacGuffins intertwining. Devlin *must* have the key to the wine cellar to find out what the mysterious bottles contain.

What follows is perhaps one of the most suspenseful moments in cinema. First the key: Alicia is seen taking the UNICA key from her husband's chain while he is dressing in the next room. As he enters, he grabs both her hands and kisses her right one; when he's about to kiss the other, which holds the key, she embraces him, drops it on the floor, and kicks it with her foot under Alex's dressing table. Next, in a wide-angle crane shot, the viewer is treated to camera zooming from a height (Hitchcock had to knock off the roof of the set to obtain it), first showing the party gathering under, and slowly focusing on Alicia's hand that holds the key. As she sees Devlin coming in, she goes over to greet him and, as he kisses her hand, she passes on the key to him.

In the following sequence the two MacGuffins cross, as, now with the key, Devlin and Alicia manage to slip down to the wine cellar where Devlin examines rows of bottles that stand up instead of lying horizontally next to each (poetic license is presumed). As he peers through the labels, one of the bottles falls on the floor and breaks, spreading a black metallic dust. He carefully gathers some in an envelope he carries with him while Alicia helps him as she can.

As they exit the cellar Alex is seen coming down the stairs with Joseph. Devlin embraces and kisses Alicia with real passion, and she swoons in his arms, whispering, "Oh, Dev, Dev . . . ," showing her suppressed feelings were held in check. Devlin explains to a stunned Alex, "I saw her before you, loved her before you, but I wasn't as lucky as you," betting that it was a lover's pleading that had brought him down there. But later in the action, Sebastian notices that the UNICA key is missing and at once realizes that he has been betrayed by his wife.

Pure Cinema

The cellar scene is visually intriguing and an example of pure cinema—where, in Hitchcock's terms, the visual element predominates and dialogue is sparse or nonexistent. Music and dialogue take a pause, and we only hear the bottle shattering on the floor and two quick reaction shots coming from Devlin and Alicia.

Pure cinema is achieved when the camera moves or surveys objects and action without dialogue or music (not without sound). Examples can be found throughout Hitchcock's work, but only two will be mentioned here. One is in *Rear Window*, when "Jeff" Jefferies (James Stewart) watches a neighbor across the yard carry his samples suitcase several times through-out a rainy night; Jeff naps, wakes, and still the man repeats his suspicious trips for what seems the entire night. This sequence becomes even more suspenseful by the total silence, save the raindrops or light thunder. Suspicions grow in Stewart's mind that he is witnessing a murder scene—which proves true. The other example worth mentioning is the attic scene in *The Birds*, where Tippi Hedren is attacked by the gulls and crows and other birds relentlessly for several minutes without any sound except the flutter-ing of the vicious birds.

In *Notorious*, Hitchcock uses several other visual/camera tricks, as when the forlorn and betrayed Sebastian—a crushed and no longer blind Oedi-pus—runs to his mama to tell her of his disastrous plight; the camera shoots from an overhead angle, capturing his forehead and wrinkled eyebrows, reflecting his awesome anxiety that he has blundered to his death. The wine cellar scene, already mentioned, is void of dialogue, as words spoken at this sequence that relies on speed would jar the sense of fear the audience is experiencing. This is Hitchcock's aim: to make the audience shudder with anxiety, as he places his protagonists in harm's way. In some cases, the cam-era simply moves like a pointing finger directing and dictating the viewer's attention to an object he must see, perhaps to arrive at a conclusion. In the famous scene in *Psycho*, after Marion Crane has been stabbed to death, she falls in the tub, dragging the curtain with her. There, the camera focuses for a moment on her dead open eye, then slowly pans to the right until it reaches the stolen money lying on a small table wrapped in a piece of paper. A simple movement like that points to the cause of her death: her greed, heedlessness, and lack of sufficient acumen to detect Norman's erratic behavior in the parlor moments before. In a like manner in *Notorious*, the camera points to Madame Sebastian's hand that moves holding the poisoned cup of coffee in Alicia's direction, depositing it next to her. Moments later, Alicia, ill but not yet knowing what happened to her, observes the alarmed exclamations of Sebastian and his mother when her poisoned cup is picked up by Dr. Anderson by mistake and instantly she knows the truth, her look of terror bringing emotional tension to a peak. Madame Sebastian knits casu-ally, and Sebastian leans against his couch pillows, his eyes averted in mock sympathy. That look of Alicia's, knowing she is doomed, is Hitchcock's con-ception of pure cinema. No dialogue could have expressed her terror more eloquently. It is a masterstroke, brilliantly rendered by Bergman.

Visual scenes abound through the movie, whether entirely devoid of dialogue or not. Hitchcock liked to photograph faces, letting the camera capture shades of feeling or thought passing through the minds of his protagonists. And in Cary Grant and Ingrid Bergman he had two of the most photogenic actors in Hollywood. During the balcony scene, when the two lovers kiss, the camera zooms caressingly from midriffs to their faces, where for two and a half minutes the camera lingers, recording their kiss, which, one could imagine, could be like a coitus interruptus, as the Production Code did not allow a kiss to last more than three seconds. Hitchcock was a trickster, especially where eroticism on the screen was concerned. Love to him equaled sensuality, and that could be evoked by a tense scrutiny of facial expressions. Today, the standard expression of lovemaking shows two individuals quickly tossing off coats, pants, and shirts and in the next second or so are seen naked in a frenzied lovemaking.

CONCLUSION

Notorious proved a bonanza for both Hitchcock and Bergman. Hitchcock found his collaboration with Ben Hecht fortuitous, while being freed from the stifling influence of Selznick, who was preoccupied with *Duel in the Sun*, an epic western with Jennifer Jones and Gregory Peck, a project that absorbed most of his time and energy (and money). Hitchcock took full advantage of this freedom and let his creative juices flow. What helped him was the contemporary theme of the fall of Germany and the consequent assemblage of Nazis in another part of the world, searching for uranium to plot the construction of an atomic bomb—while as a coincidence the first American atomic bomb had been dropped on Hiroshima. The averting of such a plot worked, helping to promote the tautly plotted movie, which premiered at Radio City Hall on April 15, 1946, and went on to become an international hit.

What helped more than anything else was the presence in the film of two of the most glamorous stars in Hollywood at the top of their professional careers, playing the dual roles of lovers and coconspirators in a treacherous spy mission. Grant, known for his lighter screwball comedies, proved equal to the task of portraying a man riven between duty and love, who earns laurels at the end for overcoming his fear of women. Bergman played her role of a Mata Hari—as she calls herself—a woman who sells her charms for a larger cause. In 1945 Bergman was at the top of her game, having behind her top movies like *Casablanca*, *For Whom the Bell Tolls*, *Gaslight* (for which she earned her first Oscar), *Spellbound*, and *The Bells of St. Mary's*—all of which were smashing popular hits. Arguably, she was better in *Notorious* than in any of the previous roles, as a woman who puts her life on the line in service to her country. Her romance with Devlin is more hard-edged and intense than any of her previous pairings, as she took on a dangerous mission and won, with Devlin's cooperation. She shows intelligence and grace and is quick to deceive adversaries while herself suffering from unrequited love and a defamation by her colleagues as a woman for sale. Bergman was now at the top of her game. It would take her ten more years before she could reach such heights of worship by any audience, as this was her last movie with Selznick. She stayed in Hollywood for two more movies and consequently embarked on her ruinous adventure with Roberto Rossellini, which caused her fall from the pedestal for nearly a decade. But her triumph in *Notorious* is a testament to Bergman's glamour, intelligence, and devotion to her art.

10

ARCH OF TRIUMPH

(1948)

★ ★ ★

Director: Lewis Milestone
Screenplay: Lewis Milestone and Harry Brown, based on the novel by Erich
    Maria Remarque
Producer: David Lewis. *Cinematography:* Russell Metty. *Music Score:* Louis
    Gruenberg
Cast: Charles Boyer (Dr. Ravic), Ingrid Bergman (Joan Madou), Louis Calhern
    (Col. Boris Morosov), Charles Laughton (Ivon Haake), Ruth Warrick
    (Kate Bergstroem), Stephen Bekassy (Alex)
Studio: Enterprise–United Artists
Released: March 6, 1948
Specs: 120 minutes; black and white
Availability: DVD (Oliver Films)

After the highly successful *Notorious*, which cemented her reputation as a
megastar in 1946, Bergman found herself unemployed, as her contract with
David O. Selznick was about to expire. Having no inclination to be tied up
in another long contract with him, she suggested to him that some of the
money he had made by loaning her out to various other studios belonged
to her and asked for a fair share. He was enraged, denouncing her and calling her "ungrateful,"[1] so their relationship, which had been so beneficial to
both, ended on a sour note. (Later they reconciled, as Bergman was not a

person to hold a grudge against her former employer and mentor.) Meanwhile, she had been approached by Maxwell Anderson, who asked her if she felt inclined to play the lead in his new play, *Joan of Lorraine*, about to open in New York later that year. Bergman always had a strong desire to play Joan of Arc, whether on film or stage, and she accepted ecstatically and signed a contract with Anderson, who came to Hollywood to visit her for

Joan Madou (Bergman) and Ravic (Boyer) are two exiles. *Enterprise–UA / Photofest © United Artists*

that purpose. Since the play would not open until the fall, Bergman took a role in a new film, *Arch of Triumph*, based on a novel by Erich Maria Remarque, directed by Lewis Milestone, who had directed the distinguished war film *All Quiet on the Western Front*, also based on Remarque's famous novel. The film was to reunite her with Charles Boyer, who had starred with her in *Gaslight*, and at least on paper, the project looked promising, so Bergman signed up. It was financed by Enterprise Films,[2] a new group that aspired to eclectic films of quality, as was indicated by the assemblage of first-rate actors and directors—Louis Calhern and Charles Laughton, among them. The result was a film ignored by audiences and ravaged by critics who found it too long with a muddled plot, a disappointment overall. But the stellar cast and Remarque's powerful message make the film not only watchable today but a must-see in the Bergman canon. She, of course, delivers, as she always did, even in lesser vehicles. Though some of Bergman's scenes were long and drawn out, she excels as a woman lost in the chaotic and catastrophic world of Nazi ascendancy and the cost of human displacement, loss of identity, and death. The film gained international fame and was rereleased in many countries from 1948 to 1975. In 1984, it was remade with Anthony Hopkins in the lead.

PLOT

It is 1938, in Paris, France, at the eve of World War II, when thousands of refugees from Czechoslovakia, Austria, and countries peripheral to Germany were fleeing, most illegally and without passports. While some found employment and stayed legally, a great many of them were deported or living in hiding. One of these is Ravic (Boyer), a doctor who lives without a passport and practices medicine illegally. In an opening scene, Ravic recalls a sadistic Nazi official, Haake (Laughton), who had tortured Ravic and his wife to learn things they knew nothing about. A flashback shows his wife dead, while he is freed after being whipped in the face by the savage Haake. When Ravic sees Haake again through a window of a Paris café, he knows a plot is afloat, so he visits Col. Boris Morosov (Louis Calhern), a Russian émigré who is the porter of a nightclub, Scheherazade, to inform him of the news. Morosov has connections and influence, and he commands respect for his integrity and the help he provides to the refugees flooding Paris.

As Ravic exits Morosov's place, he sees a woman (Bergman) in the drenching rain staggering and nearly falling near a riverbank. He holds her from falling and takes her to a bar where he offers her a drink, telling her to gulp it down all at once. When she has recovered somewhat but has nowhere to go, he takes her to his place, helps her with her wet clothes, and offers her his bed to sleep; she prefers to sleep on the couch. All this he does in a very gentlemanly manner. In the morning, as they are having breakfast, she reveals that she had left her hotel because a man, her lover, had died there. Ravic accompanies her back there, and the proprietor takes them to the man's room, where the dead man still lies. He finds money on him and encourages the woman to take it. She pays the bill, and then he finds her a hotel where she can stay for a while. There are no signs that she had anything to do with the man's death; the one thing she tells him is that he loved her but she didn't love him back. She and Ravic develop a passion for each other and are seen kissing.

Ravic is a Czech (this point of where exactly he is from is never established), a man without identity who has been deported several times, always managing to come back. His staunch ally Col. Boris Morosov, played by Calhern (also a CIA agent in *Notorious*), helps Ravic to bring the woman to his club. We learn her name is Joan Madou, of Italian/Romanian extraction, with several other bloods running in her veins. She sings a Russian song at Scheherazade, a pulsating low-key melody, something that reveals what she had been—a nightclub singer. As Bergman had no difficulty playing non-American parts, she easily adjusts to her role as a European vagrant, used to being supported by lovers but aimless and vulnerable to twists of fate. Bergman deftly changes personas with antithetical impulses and looks as beautiful and enticing as ever, although she had gained twenty pounds before she started this movie. After recovering from her homeless existence, Madou appears with Ravic in a number of places, among them on a beach in southern France, where she is seen in beach attire—even with the few extra pounds—a rare instance for Bergman who rarely shows exposed skin. There, at a casino, she draws the attention of Alex (Stephen Bekassy), a shallow, rich playboy who is smitten by her. When she returns to Paris with Ravic, however, her attitude has changed; she now wishes for more luxury, as she starts a new, and perilous, relationship with another man. Ravic is deported soon after he had tried to help a woman hurting and lying down on the pavement, saying he was a doctor. A plump-cheeked, plainclothes policeman who had followed the scene approaches him and asks for his identity papers. Despite the protests of people around him who cry out that Ravic is a hero, the policeman investigates Ravic, asks for his passport, and, getting no satisfactory answer, has him deported for several months. (Incidentally, the plump policeman is no other than a young William Conrad, who became a familiar TV figure in his seventies show *Cannon*, in which he played a private eye.) When Ravic returns a few months later, Madou has taken Alex as a lover, living in a new luxurious apartment. She has reverted to a life of loose morals, shiftless existence, and dependence, but she still loves Ravic and asks him to wait for her.

Upon his return, Ravic has also a new confrontation with Haake. Almost halfway through the film, Haake shows up with a bowler hat and cane, well dressed, having dinner at a plush restaurant where Ravic also eats. Still seeking revenge for the murder of his wife, Ravic lures him into a ride to a (supposed) palace of pleasures, and as Haake, becoming suspicious, tries to shoot him with his pistol, Ravic murders him with a wrench. In the rough cut, Ravic tears off Haake's clothes, stuffs him into the trunk of his car, and he carries him to another place and buries him and then burns his clothes. Joseph Breen, administrator of the Production Code, was apprehensive about this scene of extreme violence and forced the editors to cut it. This part of the plot seems unconnected to Ravic's passion for Madou. When she tries to reconnect with Ravic, who has been away for three months, and asks him to wait for her, he resists. Alex shoots her in a fit of jealousy, and, despite Ravic's efforts to save her, she dies, whispering, "*Ti amo, ti amo*" (I love you, I love you), "*anche tu?*" (and you?).

THEMES

A theme that stands out is displacement of persons as a result of imminent war. Thousands have fled countries such as Austria, Hungary, and Czechoslovakia, alarmed by the threat of Hitler and the Nazis. Paris has become the center of refugees, many of them crossing the border by any means possible. Many are deported, and most of those find opportunities to slip back, as the borders are open at night. The chaotic world of Paris, just a year before the war, resembles to some extent the world in Casablanca, where refugees from Europe flooded to obtain visas for America, but in *Casablanca* all the numerous small episodes click together with the main theme of love between Rick and Ilsa, and the whole is lucid and forceful. In contrast, the world of *Arch of Triumph* is murky; most of the action in the first part is photographed in the rain at night, and the various episodes seem unconnected until the complications occur around the middle of the story, where the theme of revenge takes most of the space of the movie.

Revenge is a theme that runs parallel with the theme of displacement. Early in the film, in a conversation with Morosov, Ravic says he is beyond revenge. But when he sees the face of Haake through the glass as he sits at a café, his hatred of the man revives. And his impulse to take revenge resurfaces when he sees Haake later, after Ravic has come back from deportation (his sixth or seventh). The scene of his wife's torture at the opening shots has haunted him, while his love for Madou comes in fits and starts, first a gesture to a needy stranger but modified after he sees that she is a woman untrustworthy and morally loose. The reappearance of Haake about the middle of the story awakens his hatred of the man and his determination to pay him back. The savagery of Haake's death, though justified morally, also shows Ravic as a man unable to rein in his own vicious nature. That creates an inconsistency in him, more than a hint of a flawed man whose nature has been scathed by exile and the war. Madou also leads a shiftless existence, vacillating between honest work as a cabaret singer under the beneficial wing of Boris Morosov and her aimless wanderlust, a result of displacement but also of victimization and of her own paralyzed will.

The theme of ill-fated lovers recalls stories of lovers throughout history who either fail to make good choices or are victimized by prohibitive odds that bring on tragedy. Madou and Ravic belong to that category. Ravic says that he cannot marry Madou, as he has no passport nor resources, and at any moment he can be deported. She, on the other hand, is a weakened woman; instead of choosing to have secure employment as a singer at a nightclub, she prefers a life of ease with multiple and, by and large, unworthy lovers, living a precarious life that promises nothing but the present. Her pleas with him to wait for her are also futile as he cannot promise anything on which a common life can be based.

CONCLUSION

For a movie of two hours, lots of things are either irrelevant to the plot or left unexplained. The whole plot structure seems to fall apart, perhaps as a result of multiple cuts. A wasted good performance is from Boyer, who vacillates between a perfect gentleman and an erratic and rude lover, but whose fate is to lose the woman he loves. Bergman has excellent moments as a lost woman who recovers and sparkles for a while—and displays a singing voice in the Russian cabaret—but whose talent is swallowed up by her aimless life. She whispers, *"Ti amo"* (I love you) to Ravic as she dies in a touching scene in a story, in a relationship that seems to have no aim or future. The impending invasion of France by Germany, with its massive displacements, is felt in the gloom of the picture, but it has no bearing in the separation of lovers as it does so well in *Casablanca*. The movie, despite its numerous flaws, is worth noticing, however, for its overwhelming theme of displacement, reminding us of the current problems facing Europe with the displacement of millions of Syrians, a remarkable historical parallel. Refugees—people, mostly European, flying in different directions from Nazi Germany, seeking asylum, jobs, friendly shelters, or survival by any means. Memories of the previous war with Germany made many French citizens suspicious of sheltering refugees—for example, the young policeman, played by William Conrad, whose father had been killed by Germans in the previous war. A failed movie, potentially of epic dimensions, *Arch of Triumph* finds a saving grace in its human view of two innocents trapped in tragedy during one of the world's largest convulsions.

JOAN OF ARC

(1948)

★ ★ ★

Director: Victor Fleming
Screenplay: Maxwell Anderson and Andrew Solt, based on the play *Joan of Lorraine* by Maxwell Anderson
Producer: Walter Wanger. *Cinematographer:* Joseph Valentine. *Music Score:* Hugo Friedhofer. *Editor:* Frank Sullivan
Cast: Ingrid Bergman (Joan of Arc), José Ferrer (The Dauphin, Charles VII), Francis L. Sullivan (Bishop Pierre Cauchon), J. Carrol Naish (John, Count of Luxembourg), Ward Bond (La Hire), John Emery (Jean, Duke d'Alencon, Cousin of Charles), Frederick Worlock (John of Lancaster, Duke of Bedford)
Studio: Sierra Pictures / RKO Radio Pictures
Released: November 11, 1948 (premiere, New York City); September 2, 1950 (nationally)
Specs: 145 minutes; color
Availability: DVD (Image Entertainment)

Ingrid Bergman had a lifelong desire to play Joan of Arc, the French religious icon, warrior, and martyr, and managed to do so three times—twice on the stage, *Joan of Lorraine*, the play by Maxwell Anderson on which *Joan of Arc* was based, and the 1954 Italian production, an oratorio, *Giovanna d'Arco al rogo* (*Joan of Arc at the Stake*) by Roberto Rossellini. In 1948,

Ingrid was thirty-three, playing a young woman half that age, but, with the help of the makeup department and her eternally youthful looks, she negotiated the part admirably. *Joan of Lorraine* opened in Washington, where Ingrid expressed her puzzlement as to why black people could not buy tickets for her play;[1] she was cursed and spat upon and called "nigger lover" by picketers outside the theater. Later in New York where theatergoers, she was told, were much harder to please, she won ecstatic plaudits from both audiences and critics, being called "radiant" by *New York Herald Tribune* reviewer Howard Barnes, who expressed his "gratitude and deep satisfaction" for her performance.[2] Others agreed, telling the world she *was* Saint Joan. Such praise had its benefits for Bergman: With one stroke she played her favorite character and had shown she was a superb stage actress, something that would lead to new horizons in her later career.

Meanwhile, Maxwell Anderson, encouraged by the success of his play, renewed his efforts to have it translated into a film, with Bergman as Joan, and, after negotiations with Walter Wanger, the producer, things got under way. The director, Victor Fleming, who had directed her before in *Dr. Jekyll and Mr. Hyde* (1941), joined Maxwell and Wanger and soon the trio had formed a production company, Sierra Pictures, to make this movie, while RKO would undertake its distribution. Fleming had been a prominent director in American cinema, credited with a string of successful movies in the thirties and forties, among others *Gone with the Wind* and the *Wizard of Oz*, two perennials that left their mark on American mythology.

After *Notorious* (1946), Bergman had cut ties with David O. Selznick and was venturing into independent productions such as Enterprise–United Artists in *Arch of Triumph* (1948), which failed at the box office. Sierra Pictures would also be short-lived, but Bergman's career in Hollywood was already in decline. After *Joan of Arc*, she made one more film with Hitchcock, *Under Capricorn* (1949), shot in London but set in Australia. That movie was a flop (though it contains an impressive nine-minute one-take of Bergman), to the detriment of both Hitchcock and Bergman. But post-*Joan*, Bergman was in trouble for a different reason: She had fled Hollywood, left her husband Petter Lindstrom and her ten-year-old daughter Pia, and traveled to Italy, starting her infamous affair with Rossellini. *Joan of Arc* did not go into general release until September 1950, and by that time the scandal had already broken and had a negative effect on her American audiences in spite of its eight Academy nominations and two wins. The box office returns of *Joan* barely exceeded its generous budget of $4,650,506 (about a million more than *Gone with the Wind*), and the epic was ignored in the following decades, partly because of its shortened versions and its reputation as a "big bore." The uncut version did not surface until 1998 and did not appear in pristine condition on DVD until 2004. One bright spot was that just before the movie was released, the publicity department took Ingrid to a tour of France where she was greeted by large crowds, as if the real Joan had come back to life. This adulation gave her performance the stamp of approval by consensus, and her Joan is generally considered superior to numerous others, before and after this movie. Over the years, Joan, the French national heroine, had become the object of numerous works in the arts, literature, painting, sculpture, film, theater, music, and TV.[3]

PLOT

Unlike *Joan of Lorraine*, a static play in which a group of actors react to her martyrdom, *Joan of Arc* is a long chronological narrative, epic in scope, with battles, court intrigues, and a trial and the execution of Joan at the stake. As a period piece, it is rich in color, art design, and costumes, receiving Oscar nominations for all three. It is the story of a pilgrimage of a young female, inspired by "voices" from saints, leaving her place of birth for a royal court and eventually to a trial for heresy.

The action starts with Joan (Bergman) leaving her home at Domrémy in northern France in December of 1427 at the age of sixteen against the will of her father, who has actually arranged a marriage for her. She says she is obeying her "voices," which asked of her that she travel to Chinon and the meet the Dauphin, successor to the throne of France, and to crown him King Charles VII. A friend of the family takes her as far as Vaucouleurs, where she arrives in May 1428. It is the end of the Hundred Years' War (1337–1453) between England and France, and her action is supposed to help chase out the English and their French allies and establish the divided France into one nation. At Vaucouleurs, she stands in front of the governor, Sir Robert de Baudricourt (George Coulouris), who dismisses her claim and urges her to go back to her parents. Nevertheless, enough people are impressed by her faith and help her reach the court of the Dauphin at Chinon, where one of his courtiers suggests a trick, which Charles likes and goes along with: to have Charles hide among his courtiers, placing his royal insignia on someone else, and see whether Joan can discover the pretense. Joan enters, the impostor sitting on the throne, and she slowly surveys the rows of courtiers and arrives in front of the Dauphin (José Ferrer), kneels, and embraces his feet. The effect on the audience is electric. But Charles, though impressed by her abilities, vacillates between action and inaction, concerned more about his heavy debts than a desire to go to war against the English.

After Joan wins the trust of the Dauphin, she is given military attire and leads a ragtag army—getting bigger as she is marching along—in order to lift the siege of Orleans, which is occupied by the English and their French allies, the Burgundians. Orleans is protected by strongholds outside it, one of which Joan attacks after a failed attempt to negotiate surrender, and, with the help of a strong army, she attacks the English fortress. But the attempt fails, and Joan is wounded, struck by an arrow near her heart. She pulls it out with her right hand. Her bravery impresses her troops, and they attack again, and this time they take the fortress after a bloody struggle. She enters Orleans on April 29, 1429.

The next phase of the story focuses on the trial and execution. The charge is heresy and sorcery. Joan's victories have alarmed the English and the Burgundians. The English are represented by England's Regent John of Lancaster (Frederick Worlock), Philip the Good, Duke of Burgundy (Colin Keith-Johnston), and John, Count of Luxembourg (J. Carrol Naish), the man who captured her on May 23, 1430. The count surrenders her for the

Wounded in battle, Joan (Bergman), undaunted, pulls the arrow out. *RKO Radio Pictures, Inc.* / *Photofest* © *RKO Radio Pictures, Inc.*

sum of 10,000 pounds to the most prominent of the Burgundians, Bishop Pierre Cauchon of Beauvais, played by the bulky Francis L. Sullivan, who initiates the proceedings and conducted the trial. The trial takes place at Rouen, from February 21 to May 30, 1431, and though nothing is proven, the verdict is guilty. Joan, who has been held in prison, is told that if she recants, she would receive life in prison. After some hesitation, Joan chooses to be burned at the stake, and indeed she is in a spectacular scene watched by a large crowd, many of whom are weeping and praying for her. She dies on May 30, 1431, at the age of nineteen.

THEMES

Joan of Arc is one of the few films in which Bergman does not have a romantic interest.[4] Many believed (including Fleming, who was in love with Bergman himself) that a movie without a love story, about a French girl who saved her country, would not have a box office appeal in the United States, despite the success of Maxwell Anderson's play on Broadway.[5] Bergman, therefore, carries the burden of the story on her shoulders, and though she is surrounded by scores of ecclesiastics, military men of rank, and courtiers, played by fine actors, she remains in the center of interest from the first shot to the last. Men around her generally revere her, even in the middle of a military camp, where crude soldiers swear and gamble in her presence. She speaks with authority when she tells them that they should behave as good Christians, stop blaspheming and whoring, confess, and take communion. The soldiers, impressed by the forceful words and piety of such a young woman, see her as a leader among them and pay attention to her. Joan soon has a large following in the military camp commanded by La Hire, played by a gruff Ward Bond, the sidekick of John Wayne in many westerns. He is her staunch ally who slowly forms a regular army to march against Orleans.

Bergman looks comfortable as Joan, the heroine she had played on the stage in New York for six months. Her Joan in the movie is a military genius who knows where and when to strike and also understands what personal valor, spurred by faith, can achieve. She does not like the killing of battle that will be certain to follow, so she begs the English commander, John of Lancaster, Duke of Bedford, at the fortress to surrender. When he peremptorily turns her down, she charges, leading the troops scaling the fortress and fighting along with the other soldiers. The leggy Bergman, covered with metal from head to foot, as tall as or taller than most men around her, resembles an androgynous visitor from another planet. She, like the historical Joan, wears men's clothing at the camp full of men to protect her from molestation, and in battle she wears armor granted to her by King Charles. Bergman, who had honed her skills as Joan under the stage lights, had no problem projecting a soulful and brave Joan revered by friends and admired by some of her enemies.

In her autobiography, Bergman relates an incident when she had a meeting with George Bernard Shaw, whose play *Saint Joan* premiered in London in 1923, three years after Joan's canonization in 1920. In the summer of 1948, Bergman was in London, preparing to film *Under Capricorn* with Hitchcock, when Gabriel Pascal, a Hungarian director who lived in England for many years (he produced Shaw's well-known play *Pygmalion* in 1939), asked her if she wanted to meet the famous playwright, and she said yes. They drove up to his place in Hertfordshire, where the ninety-two-year-old host opened the gate himself. Immediately he asked her why she didn't do *his* play.[6] Bergman replied that she didn't because she didn't like his play. When a bemused Shaw asked her why she thought so, Bergman explained that his Joan was not the simple French girl she had portrayed but a creature he had invented, and that her words in his play were not hers but Shaw's. She continued to tell him that the words she spoke at the trial were based on transcripts of the trial and that these were "historical documents." She did not mention a broader point that Shaw had made in his lengthy "preface" to the play, where he argues that Joan, as a woman, belonged to one-half of the human species, and as such she could be as entitled to be a military genius as any man.[7]

Maxwell Anderson's play, and subsequent screenplay, which Shaw sarcastically dismissed, does make Joan pious, obeying the voices of Archangel Michael, Saint Margaret, and Saint Catherine, but, wisely, the voices are never heard by the movie audience; they are only in Joan's mind. But the script does make Joan a quick-witted person, unfazed by men of rank who ask abrupt questions or dismiss her. An example may be her first encounter with Sir Robert de Baudricourt, to whom she says that the Lord sent her to meet the Dauphin, to which he peremptorily replies: "I am your Lord." "I was referring to my Lord in heaven," Joan readily answers. "That's a point, that's a point," Sir Robert concedes. It is her mental acuity combined with unshakable faith that makes Joan listened to wherever she goes. But her piety and ready wit would not lead anywhere had Joan not led the French army, such as it was, to many victories and made her a real threat to the English, who feared her military genius, and to the Burgundians, top heavy with high-ranking Church prelates, who saw her as a threat to the Catholic

Church. During the trial, Joan gives courageous, clearheaded answers, humiliating to her chief accuser, Bishop Cauchon, who eventually is told she is "too smart" for him and they should try her as a heretic instead.

Heresy and cross-dressing were two of the charges brought against her, but behind all these charges, the reasons for her persecution are political. The English were afraid that she would attack and take Paris, and the Burgundians would lose their prominence—and power—once the English were driven from France. As for King Charles VII, he is a weakling, more content with playing ball with the court ladies than planning another war. In the film he is shown as lazy, vain, seen chewing on a lamb leg, swirling around in his velvet royal gown and annoyed every time matters of state are brought to his attention. That of course does not sum up the real personality of Charles VII, who, historically, is credited with ending the Hundred Years' War and leading France to prosperity and power in later years. By the way, José Ferrer, as the Dauphin and King Charles, in his first appearance, won an Oscar nomination for his performance as a foil to Ingrid Bergman's Joan. He provided some structural balance in a plotless epic, giving Joan a goal, for she realizes that without his coronation her plan to free France would be unattainable. Once the trial begins, however, Charles vanishes from the scene, unable or unwilling to mount an attack to free her.

The trial, as presented in the film, shows Joan's inhuman incarceration in a dungeon at the Castle of Rouen (known today as the Joan of Arc Tower) meant for male prisoners, exposed to hunger, cold, and sexual assaults by the guards. She is kept there for months, but her spirit is not broken, and when she appears in court, in a scene reminiscent of grand opera, with dozens of prelates sitting in a circle, she is calm and ready to answer. When asked if she was in God's grace, she answers: "If I am not, may God put me there; and if I am, may God keep me," a clever answer, since either a yes or a no would be enough to convict her. She is especially effective with Pierre Cauchon, telling him in a raised voice that he is unfit to judge her and even cautioning him to be careful with what he says and does, for he will be accountable in heaven. An advisor tells a shaken Cauchon to conduct the rest of the trial in private quarters where he will not be exposed to ridicule by a fearless and intelligent adversary. After weeks of relentless questioning, a weakened Joan chooses to be burned at the stake rather than live the rest of her life imprisoned.

Her execution is a transcendent moment of martyrdom as Joan approaches a pole to which she is tied, with guards piling dry wood around it. A cross is given to her, which she holds to her chest as the flames devour her. If Bergman's skill as an actress portraying Joan was exceptional and true to the letter and the spirit of her role, it is also a blending of human and divine elements. She is the peasant girl who heard the voices that sent her to her destiny, befitting a saint; and she is also the all-too-human young girl who, while being burned, cautioned one of the guards not to come too close to the flames and hurt himself. No wonder the French greeted Bergman as being Joan while she toured France. Biographer Donald Spoto notes:

> Her performance had a quality of utter transcendence—the lighting seems to shine through rather than on her, and that is entirely due to the deep humanity she gave the maid. This is not performance of a plaster saint, but rather a recognizably human, confused woman who knows that God writes straight with crooked lines. And it is unlikely that anyone who saw the picture ever forgot her final scene at the stake.[8]

CONCLUSION

The curtain closed; the lights went out. What was the verdict? While her 199 stage performances on Broadway were before packed houses, the epic venture on the screen didn't do so well. The lengthy, expensive, lavish epic was judged by many a big bore, too many talky scenes among other things, despite Bergman's brilliant performance and its eight Oscar nominations. It was said that when Victor Fleming saw the result, he cried. That and his desperate love affair with Bergman coming to an end may have contributed to his fatal heart attack a few weeks after the movie was finished. Certainly, this was the end of Ingrid's career in Hollywood for almost a decade. But it wasn't the seal of doom for her. Like Joan's, her life had its ups and downs, and Ingrid still had some sense of irony and humor as she tells us the final episode of the Saint Joan saga. Upon her return from her France tour, a priest, Father Donceur, sent her a parcel with a small wooden statue of the Madonna. Before it arrived, the US Post Office sent her a cable: VIRGIN ARRIVING IN HOLLYWOOD. SLIGHTLY DAMAGED. LOST HER HEAD. Next day Ingrid glued the head back on, muttering, "Well, that's Hollywood!"[9]

If that wasn't a good-bye, it certainly sounded like one. Like the headless Madonna, Ingrid had to wait a long time before she could glue her own back on again.

STROMBOLI

(1950)

★ ★ ★ ★

Director: Roberto Rossellini
Screenplay: Sergio Amidei, Gian Paolo Callegari, Art Cohn, Renzo Cesana,
    and Roberto Rossellini
Producer: Roberto Rossellini. *Cinematographer:* Otello Martelli. *Music Score:*
    Renzo Rossellini
Cast: Ingrid Bergman (Karin Bjornsen), Mario Vitale (Antonio), Renzo Cesana
    (Priest), Mario Sponza (Lighthouse Keeper)
Also known as: Stromboli, Terra di Dio
Studio: RKO Pictures
Released: February/March 1950
Specs: 106 minutes; black and white
Availability: DVD and Blu-ray (Criterion Collection)

---

*"I revealed myself to those who did not ask for me; I was found by those
who did not seek me."*

—Isaiah 65:1 (NIV)

"Oed' und leer das Meer": "The bleak and empty sea"

—T. S. Eliot, *The Waste Land*

By 1948, after Ingrid Bergman had ended her association with David O. Selznick and made two more movies in Hollywood (*Arch of Triumph*, *Joan of Arc*), she went to Italy to make *Stromboli* with Roberto Rossellini, with whom she soon started an affair. It was a disastrous move, which put an end to her Hollywood career. It took seven years in exile and several films with Rossellini, by and large considered flops, until she finally made amends with Hollywood by taking up the leading role in *Anastasia*, which won her a second Oscar.

The affair with Rossellini started innocently enough. Bergman had sent a letter to Rossellini expressing her desire to make a film with him after she had seen *Rome: Open City* and *Paisan*, two films that had catapulted the Italian director to international fame after the end of World War II. Rossellini responded by writing Bergman a lengthy letter in which he explained that he had an idea for a film about a woman he had met in an internment camp near Rome, adding that he'd like to make a film with Bergman based on this encounter. Encouraged by her, he traveled to Hollywood to meet her and her husband of fourteen years, Dr. Petter Lindstrom. Things progressed but did not turn out as expected, as Bergman fell in love with Rossellini and he too was smitten. While the film was being shot, their affair caused uproar back home, especially when it became known that she was pregnant with Rossellini's child. The beloved star of *Casablanca*, *For Whom the Bell Tolls*, *Gaslight*, *The Bells of St. Mary's*, and *Notorious* was accused of betraying her profession by leaving her husband and child for a filmmaker who was already married as well as a lover of Anna Magnani. Bergman was excoriated by the press and the clergy as immoral and scandalous, and even a US senator, Edwin C. Johnson of Colorado, stated on the Senate floor that Bergman's affair with Rossellini was "an all-time shameless exploitation and disregard for good public morals."[1] The film received negative notices, but it was mostly Bergman's affair with Rossellini that incurred the wrath of the Hollywood establishment and left Bergman's career in shambles for half a dozen years. Though European critics, and especially new wave French filmmakers such as Eric Rohmer and François Truffaut, reserved judgment and even gave Rossellini nods for originality and cinematic ingenuity, *Stromboli* and several other films Bergman made with Rossellini were dismal box office flops and remained in the shadows for many decades. In recent years, however, some of Bergman's films with Rossellini, especially those of Criterion Collection's 2013 notable issue,[2] kindled new interest in the Rossellini period of Bergman's film career. Aided by this restored version and its worthwhile commentaries, *Stromboli* is now considered a classic by many, one of Bergman's most notable, if not most popular, achievements.

Stromboli was financed by Howard Hughes, the new boss of RKO Studios, after Samuel Goldwyn turned it down, fearing that Rossellini's films were too dark and pessimistic for American audiences.[3] Of course, Hughes, like everyone else, expected Bergman to come back to Hollywood, so he risked a considerable investment, believing that this foreign film would boost her international status, with profits to match. But *Stromboli*, and Bergman's part in it, fell short of such expectations. The venture was disorganized from the start, judging from Bergman's reaction to Rossellini's methods compared to the Hollywood standards Bergman was used to before she left for Italy. There was no script—just an idea of an errant woman, based on a true story Rossellini experienced. Aside from Bergman, there were no professional actors, and the crew was assembled ad hoc, mostly from the fishermen in Stromboli, a volcanic island inside a group of the Lipari Islands north of Sicily. Basic facilities for the crew were missing, and the island was a hardened black rock of molten lava, a moonscape dotted with white square hovels at the bottom of a steep hill, the active volcano itself. Since there were no doubles, Bergman had to do all the walking around and scrambling through the rocky paths and narrow village streets, just as she is seen in the film—one could identify her with the protagonist. At first she was enraged by this primitive method of filming, without sets or actors except for the locals, who had no idea of what Rossellini was trying to do. Here is how she herself describes the way Rossellini's working:

> They couldn't care less, they'd just stand around laughing, and Roberto would say, "Now you walk up that line toward that place. That's where the camera is. Understand?" and they didn't reply, "Oh, yes, this line here? Is that all right?" Then Roberto would give them an idea of what to talk about and they'd chatter away, and I'd stand there like an idiot, because I didn't speak any Italian, so I didn't know what they were saying. . . . So to solve the problem, Roberto attached a string to one of their big toes inside their shoes. Then he stood there, holding this bunch of strings, and first he'd pull that string and one man spoke, then he'd pull another string and another man spoke, so I didn't have a string in my toe, so I didn't know when I was supposed to speak. And this was realistic filmmaking![4]

Yet, despite an occasional temperamental fit, Bergman was far from unhappy with her adventure in this isolated and barren spot, thanks to Rossellini's "charm," as she herself put it. As her love affair with Rossellini progressed during filming, the scandal back in America grew to exponential

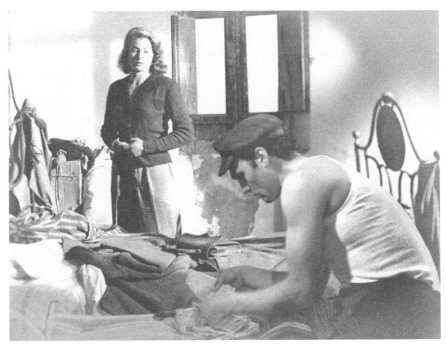

Karin (Bergman) in a tense situation with her husband Antonio (Mario Vitale) in *Stromboli. RKO Radio Pictures, Inc. / Photofest © RKO Radio Pictures, Inc.; Photographer: G. B. Poletto*

proportions, worsened by the fact that Bergman was pregnant with Rossellini's child—not unlike the character she played.

PLOT

The plot of *Stromboli* may be summarized in one line: A woman tries to escape from one bad spot to get to a better one, but she fails. She is first seen in an internment camp in Italy, where refugees from war-torn Europe were held, while the Italian authorities tried to deal with the crisis by sending them to various destinations. The woman, presenting herself as Karin Bjornsen, a Lithuanian (a Latvian in Rossellini's letter) who had escaped the Nazis and lost her husband, is now trying to gain a visa to go to Argentina. She is tall and beautiful, and her demeanor suggests an aristocratic bearing, but the authorities deny her a visa, finding her credentials inadequate for reasons that are not quite clear. She has, in the meantime, developed a liaison with one of the camp guards, Antonio (Mario Vitale), who is more than happy to marry her and take her to his native island. She follows him to his squalid village in an arid volcanic island (she had imagined any island in the Mediterranean would be beautiful), and she revolts right away, feeling trapped, unwanted, and miserable. "This is a ghost town," she tells him as soon as they set foot in Stromboli. "How can one live here?" A baby is heard crying, as to validate his answer that if there are babies there must be people. She tries to adjust, fixes her house, spends time with village children, and tries to connect with the local women, yet nothing works. She imagines that if she could get to the other side of the island, she could find the means to get away from there. But she needs money. She hopes her husband will make enough after a rich harvest of large tuna, however he takes home only small wages. She even tries to seduce the local priest, who retains a significant amount of money meant for children's charities, but he reminds her he is only a poor priest. She then approaches the lighthouse keeper, whom she befriends, manages to get money enough, and after a volcano eruption that leaves the villagers stunned, she undertakes the harsh trek climbing the mountain still emitting sulphur fumes that almost suffocate her. Exhausted, she spends a night on the mountain. She is pregnant. In the morning the sun shines, the fumes have cleared. She invokes God's mercy, and it looks as if she has been saved. The film ends there.

THEMES

The film was released in three versions. The American version in February 1950 by RKO, which had financed the project, was shorter than the other two and had a voice-over narrative and a different ending, in which Karin returns to the village and accepts her fate. The second, called the international version, was released in Europe in March of the same year. It was longer by thirty-five minutes, had no voice-over, and included more of Karin's meandering through village, stressing her desperation. It also had a longer sequence of the tuna fishing, and the encounters with the village women were longer and more emphatic, stressing her rejection by the female population of the island. The ending, as said above, was ambivalent. The third version, titled *Stromboli, Terra di Dio* (*Stromboli, the Land of God*), is shorter than the second, a few scenes were added to it, and is given in Italian with subtitles in English. Bergman herself speaks her own lines, dubbing her own voice, but her Italian lines were superimposed later, as her scenes were shot twice. The version discussed here is the second, with hints given where differences matter.[5] The film begins with an epigraph: "I revealed myself to those who did not ask for me; I was found by those who did not seek me."[6] Karin confronts the harsh conditions of living in an arid and godforsaken place, something like Dante's *Inferno*, from where there is no exit. Aside from the priest, a pious man who compassionately admonishes those around him, no one else pays much attention to her pleadings, as the harsh conditions of making a living absorb their attention and no one seems to pay much attention to God's mercy, though they offer thanks to the Virgin Mary and Jesus every time there is a big catch. The only thing that exercises its power over them is the volcano. It can momentarily shine in the sun and let them go on with their everyday living chores, or it can erupt and destroy what they have labored to build. The priest, along with everyone else, serves this alien deity.

God is totally absent during Karin's ordeal. When the priest declines to give her the money, she tells him, "You are as merciless as your God!" Her motives coincide with her total lack of mysticism. She sees only the spiky rocks, the arid and bleak sea, the white squat houses, the crude peasants, the hating women, and the well-meaning but helpless man she is tied to. Thence her total despair and her blind will to get out, no matter how. Yet, up on the mountain after a night's torpid sleep, when she wakes in the bright sunshine she seeks God's help—for her child. Mother and woman intersect each for the sake of the other; mother speaks for the child and seeks God—and, to repeat the epigraph, she was found by One whom she did not seek. Incidentally, the Catholic Church did not think that Rossellini was a true believer, and some Catholics said that he twisted the ending trying to appease them. But Rossellini never tried to answer this charge. He kept silent and enigmatic. If he was religious, it would be obvious. He let his movie speak for itself. He did say in an interview with Eric Rohmer that freedom is only found in Christianity—as Christianity is the only true road to freedom.

The Pathos of Rossellini's Letter

While Bergman's letter to him was only a few lines long, Rossellini's reply was lengthy and passionate. He explained that, entirely by chance, he saw a woman in a tightly guarded internment camp just north of Rome, approached her, and asked her a few questions. She answered in a few Italian words she knew, telling him that she was from Latvia, looking at him with her despairing eyes. Rossellini was pushed back rudely by a guard, but he returned a little while later having obtained permission to talk to her. But he was told by the other women that she had married a soldier from the

Lipari Islands and left the camp. The Lipari Islands are volcanic rocks, nearly uninhabitable, where enemies of the Fascist government were confined during the war. Rossellini imagined the rest of the story, as follows: This woman arrives there with her new husband and realizes that she has walked into another trap from which she cannot escape. She hopes for a miracle, not realizing that one is beginning to happen inside her. "She understands the mighty power of he who possesses nothing," says Rossellini, who compares her to Saint Francis (as he does in *Europe '51*). The woman is joyous in her heart in understanding this, and that is what saves her. Based on that description of a potential scenario, Rossellini begged Bergman to forgive his enthusiasm, hoping she would be interested in making the movie.

On the surface, the similarities between the Latvian woman in Rossellini's letter and Bergman's Karin in the movie are striking. Both women are entrapped, first held in a camp and then, as a means of escape, are married to a man who takes them to an ungodly place, a volcanic island cut off from civilization from where there is no exit. Although Rossellini's Latvian woman disappears from view and has to be invented by him for the rest of her tale—and her hypothetical transformation—his vision of her becomes the basis of Karin's tale. But a closer comparison of what Rossellini saw in the camp and what appears on the screen reveals a substantial difference in the two women. To be specific, let us quote Rossellini's words, as he first visited the camp:

> At the further end of the field, behind the barbed wires, far away from the others, a woman was looking at me, alone, fair, all dressed in black. Heeding not the guards, I drew nearer. She only knew a few words of Italian and as she pronounced them, the very effort gave a rosy tint to her cheeks. She was from Latvia. In her clear eyes, one could read a mute intense despair. I put my hand through the barbed wires and she seized at my arm, just like a shipwrecked person would clutch at a floating board. The guard drew near, menacing, I got back to my car.[7]

The rest of Rossellini's letter is his projected fantasy of how this woman would fare as she was taken by her husband to the Lipari Islands. As he laid down her story in his imagination, Bergman would behave like the Latvian woman he had seen in the camp, or at least he would expect Bergman to keep his view in mind. Aside from her objections to the filming conditions, Bergman had no misgivings as regards her identity and let Rossellini guide her during filming. But as soon as she appears on the screen, one can see that the Bergman persona, with all the baggage she carried from Hollywood, would be practically the antithesis of the Latvian woman. The latter is sketched quickly with a few brushes—"alone, fair, all dressed in black . . . in her clear eyes, one could read a mute intense despair"—leaving the reader with the image of irreversible loss. Is it possible for that woman to go to a hellish island and be regenerated? In Rossellini's imagination it actually happened: "She saw the mighty power of possessing nothing . . . and in reality she becomes another Saint Francis."[8]

Bergman does not appear to be such a person. From the start, she seems to be scheming alternatives. When she is refused a visa to Argentina, she takes it calmly, and she is next seen leaving for Stromboli as if she had scored a victory. When she sees that she has walked into another trap, she becomes hostile, negative, and egotistical. She has a strong sense of class and sees her husband and his environment as unworthy of her. "You are my husband," she says to him, "but I am different." She reminds one of many déclassé Europeans, before and after the two World Wars, who roamed throughout Europe trying to survive by means fair or foul. Bergman had already played such a role, Joan Madou in *Arch of Triumph* (1948), an aimless refugee in Paris shortly before World War II. She played Karin following a period of Hollywood splendor, playing heroines who for the most part showed decision and purpose—Ilsa Lund, Paula Alquist, Alicia Huberman, for instance—classy women who fought adversity and won. In *Stromboli* Karin is both angry and desperate. She remains so throughout the movie, blasting her husband for bringing her 30,000 lire, equivalent to 20 dollars, angrily dismissing the local women after they refuse to come into her house, and excoriating the priest for not giving her the money entrusted to him. She is not a woman to be put down by the local environment and makes demands to the very last, even offering her favors to the lighthouse man to get the money to escape. Although she has moments when she is sincerely trying to adjust, she is bitter, angry, and dismissive of everyone around her, unable to have her way. One can argue that she walks deliberately into a certain path of destruction. What of her conversion? It comes with the morning sunshine, as she becomes aware of the beauty of her, while the instinct of motherhood awakens in her. At that moment, the image of a Hollywood beauty is wiped out and one sees the morally errant woman turning into a humble, though not humiliated, human being. A Saint Francis? As her conversion is not a moral decision but a freedom from total loss to inner freedom, the viewer is left with the freedom to decide for him- or herself.

Karin's loneliness comes mostly from the striking differences between her and the villagers, especially the women. They dislike her at first sight, avoid her, and gossip behind her back. When she asks one who speaks some English, the woman tells her that she lacks modesty. "You are not modest," she tells her. This is not surprising. Physically, Karin is tall and beautiful and looks as if she comes from a high-class background; the lack of makeup and a streak of gray hair often tussled by the wind as she wanders through the narrow streets or sits on a rock make her look like a creature who arrived from a different planet, while the village women are short, and they invariably wear black as if in permanent mourning. Most importantly, she attracts men, and she flirts openly with the lighthouse man, provoking her husband's rages of jealousy. With all this, she is far from gregarious, even with the few men she consorts with. She is seen eternally walking the labyrinthine street villages, walking to the beaches where she sits on rocks and surveys the empty sea. Her only company is an occasional mixing with children. On one occasion, as boys at the beach are trying to catch an octopus, she wades into the water, pulling up her skirt a bit, playing their game. When the lighthouse man comes in and uses a glass-bottom barrel to find and catch an octopus, she becomes a bit too friendly; then she looks above and sees a throng of women watching her. Even the men are after her, not aspiring to make passes at her but because they consider her husband a weak man who is unable to control his foreign wife's whims. When she goes to a woman with a sewing machine to have her dresses repaired, men gather outside in a mock serenade, as this seamstress has a bad reputation. When Mario shows up a few moments later to take her home, they call him a cuckold (*cornuto*). Shame falls on both of them. She has dragged Mario into her outcast status. When she attempts to escape both the villagers and her husband, she finds herself even more alone at the side of spuming volcano. With nothing left her, she invokes God's mercy.

Rossellini's Documentary Style: Neorealism

Along with a group of other postwar Italian filmmakers (Vittorio De Sica, early Federico Fellini, Luchino Visconti), Roberto Rossellini was labeled a "neorealist," as the leader of a movement that viewed cinema as a reflection of the harsh realities of life. The war had left Italy a poverty-stricken country, especially after the Allied invasion and the retreating Germans. *Rome: Open City*, Rossellini's masterpiece, brought these realities to the attention of the world and to his own countrymen. The aim of neorealism is to imitate reality as closely as possible. Use the simplest means, real people instead of actors when possible; photograph real neighborhoods, real houses, real landscapes, no matter how ugly or unglamorous; show how people really live; avoid Hollywood glitter; above all, don't think of cinema as a medium for escapism. Make people think about their lives, concerns, troubles, joys, tragedies. Neorealism should also provoke thought and reflection and aspiration, even when aspiration fails.

Poverty-stricken Italy was the perfect subject for *Open City*. An intruder into this world is the subject of *Stromboli*. Rossellini wanted to represent this world with his own spare (not entirely out of necessity) means. He made no attempts to embellish the environment into which his protagonist, Karin, entered. There were no sets built; the people of the village were used as extras; there were few long shots so the camera could stay close, but no close-ups either, just medium shots. For the first time, Bergman's face does not cover the entire screen. She is shown walking into the city lanes, near the shore, climbing, talking at full-body length. If a close-up is necessary, she is shown from the waist up. Rossellini did that deliberately, knowing that close-ups are used to mark a critical turning point in the story, an artificial photographic enhancement usually reserved for leads. Incidentally, *Stromboli* reveals Bergman's natural beauty as no film has before or after. Lack of makeup, a natural pallor, and a streak of gray hair give a new, exotic look to Bergman. Rossellini had the sense not to give a haircut to his beloved actress, letting her be as if nature, an ugly nature and a hostile sea, let his siren enhance the arid landscape.

General views prevail that Rossellini offers gratuitous documentary scenes in his films, particularly in *Stromboli*. The film employs no sets; actors are recruited from the peasant population, positioned in various special arrangements while the film is being shot, and told what to say. But certain sequences seem to be there in and of themselves, as, for instance, the tuna fishing episode. The scene is impressive as it is, photographed by Rossellini himself. Nets are cast by fishermen on boats, who wait for hours until they feel the bites of the cast lines and know a school of tunas is approaching. Then the boats form a circle, pulling up the nets, trapping a large school of tunas, and pulling them up into the big boat, using hooks to haul in the large animals, some three times larger than a human being. They are thrown into piles, writhing and choking as they expire. Rossellini expends camera space describing the death throes of the murdered animals. Rossellini rejected this idea that the scene is being a mere documentary, saying it is part of the story. This idea can be validated by making two points: (a) Karin/Bergman is present during this ritual, and we see speckles of foam flying to her face; she is trying to guard herself with her hands as if bees were attacking her. Like the tuna, she is trapped within space she desperately wants to escape. She may even die in the effort; and (b) Karin also sees this fishing activity as a means of profit for her husband, who says he is always underpaid because of his foreign wife, as the large fish crop would earn him enough for her, or for both, to escape.

Stromboli is rife with symbols, which in effect add a layer of meanings to the movie. The ferret (a polecat) is trained by Karin's husband, Antonio, to catch rats and rabbits, needed as bait for the fishing expedition. But Karin turns her face with disgust as the violent ferret tears the small rabbit to bits. She becomes sick after witnessing the captured tunas, agonizing as they are trapped, beyond escape. She is trapped herself, both by man and nature. The volcano is the most potent symbol in the movie: Man's cruelty derives from the necessity of living under its power, which is both omnipresent and mindless. The inhabitants are subject to its unpredictable whims, forced to obey and adjust, accepting it as their supreme deity, one they cannot appease with prayers. Karin's daring attempt to cross it only ends with a complete surrender along with a cry of recognition: God is unknowable—or indifferent—and only to be found in a morning ray of sunshine.

CONCLUSION

In *Stromboli*, there is only one lead, Karin, who holds the attention of the audience from beginning to end, being in almost every shot of the film. What is it that she wants? That becomes evident almost immediately, as soon as we see her at the camp. She wants to get out of there to go somewhere else, but once she is somewhere else, she again wants to escape, and that becomes her motive in the entire film. In the war she had lost everything—her family, her husband, and the life of privilege she was born into. She is displaced in the full sense of the word. But where exactly she wants to go is not clear, at first or later. The island where she ends up is worse than the camp, as she is married to a man who does not suit her. She tells him, "Though I am your wife, I am different." Her motives are defined by the idea of escaping. She will not cease and desist, though the man she chose is generally compliant, tries his best, but fails to satisfy her. So as soon as she is there, she wants to go elsewhere, to find herself with people equal to her. This becomes the motif of the film and that affects the point of view of the viewer, who seems stranded with her in a hellish spot, barely fit for human habitation as it is. As she is trapped on this spot, so is the viewer. When finally Karin summons the courage to go away—presumably to the other side of the island—she has to battle the forces of nature, and, exhausted and alone, she lies down to die. But the morning brings sunshine, awareness that she is carrying a child, and a wish to God to be saved. When Rossellini was asked where he would have her go, he answered that he didn't know; he said that would have been the subject of another film. The important point, he stated, is that the character came to a turning point— and to say something more would be superfluous, even arbitrary.

EUROPE '51

(1954)

★ ★ ★

Director: Roberto Rossellini
Screenplay: Roberto Rossellini, Sandro De Feo, Mario Pannunzio, Ivo Perilli, and Brunello Rondi
Producer: Roberto Rossellini. *Cinematographer:* Aldo Tonti. *Music Score:* Renzo Rossellini
Cast: Ingrid Bergman (Irene Girard), Alexander Knox (George Girard), Ettore Giannini (Andrea Casatti), Giulietta Masina (Giulietta, detta Passerotto), Sandro Franchina (Michele Girard), Alfred Browne (Hospital Priest), Antonio Pietrangeli (Psychiatrist), Giancarlo Vigorelli (Judge)
Also known as: The Greatest Love
Studio: Ponti–De Laurentiis Cinematografica
Released: November 3, 1954
Specs: 109 minutes; black and white
Availability: Blu-ray (Criterion Collection)

Europe '51, Bergman's second film with Rossellini, is, like its predecessor *Stromboli*, about a failed marriage and a final epiphany, but in a very different context. In *Stromboli*, Bergman marries the first available man in order to escape a displaced persons' camp. Her husband is a fisherman who barely scrapes a living, keeping her captive on a volcanic island until she rebels and runs away. In *Europe '51*, Bergman plays a socialite who abandons her husband, relatives, and friends to dedicate her life to the suffering poor classes, embarking on an apostolic-like mission in order to cleanse herself from guilt and self-hatred. She is declared mad and detained in a psychiatric ward for what seems the rest of her life.

The film, like the ones to follow with Rossellini (*Joan of Arc at the Stake* [1954], *Journey to Italy* [1954], and *Fear* [1955]), failed with both critics and audiences, hastening Bergman's downward spiral for the next few years. However, like *Stromboli*, *Europe '51* has in recent years received considerable attention from scholars and commentators, whose remarks, among other things, help to illuminate Rossellini's approach in directing Bergman. With just a few films, Rossellini deliberately abolished Bergman's image as a Hollywood superstar. For one thing, with *Europe '51* he demonstrated Bergman's ability to take on roles that reveal catastrophic self-conflicts, unrelieved by the prospect of a union with a glamorous costar—so familiar to her fans during her Hollywood era. Bergman, by now adjusted to Rossellini's methods, acted this part extremely well, proving that she had no need of a Gary Cooper or a Cary Grant to shine on the screen. The au-

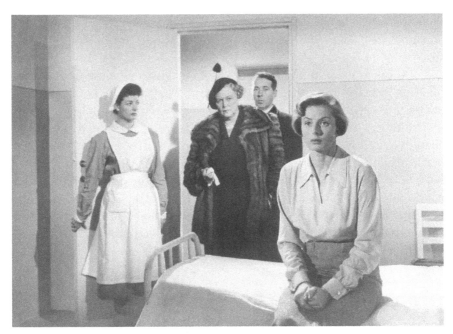

Irene Girard (Bergman) in her final isolation in the psychiatric ward. *Ponti–De Laurentiis Cinematografica / Photofest © Ponti–De Laurentiis Cinematografica*

diences, of course, used to seeing her being paired with another superstar, did not like her metamorphosis, thence her descent in public opinion—and her seven-year exile from Hollywood.

PLOT

In *Europe '51*, Bergman is Irene Girard, the wife of a wealthy industrialist, George Girard (Alexander Knox), who lives in Rome, surrounded by high-society friends and acquaintances. She has long adjusted to this life, busy with dinner parties and social obligations. She and her husband have a twelve-year old son, Michele (Sandro Franchina), who complains that he is alone and neglected, as his father is too involved in business and his mother tied up with social obligations. The mother tries to quiet the boy, but, during a dinner party, the boy falls down the stairs and breaks a leg. They rush him to a hospital, and the prognosis is hopeful: only a fracture, but the boy dies of a blood clot. After some inquiries, it is determined that the boy had committed suicide.

Devastated, the mother feels guilty of her neglect of her child, and, to relieve her guilt, she starts visiting poor neighborhoods, discovering how the underprivileged live. Soon, she finds herself helping them, but she understands that some of them are happy to live as they are, while others are susceptible to disease and crime. She devotes most of her time mingling and tending to them, to the displeasure of her husband, close friends, and relatives. When she urges a young man who has robbed a bank with two others to escape and go to his freedom, she is accused of helping a fugitive of justice. That gets her into trouble with the police, who do not bring charges against her, but with the advice of a psychiatrist and the consent of her husband they agree to commit her to an asylum. She behaves peacefully, but when asked why she was being antisocial she explains that she did not do this out of love but because of self-hatred for the life of indifference to others she had lived. She remains at the ward; her husband and mother depart, but underneath her barred window she hears some of the people she had been friendly to call her a saint.

THEMES

Europe '51 came in several versions.[1] The first version, appearing as *Europa '51* at the Venice Film Festival in 1952, was in Italian, as was the one,

almost identical, shown in Italian movie houses at the time. The locale of
that film was in Paris, and the film contained scenes showing the political
turmoil related to Italy's political left in collision with the Christian right.
Rossellini made changes to the international version, renamed it *Europe
'51*, and changed the location from Paris to Rome, dubbing the dialogue in
English. Another version was shown in the US, *The Greatest Love*. In the
international version, *Europe '51*, discussed here, some scenes considered
leftist propaganda were cut or shortened, as, for instance, Irene's visit to the
factory, which was considered a criticism of the brutal conditions the Italian
working class had to work under. This version was "cleaned up" of politics,
concentrating instead on Irene's plight as she plunged from her high social
status, practically changing identity and becoming a Christian, one who does
not conform to the established practices of Catholicism. This version of the
film sheds its presumed objective of advancing Socialism, Italy's Communist
Party, which was not Rossellini's true aim; neither was it meant to show his
heroine as an advocate of the Christian Democrats then politically aligned
with the dogmas of the Catholic Church. Ideologically, the film was pulled
in two opposite directions though it contained elements of both. Eventually
Irene's persona was divested of both Socialist and Catholic ideologies, thus
becoming a projection of Rossellini himself. By making Bergman's Irene the
main concern of the story, Rossellini allowed the viewer to perceive her progress—or descent, depending on one's point of view—as a series of rejections
of her social status, wealth, manners, and the divergent politics of the times.

Politics, however, is not entirely eradicated from the film, and *Europe
'51* remains Rossellini's reproof of the social inequalities of the postwar era.
When Andrea (Ettore Giannini), Irene's cousin, returns from a trip (he was
absent during the tragedy), he talks of a Socialist solution that would lift the
lower class out of poverty with government intervention. It is the war that is
to blame for the postwar era's social upheavals. Young Michele, he tells her,
lived through the war, the bombardments, everyday dangers that unsettled
his psyche and led to his suicide. As for the present, although nothing can
relieve her sorrow, Andrea suggests that visiting some of the poor families
could at least give her a motive to see his point of view. Irene listens to his
advice patiently and visits poor neighborhoods, making friends with those
in need, but in her heart she does not believe that the government can be
the solution to poverty. Commentators, like Adriano Aprà, attribute this
change to Rossellini's rejection of the Communist Party, then dominant
in Italy. Italy's prime minister, Giulio Andreotti, a Christian Democrat,
had sent a letter to Rossellini asking him to drop the leftist platform he
thought Rossellini was adopting. This is one reason the international version

embraces Irene's rejection of Andrea's advice, especially after her visit to a factory, where the conditions of working horrify her. The idea of raising the wages of those workers would not lead to paradise on earth, as Andrea had asserted, because it would not solve the social problems of poverty and need.

As in *Stromboli*, Rossellini describes a woman who while in distress discovers God: She is a modern Saint Francis, who gives up wealth and privilege to reach the poor, the sick, and the needy. Rossellini did not conceal his admiration for Saint Francis, having already done a film about him, *The Flowers of Saint Francis* (1950). Irene embraces the unfortunate, but for reasons different from Andrea's. Andrea, a publicist, retains his social status and uses his influence to convince others—mostly the government—that action must be taken to relieve the poor class. To do that, he is not giving up his social status as he is not himself charitable; as a journalist he works abstractly, not personally, though he would help someone to get a job. Irene, on the other hand, leads by example, and, to her surprise, she finds that some residents in the underprivileged neighborhoods live happily as they are. An example is Giulietta, played by the wonderful Giulietta Masina, Fellini's wife, who is a woman taking care of six children, three of them not her own. Irene becomes friendly with her during her repeated visits to the poor slum of Rome, learning in the process that happiness can come at all levels of the social ladder if one can accept life as it is.

While at the asylum, Irene is subjected to various interrogations, one by a judge who is trying to determine whether she is sane. A priest speaks to her in friendly tones, trying to elicit a confession. He is curious to know if she is infatuated with another man. She denies it and explains to him that one can be happy regardless of one's social position: "God made them as they are," she asserts calmly. "It is love that can move mountains." The priest speaks in generalities (as a priest also does speaking to Anna Magnani in *Rome: Open City*), as he believes it is his duty as he makes his rounds in the psychiatric asylum. When he hears the lines she speaks, he asks her if she took those from the Gospels. In the international version, Irene's scene with the priest is shortened, in order to, as Elena Degrada explains, "make her less saintly and the priest less obtuse."[2]

While in *Stromboli* Bergman looked openly erotic, in *Europe '51* she is photographed to look monastic, wrapped in long overcoats, while her face is shown to reflect the radiance of a saint. It is to be noted that at that time Bergman was pregnant with the twins, Isabella and Ingrid, and she was hoping the filming would end before her baby bump would show. Since the film was shot mostly at the Ponti–De Laurentiis Studios, lighting was controlled and helped set the tone/mood of the film. Bergman's face was brightly lit, or diagonally lined by shadow, to express the divided state of her mind. As her face was the only visible part of her, it was lit brightly to express her moods. These photographic tricks reveal her state of mind as she was being pulled in two directions: the established societal order she belonged to and the life of engagement with the needy that compelled her to abandon her social circles.

As soon as she learns from her cousin Andrea that Michele's death was a suicide, Irene falls into a deep depression and refuses to eat, staying in her room all the time, despite the pleadings of George, her husband, who thinks she should try to come back to her "normal" life. He is seconded by his mother-in-law, Irene's mother, who has flown all the way from America to console her daughter. Irene, however, resists all their attentions, saying to them that she is "not mad," that she needs to deal with this sorrow in her own way. Her husband, like her family, is not much help, insisting that she is being stubborn, something, her mother explains, she was since she was young, doing only what she wanted, not taking advice. Having nowhere else to turn, Irene isolates herself from her social environment.

Language in the film was controlled to show the political realities of the times. The men who will determine her case are a judge, a lawyer for the family, and a doctor at the asylum. The latter, impressed by Irene's ability to "cure" a patient from her attempt to commit suicide, asks her if she felt an inner strength, which enabled saints to do the same. But for Irene this was simply an act of love—not a miracle. When the judge speaks of the relativism of the times, as everything is twisted to reflect sociopolitical and religious positions, he simply reveals Rossellini's exposure of those who fail to comprehend Irene's simple desire to love others, mistaking it for propaganda that takes various forms, as the political factions of the day, including the Christian Democrats who were unable to communicate with each other. In *Europe '51*, there is a collision of these ideologies, which pass by as a woman is committed to an asylum for the insane when her very simple language is misinterpreted for political or religious dogma. In some ways, this is similar to George Orwell's "double-speak," or today's "alternative facts." When the priest says, "Yes, we must all love but there are rules," he means that Irene's ties with her family and friends are broken in order for her to help the poor, implying that love in this case does not count. Doctor, lawyer, judge, priest—they all think that way. In the end, Irene's incarceration to a mental ward is a failure of communication. Politics, medicine, law, religion have all failed to communicate with her, or she with them. But she sees, much more clearly than they, that any attempt to make them understand is futile—and she remains silent.

CONCLUSION

This movie was a unique challenge for Bergman, even as she had played a nun and a saint both on film and stage before. In *Europe '51*, she had to align herself perfectly with Rossellini's views of the world, views that show that he had adapted and adjusted to the realities of the 1950s, the Cold War era, which had gone past the realities of the post–World War II era of neorealism, which had concentrated on the wreckage Fascism had left behind in Italy. Another front had opened, one that showed that the world was being pulled apart by two new forces—Communism and the political/religious right. Rossellini had borrowed elements from both of these forces, only to show how inadequate they were to deal with Italy's—and the world's—needs, thence his title, *Europe '51*. Instead, he furthered the idea of Saint Francis revisiting the earth, this time in the form of a woman who leaves friends and relatives and her high social status, having turned to love as an antidote to misery and political chaos. It is a testimonial to Bergman's skill that she did not allow this projection to become a mawkish, tearful degradation of her image. In a power shot, showing her face behind bars, with her friends in tears waving at her, calling her "a saint," she indeed projects the dignity of a saint. Thus, by having a beautiful woman fall from her high social status to what amounted to an incarceration, Rossellini showcased the paradox of her sainthood: the highborn, most sensitive, and most intelligent make the best saints.

ANASTASIA

(1956)

★ ★ ★ ★ ★

Director: Anatole Litvak
Screenplay: Guy Bolton and Arthur Laurents, based on the play by Marcelle
    Maurette
Producer: Buddy Adler. *Cinematographer:* Jack Hildyard. *Music Score:* Alfred
    Newman
Cast: Ingrid Bergman (Anna Koreff / Anastasia), Yul Brynner (General
    Bounine), Helen Hayes (Dowager Empress Maria Feodorovna),
    Akim Tamiroff (Boris Chernov), Martita Hunt (Baroness Elena von
    Livenbaum), Natalie Schafer (Irina Lissemskaia)
Studio: Twentieth Century Fox
Released: December 14, 1956
Specs: 105 minutes; color
Availability: DVD (Twentieth Century Fox)

By 1955, Bergman's marriage to Roberto Rossellini was on the brink of collapse and her career seemed ruined forever, when an apparent savior came
along: Jean Renoir, who a decade earlier when Bergman was at her Hollywood peak had refused to do a movie with her when she asked him, saying
he would wait "with a net" to catch her when she was going down.[1] The
movie, *Paris Does Strange Things* (*Elena et Les Hommes*), had luxurious
sets and costumes, featured famous stars like Mel Ferrer and Jean Marais,

with Bergman smiling, flirting, and dancing, but doing little else. The elegantly filmed *Elena* did not capture the attention of American audiences then or later, but it did give Bergman some space with hostile audiences, while hastening her rupture with Rossellini. But her next film, *Anastasia*, revived her career in film and netted her the New York Film Critics Award and an Oscar for Best Actress. The film had the sweep of a historical epic as it recounted the myth of the survival of Grand Duchess Anastasia Nikolaevna, daughter of Tsar Nicholas II and Empress Alexandra Feodorovna, whose entire family had been assassinated at the aftermath of the Soviet Revolution in 1918. Financed by Twentieth Century Fox with a generous budget of more than $4.5 million, *Anastasia* featured luxurious sets and costumes, a rousing music score by Alfred Newman, and photography by Jack Hildyard, offering audiences a grand re-creation of the era of Russian exiles in Europe who yearned for a return to their former glory.

As usual in her major films, Bergman carried the weight of the protagonist with distinction, bolstered by an equally distinguished supporting cast: Helen Hayes, Yul Brynner, and veteran actors Akim Tamiroff, Martita Hunt, and Natalie Schafer. The film was a huge popular success both in Europe and across the Atlantic. Critics praised and audiences went to see, intrigued by the prospect of a beloved actress who had come back to the fold. Even Senator Edwin C. Johnson, who had denounced her on the Senate floor seven years earlier, joined the chorus in praise. Her Oscar was accepted by Cary Grant, who soon rejoined her for a new movie, *Indiscreet* (filmed in England), which further restored her image and renewed her ties with Tinseltown. Bergman had now come full circle, but she chose her roles as she willed from that point on and she never again allowed outsiders to dictate what she would do next. Her marriage to Lars Schmidt, a Swedish producer, in 1958, kept her in Europe for most of the next decade, and though her visits to America were rather sporadic, her ties to Hollywood now rested on firmer ground. Still looking young and beautiful in her early forties, Bergman projected a cosmopolitan air that earned her new friends and kept her in demand in all acting fields. Her golden age in the 1940s Hollywood, however, never returned.

PLOT

The opening shots of *Anastasia* show crowds exiting the magnificent Russian church in Paris, while a chorus is heard singing Easter hymns, celebrating the Russian Easter. An errant woman (Bergman) is seen pausing before a picture of the Romanov royal family, then walking toward the riverfront, apparently ready to fall into the river. A man pulls the woman back and takes her to a basement where two other men are waiting, apparently interested in her identity. The man is General Bounine (Brynner), head of a group who brawl over the cost of transforming this woman into a credible facsimile of Grand Duchess Anastasia. One of his partners is Boris Chernov, played by Tamiroff, a bit of a buffoon no matter what he plays; he adds a comedic touch to this motley group. Chernov is a cheat, financing the enterprise by using investments from the well-to-do exiles; the other man, Piotr Petrovin (Sacha Pitoeff), keeps tabs on operations. Bounine knows that Anna Koreff,[2] the woman he has brought in, is not the grand duchess, but, since the group is financially stressed by the long search to find her, he declares that even if the real Anastasia does not exist, they have no option but to train Koreff to behave and look like a duchess. They have eight days to accomplish their task; otherwise, they will go to jail for fraud. If all goes well, the 10 million pounds that has been deposited in the Bank of England by the tsar will be released to her, and of course a large part of it will be theirs, they assume.

After a few days of intense training, Koreff accomplishes the task of walking straight, dancing the waltz, memorizing names of those she was supposed to know at seventeen, and recalling the various places she had lived in the ten-year interim, mostly hospitals and asylums for the mentally ill. As she suffers from amnesia, she is confused about where she had been and has a hard time recalling the sequence of events of her shiftless life. But after careful tutoring from Bounine, Koreff appears before a group of Russian émigrés, headed by Irina Lissemskaia, played by Natalie Schafer (who later embodied the charmingly nutty Mrs. Howell in the popular TV comedy *Gilligan's Island*). The aristocrats she has assembled, however, seem far from convinced that Bounine's protégée is Anastasia and dismiss his claims and those of his coconspirators.

The plot takes a dramatic turn when Bounine decides to travel to Copenhagen to try to present Koreff, who had been uncomfortable throughout the process of her transformation, to the dowager empress. The latter is set against such an encounter, having faced many pretenders for a long time, but Bounine finds an ally in the unsexy and vain Baroness Elena von Livenbaum, wonderfully played by Martita Hunt, who has entertained thoughts of a liaison with the handsome Russian general. The dowager empress, given with regal command by Helen Hayes, finally accepts to meet the pretender, and during an emotional encounter with Koreff, Koreff coughs violently. When the empress asks her if she is ill, Koreff explains that she had always coughed in moments of emotional stress. Suddenly the empress yields and embraces her granddaughter, recognizing her as the Grand Duchess Anastasia. She is to be presented to a large group of upper-class Russians and be officially accepted into their circle as such. Meanwhile, Prince Paul von Haraldberg (Ivan Desny), a pauper cousin of the empress, has been charmed by the stunning looks of Koreff, and, entirely convinced she is Anastasia, he plans to propose marriage. But the dowager empress, who knows Bounine and who can read hearts, suspects that he and her granddaughter have fallen in love. As preparations for a grand ball are under way, the empress prepares to go in and announce to the crowd that Anastasia and Bounine have gone away together. The "play is over," she says, and the movie ends.

THEMES

The main theme explored in *Anastasia* is loss of identity. Anna Koreff is the fictional name the moviemakers chose for Anna Anderson, a real woman who had excited the curiosity of many, including the Russian exiles in the West. Anderson had claimed she was Anastasia, but she lived a life so erratic that her claims, though provocative, lacked real substance and were looked upon with suspicion. Many, however, believed that there was something to the myth that the youngest daughter of Tsar Nicholas II and Empress Alexandra had survived the massacre of the family. The movie, a period piece, was set in 1928, ten years after the royal family had been shot; but in 1956, when the movie was being made, Anderson was living in Germany in a hut in the Black Forest hidden from public view, away from the curious, but still a reminder to those desperate to have a living member of the dethroned dynasty who could reclaim past glories. It is upon such shaky historical grounds that the image of Anastasia was created by the filmmakers, who left the question of her identity ambiguous, either because they believed it to be true or were deceived by Anderson's uncanny memory of details that no one but the actual Anastasia would know. The historical question of Anderson's identity was not resolved until late in the twentieth century when DNA evidence proved that she was a fraud.[3] But at the time the movie was made, the myth of her being Anastasia was very much alive. Koreff goes to Copenhagen to meet the empress with the name Anderson in her passport.

Another major theme of the movie was that of displacement. The Bolshevik Revolution of 1917, which overthrew the Romanov dynasty, was a monumental historical convulsion that caused the massive displacement of Russian people from all walks of life but mostly those connected with the royal family. In the opening shots of *Anastasia* the viewer sees crowds outside of the Russian church in Paris (the filming took place in London), attending services or milling around, some being vendors, cabdrivers, or menial workers trying to survive. Ingrid Bergman had already played displaced persons in *Casablanca*, *Arch of Triumph*, and *Stromboli* before tackling *Anastasia*, so she was familiar with this type of role. But while in the previous movies she had been a fictional character, here Bergman was asked to represent an image believed by many to be a missing living figure of a lost royal dynasty. The Romanovs had been in power in Russia for three centuries, and many of those who had been displaced after the royal family's execution, especially those who had been able to retain some of their wealth and status, were thirsting for reassurance that a member of the Romanov family had survived. The group of prominent aristocrats who met Koreff in the film felt wary of her presence, having seen many pretenders before, but they were also eager to find a princess savior who would meet their aspirations. Thus Koreff, a displaced person herself, became a new focus of interest of a large group of displaced persons, renewing hopes of a return of a dynasty, hopes that lasted for decades.

The Pygmalion myth has been brought up by various *Anastasia* commentators,[4] and it is worth mentioning. Pygmalion, a Cypriot sculptor, had made a statue of Galatea so beautiful that he fell in love with it. As is well known, *Pygmalion* was also the title of a play by George Bernard Shaw, which was filmed in 1939 and again as a musical stage play, *My Fair Lady* (1956), filmed in 1964. General Bounine undertook to transform a woman from the streets, as Professor Higgins did with Eliza Doolittle, a flower girl, betting that if he taught her to speak proper English he could pass her as a duchess. But while Shaw's play was a comedy and light in tone, *Anastasia* was a historical melodrama featuring a woman who seemed unstable and suicidal, an image that would fit Koreff, Bounine's creation, rather than the endearing gamine invented by Shaw and his stage and film imitators.

Nonetheless, Bounine had a comparable task to perform: taking a bedraggled, shivering with cold, and disoriented woman and transforming her into a lost princess. Yul Brynner had won an Oscar in 1956 for his role in the film version of *The King and I*, a Broadway musical in which he had appeared as King Mongkut of Siam for more than forty-five hundred performances. At the time he played General Bounine in *Anastasia* he was at the peak of his career, having also appeared in the blockbuster epic *The Ten Commandments* as Rameses II. One can add that two years later, 1958,

Anna Koreff/Anderson (Bergman) pleads with Dowager Empress Maria Feodorovna (Helen Hayes) to recognize her as her granddaughter Anastasia. *Twentieth Century Fox Film Corporation / Photofest © Twentieth Century Fox Film Corporation*

he also played Dmitri Karamazov in *The Brothers Karamazov*, directed by Richard Brooks—so he was used to playing characters larger than life. His General Bounine was a tense-muscled and domineering character firmly planted on the ground with open legs and crossed arms, his gaze meant to mow down any opposition. He seemed to be motivated not just by the prospect of ill-gotten gains but also by his passion to accomplish something nearly impossible: to make a credible princess out of a drifting and amnesiac woman found in the streets. More importantly, he had to present her to a group of aristocrats highly suspicious of pretenders, whom they regarded as fronts put up by impostors aiming to get their hands on the duchess's large fortune.

The most difficult task Bounine confronted was presenting the fake Anastasia to the dowager empress, and for that he and his protégée had to travel by train to Copenhagen (a second unit had filmed the parade scenes in Copenhagen), where the empress resided. When Bergman's Koreff was issued a passport bearing the name of Anna Anderson, permission had to be obtained from Anderson herself. The encounter with the dowager empress was staged with unparalleled skill. Both Bergman and Hayes had been experienced stage actresses (at the time Bergman was doing *Tea and Sympathy* by Robert Anderson, in Paris), and the scene between them sparked with tension. But by that time Bergman's character had even exceeded Bounine's expectations, and she truly started believing she was Anastasia. So her pleading had an authenticity that even the unbending empress, who had much experience in countering fakes, was moved to tears. The scene between empress and granddaughter is exquisitely staged, evoking to its fullest extent the pathos of recognition. Helen Hayes's performance gave the movie its extra polish, creating the illusion that a regal personality had passed on the scepter of royalty to the next generation.

Romance has also surfaced, as the empress senses that Bounine and her granddaughter have fallen in love, so she becomes the deus ex machina by staging their flight. It might be supposed that the empress provided them with a proportionally generous wedding gift. This is where the film leaves us bereft of a grand romantic emotion. The romance is somewhat lackluster, as Bounine serves better as a tutor, unbending and dictatorial until the very end, when his jealousy becomes obvious as he bows out of his protégée's good fortunes, leaving her to be wooed by the aristocratic breed of Prince Paul—himself a pauper in the empress's retinue. Also, Bergman and Brynner lack romantic chemistry, never seen courting and kissing or even liking each other as in the romantic encounters between Brynner and Deborah Kerr in *The King and I*.

CONCLUSION

Anastasia was a landmark in Bergman's career and in some ways for American cinema. When she left Hollywood, the McCarthy era was beginning to take hold, which meant that many writers and directors moved abroad or wrote under cover names, and it was easy in postwar, increasing puritanical America to revile a wayward woman who had followed her desire to make a movie with an Italian director, leaving husband and child behind. But in seven years, things had changed; it was not that morality was getting tolerant (it took the sixties for that to be accomplished), but actors, directors, and stars went abroad to make movies as the hold of the studios on them was breaking up (Gregory Peck in Paris for *Roman Holiday*, Kirk Douglas in Italy to do *Ulysses*, Cary Grant to the Riviera to do *To Catch a Thief*— to cite a few examples). Bergman's triumphant comeback was a sign that American audiences were ready—if not eager—to welcome a star who had done "penance," in the words of Ed Sullivan, a popular television host who had thought of inviting her to his show. When Bergman arrived in New York to receive her New York Film Critics Award, crowds were waiting for her at the airport, and she was mobbed wherever she went for the few days she stayed there. Professionally, Bergman had grown by her association with Rossellini, having been exposed to harsh conditions of shooting in the volcanic island of Stromboli and elsewhere in Europe. She had, indeed, become a European actress, welcome to do work on the stage, TV, and film on both sides of the Atlantic. When after the success of *Anastasia* Twentieth Century Fox offered her a contract to do five movies at $1 million apiece, Bergman rejected the offer on the grounds that she did not want to be "indentured" to a studio again, and she let the lucrative offer go.[5] From now on she could pick her own roles, depending on her own inclinations. She had gained the maturity and sense of purpose that allowed her to choose wisely, and that is what she did for the rest of her life.

⓯

INDISCREET

(1958)

★ ★ ★

Director: Stanley Donen
Screenplay: Norman Krasna, based on his play *Kind Sir*
Producer: Stanley Donen. *Cinematography:* Freddie Young. *Music Score:* Richard
    Bennett
Cast: Cary Grant (Philip Adams), Ingrid Bergman (Anna Kalman), Cecil
    Parker (Alfred Munson), Phyllis Calvert (Mrs. Margaret Munson),
    David Kossoff (Carl Banks), Megs Jenkins (Doris Banks)
Studio: Grandon Publishers Ltd.
Released: June 26, 1958
Specs: 100 minutes; color
Availability: DVD (Olive Films)

Indiscreet came when Ingrid Bergman was breaking ties with Rossellini and had already made the acquaintance of Lars Schmidt, who would soon become her third husband. It was a transition period for Bergman, who had already won an Oscar with *Anastasia* (1956) but had not fully reconnected with Hollywood. Cary Grant, who had accepted her Oscar for *Anastasia*, had remained her true friend during Bergman's exile from Hollywood. When Bergman arrived in London in the fall of 1957, Grant was there at the airport to help her escape the relentless scrutiny of the press corps and hustled her to her hotel and to safety.

The movie had been based on a play, *Kind Sir* by Norman Krasna, which had a successful run in 1956 and was now coming to the screen, produced and directed by Stanley Donen, who invited Bergman to come to London to star in it opposite Grant. *Indiscreet* is a frothy romantic comedy, which proved an antidote to the tragic heroines Bergman had played for a decade, from Joan Madou in *Arch of Triumph* to Saint Joan in *Joan of Arc* (1948), to Rossellini's succession of bedeviled heroines who found themselves in gloomy circumstances, torn by conflicts beyond human endurance. In refreshing contrast, Bergman's Anna Kalman is a rich and successful actress of the stage—something that suited Bergman's temperament—a mature woman beautiful, admired, and . . . single. In the film, she is courted by the emperor of charm, Cary Grant, who had been her partner in *Notorious* (1946) and had already conquered countless screen queens, including Grace Kelly in *To Catch a Thief* (1955). The cast also included Cecil Parker, an English character actor cut to measure for absurd situations (opposite Danny Kaye in *The Court Jester*), and Phyllis Calvert, star of many romances on the English screen, playing Anna's sister and counselor. The

Philip Adams (Grant) and flirtatious Anna Kalman (Bergman) in one of their love encounters.
Warner Bros. Pictures / Photofest © Warner Bros. Pictures

film was photographed by Freddie Young, who later collected Oscars for his work for David Lean, and Bergman is shown in brilliant color, looking splendid in the gowns designed for her by Christian Dior. Most importantly, Bergman proved herself a sparkling comedienne, expert in timing and clever repartee.

PLOT

The plot of *Indiscreet* is the essence of simplicity. It is about a famous actress, Anna Kalman, beautiful, talented, and adored by her fans, who is returning from a vacation in Majorca. She is wealthy, easily being able to afford a suite and two servants in a luxury London hotel, and she has a loving sister and an accommodating brother-in-law. But she lacks what she yearns for as a beautiful woman a step short of middle years: a love interest. She arrives with a retinue of men carrying trunks and tries to soothe her nerves by applying face cream. When her sister Margaret comes in and asks her what happened to the handsome colonel she was dating back there "who looks like a Greek statue," she replies, "And he talks like a Greek statue." Then, luck intervenes. The door opens, and the incarnation of male elegance makes his entrance. Cary Grant, in his early fifties, looks as attractive as ever, the gray in his temples having been touched up, some wrinkles in his face smoothed, his smile just winning as ever, and his black eyes darting flames aimed to melt hearts. She is obviously smitten and makes the first move when the man, Philip Adams, is about to exit the hotel.

They are all invited to hear him in a speech he is going to give at a state dinner. He is an important economist, stationed mainly in Paris, and courted eagerly by Alfred Munson (Parker) to become a member of NATO. His interest, however, is centered on Munson's sister-in-law, who is more than eager to get to know him. That happens, and the NATO business is laid aside in the movie plot. The attraction is mutual, and then things take their course.

After weeks of an affair, the secret spills out as Anna's brother-in-law, Munson, learns that his colleague is not married and passes that secret on to his wife Margaret (Calvert), who in turn cannot help revealing the secret as the three of them are ready to go to a party. Anna storms out of the room enraged, shouting, "How dare he make love to me and not be a married man!" At the party, things get out of hand, as Philip, a bit on the tipsy side, starts dancing on his own, tries to tip his heels, almost falls, and also succeeds in showing his bowlegs—as indeed Grant, a former acrobat, was bowlegged. Not to be outdone, Anna, holding her skirt, tiptoes away, all class, splendor, and elegance, easily dazzling the amazed crowds.

Back home, in a controlled rage, Anna devises a plan to extract revenge on the duplicitous Philip. She has two domestics, Carl Banks (David Kossoff) and his wife Doris (Megs Jenkins); Anna cajoles Carl into playing a part, and he reluctantly complies. Tomorrow at midnight, she says, he is to open her bedroom door, in his pajamas, show himself, and shut the door again, in seconds. The plan works—though for a moment it looks like a comedy of errors—Philip gets outraged (not really), and the end shows that this was only a lovers' quarrel, as the plan is to get married.

THEMES

The main point of *Indiscreet* is to showcase Ingrid Bergman in a role that she had never really played: a woman known for her beauty, high social status, with no troubling clouds over her head—except some puffy ones that can easily disperse. The film also achieves technical excellence. Photographed by Young, two of the screen's most glamorous heroes stay center stage almost throughout the movie. Young photographs Bergman in full frames—as she swishes through a door, for instance, in a long gold gown, ready to go to a party. In rich-colored gowns, black or white or deep purple, Bergman in Technicolor looks regal and is attention grabbing. And of course, there are the close-ups: Young takes advantage of her photogenic face and photographs it from all angles, full face, from the right or left, and lovingly lying on a pillow holding the telephone. Young also introduces the split screen, known at the time in art house cinema (and reintroduced a few years later in *Pillow Talk* and other comedies in the Rock Hudson–Doris Day movies), in which two persons talk through the telephone but in two frames joined imperceptibly in the middle. The trick was not to show two people, whether married or not, on the same bed, as the Hays Code was still in effect in the late 1950s. Young devised two square frames, joined—and splitting the screen—in which two persons holding a telephone are talking to each other. Both are in bed, in cozy relaxation, whispering little nothings to each other, as in sexual foreplay. The photographer timed their movements, so their faces look at each other's, their bodies roll closer and closer to each other, and their hands wander off toward the other; for instance, when Grant's hand extends toward Bergman's backside, she draws up the bedcover over that part, as if avoiding his salacious touch. At another point, their hands reach toward the same position in both frames, and the illusion is created that they have really touched.

The dancing scene is also suggestive of a mating call. If one doesn't sing, like a bird—a thing that can only be done vocally by humans—one dances. Dancing is giving up one's inhibitions and is done by any race, in any culture, and regardless of one's status. Poor or rich, people dance. In the higher societies, people dance in designer costume, in tuned notes, possibly classical, while middle or lower classes use the banjo, mandolin, guitar, or drum to excite their senses and get to move about uninhibited. In *Indiscreet*, Grant's dancing is hilarious; his happiness and excitement about his relationship to Anna is infectious, as is hers for him. They are neither Fred Astaire nor Ginger Rogers, and both totter and fall, losing their balance and looking a bit ridiculous, but Donen, the consummate choreographer and director of dance musicals, trained them to be mannered aristocrats loosening up.

CONCLUSION

Indiscreet is one of the several films of that era that poked fun at society. *Peyton Place* (1957), a popular movie melodrama, shocked many of the fifties audiences because of its portrayal of society's hypocritical treatment of love affairs. Philip has made no commitment of staying monogamous, therefore he remains "indiscreet" in telling Anna that he is married so he can dally harmlessly with her with no injury—he imagines—to anyone. Anna is surrounded by a loving sister, who sees Philip's approach coming close to her sister's heart and knows that a married woman has secured a future. But don't expect for a moment that Anna will become a homey housewife to cook and iron for Philip. *Indiscreet* is a comedic fantasy, and as critic Lucy Fisher puts it, "portrays the actress role-playing offstage."[1] Anna will continue to be the same woman, married or not, on stage or in life. High-class beautiful ladies can do that, and of course so can handsome men who fall into traps laid by themselves, as Grant, picking up a bottle of champagne, says: "I'll swizzle it with my nose."

16

THE INN OF THE SIXTH HAPPINESS

(1958)

★ ★ ★ ★

Director: Mark Robson
Screenplay: Isobel Lennart, based on the novel by Alan Burgess
Producer: Buddy Adler. *Cinematography:* Freddie Young. *Music Score:* Malcolm
    Arnold
Cast: Ingrid Bergman (Gladys Aylward), Curt Jurgens (Capt. Lin Nan), Robert
    Donat (Mandarin of Yang Cheng), Moultrie Kelsall (Dr. Robinson),
    Athene Seyler (Jeannie Lawson), Burt Kwouk (Li), Ronald Squire (Sir
    Francis Jamison), Peter Chong (Yang)
Studio: Twentieth Century Fox
Released: December 19, 1958
Specs: 158 minutes; color
Availability: DVD (Twentieth Century Fox)

The Inn of the Sixth Happiness was Bergman's second major movie with Twentieth Century Fox, whose executives saw the advantages of spending lavishly on an epic blockbuster that featured their rehabilitated star. After *Anastasia*, Bergman had not remained idle, making *Indiscreet* with Cary Grant, in color and splendid décor but light in substance. *The Inn of the Sixth Happiness* was a major undertaking, requiring expensive sets, thousands of extras, and filming on location in Snowdonia, North Wales, subbing for the Chinese mountains. The film recounts the life and achievements of Gladys Aylward (1902–1970), an English missionary who went to China on her own volition as World War II was approaching and the Japanese were already attacking China, then under the nationalist leader Chiang Kai-shek. Aylward's journey to China had just been recently recounted in *The Small Woman* (1957) by Alan Burgess, on which the scenario of *The Inn* was based. Aylward is said to have strongly objected to Bergman's taking the role—and name—of her Chinese mission, as she herself was a devout Christian, void of romance (she said she had never kissed a man), and innocent of any scandal. But the moviemakers trusted Bergman to bring the role to life—and they were right. The story worked well, as Bergman approached the project with her usual rigor, though initially hesitant to play a missionary after she had already played a nun and a saint. She again demonstrated her ability to adjust to any role that came her way, no matter what the context. As her biographer Donald Spoto observes in his commentary on this film, Bergman had done movies in widely divergent roles and in five languages: Swedish, German, English, Italian, and French. No other actor, he adds, had achieved as much, to his knowledge.[1]

Gladys Aylward (Bergman) leads children to safety through treacherous mountain territory.
Twentieth Century Fox Film Corporation / Photofest © Twentieth Century Fox Film Corporation

PLOT

Gladys Aylward (Bergman) is first seen applying for the mission to China at the London office, directed by Dr. Robinson (Moultrie Kelsall), but she is told that she lacks the educational background needed for a missionary. She decides to go on her own, so she sets to work as a domestic at the residence of Sir Francis Jamison (Ronald Squire), who is impressed by her singleness of mind and allows her to read books on China from his library. Equipped with passport and ticket, Gladys takes the less expensive route to China, the Trans-Siberian Railway, crosses two continents, and she finally arrives in Tientsin and is then transported by mule to Yang Cheng, the province where the Mandarin of Yang Cheng (Robert Donat) rules. Gladys is warmly received by the assistant to the mission, Jeannie Lawson (Athene Seyler), who lives in the Inn of the Sixth Happiness. When asked what the name means, Lawson, a hardworking elderly woman, replies that in Chinese folklore there are five stages of happiness one can attain: wealth, health, longevity, virtue, and a painless death; but the sixth must be found inside the heart by the individual himself.

At first, Gladys finds the environment strange and even hostile. There is a prison rebellion, in which she is almost decapitated by one of the inmates, but this ends in friendship with Li (Burt Kwouk), leader of the revolt, who becomes her loyal follower. To test her, the Mandarin demands that she put an end to the practice of local women to bind the feet of their female children so they are unable to run when grown up, a sign of subjection of the female to the male. Gladys conforms and gradually adjusts to life in the village by changing her Western dress for the local attire, a blue gown with pants that cover her body from her neck to her ankles. Aside from the motherly Lawson, she gains the friendship and assistance of the genial Yang (Peter Chong), the inn's cook and improviser of biblical stories to help her teach Christianity to the children, though not a Christian himself.

But signs of trouble develop. Jeannie Lawson, already weak and in ill health, dies in an accident, leaving Gladys in charge of the school. The Mandarin, old and in poor health (as was Robert Donat, who played him), is unable to mount resistance when the Japanese planes attack and destroy the village, killing many. Japanese soldiers invade, and Gladys runs for her life, hiding in a cemetery to escape arrest. Meanwhile, a man has come into her life, Capt. Lin Nan (Curd Jürgens—billed as Curt Jurgens), tall and handsome, and barely looking Chinese. He explains to her that his father was Dutch but, as he could not live in Denmark because of his mother's Chinese blood, he wholeheartedly chose to return to China and defend his country against imperial Japan. When the Mandarin, who is an affectionate father figure, invites both Gladys and Lin to his palace, she appears in a splendid red robe of Chinese design he had given her as a gift. Bergman's beauty shines as she enters his chamber, dazzling Captain Lin who finds her irresistible, and soon the two are in love. But war separates them, as Lin has to return to his troops, and Gladys, now with a Chinese name, Jen-Ai ("loved by the people"), and Chinese citizenship, undertakes to lead the fifty children of the village, with fifty more who joined from neighboring areas, over the mountains to the next province where they can be evacuated to safety. Before she leaves, in a small ceremony, the Mandarin is converted to Christianity. (Robert Donat struggled to dub his own voice, as he was suffering from severe asthma and died shortly after the shooting was finished.)

The twenty-five-minute sequence showing the trek of Gladys leading the children to safety is one of the most memorable sequences in film, compared by commentators to that of Moses leading his people to the Promised Land. The group had to survive hunger, cold, lack of basic medical supplies, and the Japanese attacks. They pass dangerous mountain peaks in the inhospitable terrain, climbing through rocky paths or crossing torrential streams, losing their valuable guide Li, who is killed while trying to divert the attention of Japanese attackers threatening the children. Gladys perseveres and reaches Sian, the town from where they will be transported to safety. There she rejoins Dr. Robinson, who, astonished, recognizes the woman who he thought a long time ago was unqualified to be a missionary. When asked to remain there, Gladys replies that she is going back to Yang Cheng, "back home," she says looking at the ring Captain Lin had given her.

THEMES AND MOTIVES

The film defines missionary work as a personal experience rather than as a mission directed from the outside. Modeled after Gladys Aylward the historical figure, Bergman's character is not associated with any particular denomination and goes to China on her own volition. She believes in her mission intuitively and passionately, as someone who is guided by her heart, as if an inner voice of God. By that definition, she would have attained the "sixth happiness" as defined by Jeannie Lawson. Her missionary work is unquestionably her only purpose in life and she continues it to the end of her life. Objections arose whether Bergman, still considered a sinful woman in the minds of many movie fans, should play Aylward, a woman who was

small and feisty and had a cockney accent and a "pit bull" disposition. But
these objections were overruled by the top men at Twentieth Century
Fox—Spyros Skouras, president, and Buddy Adler, producer—who took
the risk, confident that Bergman would not disappoint. Their trust in her
proved fortuitous. In her early forties, Bergman looked matronly after three
pregnancies; three children with Rossellini—Robertino and the twins Ingrid and Isabella—and of course Pia Lindstrom, her first daughter with Dr.
Petter Lindstrom, now eighteen and a college student. But Bergman was
still beautiful and youthful looking, and her star power had again reached a
zenith after a seven-year hiatus. She had always approached any role with
utter commitment, and when she decided to play a missionary she trans-
formed herself heart and mind into one. Audiences did not seem to be
affected by her past indiscretions, as the film proved very popular. Though
the real Aylward was fluent in Chinese (in fact, when she went back to
England many years later she had forgotten her English), the producers
decided that almost the entire dialogue should be in English. As Aylward,
Bergman is never seen in a church or chapel, never practices religious rites,
only supervising the overzealous Yang who, in a comic scene, preaches that
Noah visited the birth of Christ in Bethlehem. When Bergman coughs disapprovingly, he changes his tune saying that Noah, like many early biblical
figures, lived hundreds of years. Bergman had already played a saint in *Joan
of Arc*, and in one scene in *The Inn of the Sixth Happiness*, when one of the
prisoners is holding an ax over her head, she extends her hands pleading, a
look in her face much reminiscent of Joan's.

Bergman's screen persona had often been defined as "vulnerable"; that
is, of a woman assailed by misfortune, of being victimized or even killed.
Bergman had played several roles in her younger days as a vulnerable person: Ivy Peterson in *Dr. Jekyll and Mr. Hyde*, Paula Alquist in *Gaslight*, and
Alicia Huberman in *Notorious*, to use a few of the best-known examples.
Her vulnerability was a result of either exterior menace, as in the case of
Hyde, or of a personal flaw, as in her embodiment of Joan Madou in *Arch
of Triumph*, where she appears reckless in the choice of lovers. But Bergman by and large outgrew her vulnerability both in life and in the screen
roles she chose to play after her separation with Rossellini. In *Anastasia*, as
a suicidal and amnesiac woman, she proves equal to the task of becoming a
princess under the guidance of Bounine. In *The Inn of the Sixth Happiness*,
she shows a steely determination to achieve her goal from the start. There
seems to be no power on earth that will stop her from achieving her goal:
She is poor, uneducated, and unqualified to become a missionary, in the
views of those who would not have sent her to China. She is at the bottom

of the social scale, but not weak or easily intimidated. When rejected, she decides to go on her own, and her iron will carries her through the most unlikely adventures when she gets to her destination. Though she finds it hard to communicate with the natives, who call her "the foreign devil," Jen-Ai (her given Chinese name) takes over the management of the inn, establishes a better relationship with the Mandarin who had been cautious of foreign influence, and manages the inn ably until the Japanese attack. When she undertakes to drive the children over the inhospitable mountains, she and the children cross a torrential stream in their path, hanging on a rope and almost freezing to death afterward. She then urges them to sing "This Old Man" while they are warming themselves by the fire. She is the mother of the young crowd, and they are equally devoted to her and trusting her to lead them through treacherous routes to safety.

Her only vulnerability is shown in her passion for Captain Lin. The historical Lin (Linnan in Burgess's book) was not a half-breed, but wholly Chinese, and in the real story of Gladys Aylward he and Gladys did not have a romantic relationship. But any Hollywood invention that features a beautiful heroine begs for a male of equal "sex appeal." Curt Jurgens was an established actor (though mostly in European films), solid looking and handsome, and taller than Bergman, which solved some logistical problems when he stood next to her (he didn't have to stand on stilts as did the likes of Charles Boyer and Humphrey Bogart). Jurgens looked anything but Chinese, thence the invention that his father was Dutch, but the makeup people still had to pull his eyebrows back and use eye shadow to make him look Asian. And he and Bergman kiss, and that's obligatory for lovers. Also, their story does not end with the end of the trek. When Gladys/Bergman delivers the children to their destination, she looks for a reunion with Lin. One can say that vulnerability did not lie with Bergman's character, but with the scriptwriters who could not resist bringing their star within the sphere of a romantic liaison. Did it work? Very much so. The romantic subplot made Bergman desirable not only as one of pure soul, but as a woman who, despite her enforced plainness of garb, could not entirely suppress (nor would the audience want her to) the fact that she was very beautiful. Audiences would expect Bergman to show her beauty at some point in the film, and Buddy Adler and Isobel Lennart, producer and screenwriter, respectively obliged. A beautiful heroine is also expected to be in love at some point, and once she is she becomes vulnerable, having left the straight and narrow path of missionary sanctity for the uncertain vicissitudes of love. Thus, the movie gains in momentum, since the lovers are expected to be reunited at some point in the future. Moviemakers, as novelists before them, understood the longing of audiences (or readers) for happy endings as part of human nature.

Movies of epic length require adventure and spectacle in addition to romance and theme orientation. The epic form had come in the 1950s as a countermeasure to television, which had lured millions of viewers away from theaters. The epic offered what a small TV set could not: a wide screen, "casts of thousands," color, and epic battles where heroes defeated villains. The biblical epic (often called "sword-and-sandal epic"), mostly borrowed from biblical stories, some set in Roman times such as *The Robe* (1953) and *Demetrius and the Gladiators* (1954), was coming to its peak at the end of the decade, and by 1958, MGM was at work on *Ben-Hur* (1959), the most magnificent of them, which ended up winning eleven Oscars.[2]

The Inn of the Sixth Happiness was filmed at the Borehamwood MGM Studios in England, where a set of a full-size Chinese village was built with much attention to detail by art director John Box, who made it look convincingly real. A gold-painted statue of Buddha added a touch of mysticism to the venture, and the rugged mountains of Wales subbed nicely for Chinese landscapes. After the initial London scenes, almost the entire action was shot outside, enhanced by the splendid photography of Freddie Young, who was later to photograph David Lean's *Lawrence of Arabia* and *Dr. Zhivago*. Outside shooting required huge physical efforts on the part of the participants. Bergman, a strong woman, already tested in the rocky ravines of the volcanic island of Stromboli, showed that she was more than equal to the task, running around the village, answering emergencies, and undertaking the epic trek of guiding a large group of children across treacherous terrain. Bergman's Aylward was truly an epic heroine who dominated her environment from start to finish, winning the admiration of an astonished Dr. Robinson, who had thought her "unqualified" several years earlier.

CONCLUSION

In his review of the epic, Bosley Crowther noted that Ingrid Bergman's "capacity to convey a sense of supreme sincerity with little more to work with in the way of a character than a simple and wholesome façade is touchingly demonstrated in *The Inn of the Sixth Happiness*."[3] London's *Daily Sketch* wrote that the picture "touched greatness," and that this was Bergman's "finest performance of her life."[4] On the whole, Bergman's film career was fully rehabilitated, and she indeed relished it in her glory. But she did not forget the woman she had been asked to impersonate in the movie: Gladys

Aylward. She wrote her a letter, expressing her admiration and gratitude, stating her regrets for the alterations in her character that that film had demanded. She did not receive an answer from Aylward. It took Bergman ten years (1970) before she could go to Taiwan (then Formosa), where Gladys Aylward had taken refuge after she had fled Communist-ruled China and had established an orphanage. Alas, Bergman arrived ten days after Aylward had died. But in Aylward's cupboard Bergman found a scrapbook of clippings from the movie that the little London woman said she did not like. As the orphanage was in poor condition, Bergman launched a campaign to ensure that sufficient funds were raised for its preservation and progress. Contributions poured in, among them from the Variety Club of America, which became one of its most generous benefactors.

Having now achieved full reconciliation with America, Bergman continued doing independent work in England and in Europe onstage and in television, with a few movies in between. Her actual return to Hollywood did not occur until 1969, when she appeared in *Cactus Flower* with Walter Matthau and Goldie Hawn. She later appeared in Sidney Lumet's *Murder on the Orient Express* (1974), which gave her a third Oscar. Her career had expanded to its fullest, and whether she stood before a camera or commanded a stage, she gave her audiences or viewers a fully formed creation of art and beauty. She had also shown herself a woman with a big heart devoted to humane causes beyond art, proving herself a humanist and a philanthropist.

GOODBYE AGAIN

(1961)

★ ★ ★

Director: Anatole Litvak
Screenplay: Samuel A. Taylor, based on the novel *Aimez-vous Brahms?* by
    Françoise Sagan
Producer: Anatole Litvak. *Cinematography:* Armand Thirard. *Music Score:*
    Georges Auric
Cast: Ingrid Bergman (Paula Tessier), Yves Montand (Roger Demarest),
    Anthony Perkins (Philip Van der Besh); Jessie Royce Landis (Mrs. Van
    der Besh), Jackie Lane (1st Maisie), Diahann Carroll (Nightclub Singer)
Studio: United Artists
Released: June 29, 1961
Specs: 120 minutes; black and white

In 1960 Ingrid Bergman had not made a movie in two years, having been busy with stage productions after her marriage to Lars Schmidt in 1958. But when Anatole Litvak, who had directed her in *Anastasia*, asked her to take part in his upcoming movie, she accepted the role and a return to the silver screen. The movie was based on a novel by Françoise Sagan, *Aimez-vous Brahms?* and issued as *Goodbye Again* for American audiences. Sagan's novels, since her first one written when she was eighteen—*Bonjour Tristesse* (*Good Morning Sorrow*, 1954)—had set a trend in Europe for ambiguous relationships between men and women and the dissolution of marriage in modern times. This was also a time when foreign movies, mostly French and Italian, flooded not only art houses but were shown in packed movie houses across the country. The names of Federico Fellini, Michelangelo Antonioni, François Truffaut, and Jean-Luc Godard—whose *Breathless* was a smash hit (according to Andrew Sarris the "most passionate of the New Wave

Paula Tessier (Bergman), a woman of class, repels the advances of playboy Philip Van der Besh (Anthony Perkins). *United Artists / Photofest* © *United Artists*

films")—became familiar in the landmark year 1960, which affected politics, art, and literature in new and unforeseen directions. It was a youth movement, as young stars had taken over the screen, and names such as Monica Vitti, Brigitte Bardot, Sophia Loren, Jean Seberg, and Audrey Hepburn in America, to mention a few, had attracted youthful audiences.

In the sixties, middle-aged actresses were kept in the background, quietly taking on secondary roles or turning to television for work. Ingrid Bergman was forty-five at the time, reunited with Hollywood after *Anastasia*, but ready (and willing) to take roles of a middle-aged woman. She still looked younger than her years and was still very beautiful. Yet she was going against the grain, turning to the stage where acting takes precedence over looks, but not minding playing a middle-aged woman in love with two men. The movie, despite its vigorous cast, did not do as well as expected in the US, but it is still worth noticing for its elegance, for its ambiguity, and, as always, for a solid performance by Ingrid Bergman. Another member of the cast, Anthony Perkins, fresh from his schizophrenic murderer role in Hitchcock's *Psycho*, won a prize for his performance in *Goodbye Again* at the Cannes Film Festival that year. Yves Montand, a singer-actor and titanic figure in French cinema since his triumph in *The Wages of Fear* (1953), also delivers as a jaded Parisian who likes his steady date but also his philandering perambulations, as it was thought a man of the world should behave during the eruption of loose morals of that decade. Overall, Bergman stood her ground as a woman in conflict who battles with moral friction that comes with the territory when one is so beautiful, intelligent, and seemingly above the fray.

PLOT

Bergman plays Paula Tessier, a middle-aged woman who runs a fashionable design shop in Paris, living a comfortable life and enjoying the friendship of some of her customers, one of whom is a rich American, Mrs. Van der Besh (Jessie R. Landis), whose twenty-five-year old son, Philip (Perkins), a lawyer, is staying in Paris and is known for his drinking habits and neglect of work and future. He falls passionately in love with Paula, but she is already involved seriously with a business executive, Roger Demarest (Montand), whose infidelities she tolerates, as she truly loves him and expects to marry him eventually. He is seen with other women, whom he calls his "Maisies," giving them numbers: #1 played by Jackie Lane, #2 Jean Clarke, and #3 Michèle Mercier. He is bedding them at will during "business" trips, or on weekends, but he is always ready to return to steady love of reliable Paula.

Young Philip, dashing and smirking and crashing into bars and being carried out drunk, is the epitome of youthful decadence, but as a character he is likeable and becomes Paula's fixation after a while. His attentions, charm, and willingness to do anything for her, including giving up drinking (it does not last long), finally overcome her resistance and they become lovers. His mother disapproves, and so does Paula who sees no future with him, and he eventually comes to his senses and gets ready to leave for New York where his future lies. Paula reunites with Roger and asks him to marry her if their relationship is to continue. He says yes; they marry and they start a happy life, but not "happily ever after." Roger resumes his trips, mostly around Europe, and Paula seems resigned to her lot.

THEMES

Essentially, this is a story of a doomed triangle. Bergman had been in triangles both in life and in the movies, so her performance is delivered with pinball precision. One could go back to *Casablanca*, where two men are vying for her love. Or to *Anastasia*, where two men are at her heels, but she chooses the more unlikely. The difference was that on those and other previous occasions, Bergman's character fights for her choices. In *Gaslight*, she comes through, escaping madness when another man comes to her help, and so she does in *Notorious*, when, against tremendous odds, she finds the will to walk down the stairs of the Sebastian manor accompanied by the lover who rescued her. Even in the pessimistic Rossellini films, she showed the will to go against odds to become the independent woman she wanted to be. Beautiful, and strongly built, the tall Swedish actress never appeared timorous or indecisive in most of her roles thus far. Whether garbed in armor, as Saint Joan, or climbing the lava-strewn hillsides of Stromboli, she dared to provoke whatever odds were found in her path. In *Goodbye Again*, she is stoic. Two men pursue her, but one is an endearing yet shiftless youth, barely weaned from a daffy mother (is there any other role to play by the redoubtable Jessie Royce Landis?), the other a hedonistic philanderer used to paying generously his "Maisies" for sex favors, while also expecting stability from his steady mistress, returning to her from his sexual interludes. This conflict of a love triangle is unique in Bergman's canon. She is passive throughout, unable to extricate herself from either relationship, having to settle with an erratic love life. In some ways, *Goodbye Again* resembles Antonioni's *L'Avventura*, in which Claudia (Monica Vitti) has to settle with a betraying lover. "Love, love, what is it?"

shouts Demarest to one of his young Maisies he had bedded the previous night, to which she answers: "Are you here to examine my vocabulary?" Even Demarest is fatigued mentally with the lie he lives. Love has been reduced to an accommodation.

What enriches the thematic motif in *Goodbye Again* is its music. The score is by Georges Auric, complemented by music by Johannes Brahms and the popular song "Love Is Just a Word," sung by Diahann Carroll, whose career as a television star and singer was being launched at that time. When Philip, at first disappointed by Paula's refusal of him, visits a bar to drown his sorrow in drink, he hears the nightclub singer sing "Goodbye Again," which became the title of the American version of the film. At one of their earlier meetings, Philip and Paula are seen standing in front of a symphony hall where one of Brahms's symphonies is to be played; and on subsequent occasions, melodies from Symphonies no. 1, fourth movement, and no. 3, third movement, are heard on the soundtrack. Brahms's music is first heard when Paula is preparing to go out to a concert with Philip, and she is asked by her French maid, Gaby (Uta Taeger), "What these Brahms are?" In reply, Paula tells her to put a record on the gramophone where strains of the music of Brahms are heard. During a concert she attends with Philip, Paula has a flashback of her first encounter with Roger (pronounced Rojér in the film). She was sitting at an outdoor café, Roger was at another table nearby, and as a company of dragoons was marching by to the tune of the music of Brahms, they became acquainted. That was five years ago; Paula was approaching middle age and was susceptible to an attractive man's attentions. Now, as the relationship is resolving, she recalls that first electric moment when lovers connect. In her mind, the phrase "Aimez-vous Brahms?" represents an emotion, that of love. It could have been supplanted by the phrase "Do you love me?"

The European title *Aimez-vous Brahms?* was discarded as incomprehensive to American audiences, though not all American viewers were happy with the change. Bosley Crowther called the score "as elegant as the setting," adding the music works cited were "the most respectable thing in the film."[1] Were that to be entirely true, one would have to discard the argument that this is a love story, a definition of love as it were. All members of the triangle struggle to understand what the word means. The singer says it's just a word, and Demarest himself asks one of his Maisies to explain it to him. She replies that that's a word one could use at night, but not in the morning when it's pay time. Demarest pays his mistresses for their favors—an easy way out for a man void of an emotion he fears. He remains uncommitted; he wants love but is unable to give it fully, and when he gets his way and marries Paula, he remains a man corroded by habit. Yves Montand renders his character Roger with chilling efficiency. One of France's top actors, he could be as ambiguous as Marcello Mastroianni and just as engaging, whatever his mask. Established mostly as a tough guy, but also a romantic lover when he need be, Montand as Roger overwhelms Paula with his attentions. Eventually, during a dance with a Maisie, as Paula dances with Philip, he holds her hand, and that sparks a reunion. Philip also sees him in the same dance hall, understands that Roger will never be wiped from her mind, and packs off for New York and a new life. A hasty marriage follows, and Roger and Paula are seen exiting city hall, from which other newlyweds emerge. Is this a happy ending? No! As Paula is getting ready to go out with her new husband, the phone rings, and Roger announces he is going (sorry!) on one of his trips. Paula understands. She is seen sitting opposite her mirror, removing her makeup with face cream, while a strain from Brahms's third movement of his Third Symphony soars—sad, passionate, even tragic, as the curtains close, wiping off Paula's image from the screen.

CONCLUSION

Not much else can be said of this sensitive movie, which shows Bergman at one of her most delicate moments. Not entirely a heroine, she still remains the center of the movie, a beautiful, elegant society woman who knows how to love but not how to choose wisely. She dates Philip on the rebound, knowing that such a relationship has no future. Tall, lanky, and charming, Anthony Perkins delivers a passionate performance, just on the heels of his Norman Bates in *Psycho*, shedding his monstrous side and retaining the charm. Love, the theme of the movie, turns out bittersweet, accepted as an adjustment, simulating, perhaps the diverse personalities of its main characters: French, American, and Swedish, a blend of lovers, each adding a special note to the most used word in any language: love. Is it? Not a dreamy feeling certainly, but rather an adjustment to life. Pedantic definition, perhaps, but if you love Brahms, you may take it as it is.

18

THE YELLOW ROLLS-ROYCE

(1965)

★ ★ ★

Director: Anthony Asquith
Screenplay: Terence Rattigan
Producer: Anatole de Grunwald. *Cinematographer:* Jack Hildyard. *Music Score:*
    Riz Ortolani
Cast: Ingrid Bergman (Mrs. Gerda Millett), Rex Harrison (Lord Charles
    Frinton—The Marquess of Frinton), Shirley MacLaine (Mae Jenkins),
    Jeanne Moreau (Lady Eloise Frinton), George C. Scott (Paolo
    Maltese), Omar Sharif (Davich), Alain Delon (Stefano), Art Carney
    (Joey Friedlander), Joyce Grenfell (Hortense Astor), Carlo Croccolo
    (Michele), Wally Cox (Ferguson)
Studio: MGM
Released: May 13, 1965
Specs: 122 minutes; color
Availability: DVD (Warner Bros.)

The Yellow Rolls-Royce was made when Ingrid Bergman had been spending
more time in stage productions than screen appearances, such as Ibsen's
Hedda Gabler, which she performed in London and subsequently in French
in Paris. There had been also a seventy-five-minute TV version of the play,
in which Bergman showed equal ability in smoothly transferring from
stage to screen, and vice versa. After her success with the Oscar-winning

Anastasia, as her marriage to Roberto Rossellini had been annulled, Bergman had formed a relationship with Lars Schmidt, a Swedish producer and impresario whom she married in 1958. Schmidt had a decisive effect upon her career orientations as well as on her personal life, encouraging her to spend considerable time for leisure in their new Swedish home or traveling with him to the Far East.[1] By 1963, as she was approaching fifty, romantic roles were harder to get, while her stage appearances flourished. In 1964, when screen audiences had been treated to such megahits as *My Fair Lady*, *Who's Afraid of Virginia Woolf?*, and *Barefoot in the Park*, Bergman was offered the role of Gerda Millett, a rich American dowager in *The Yellow Rolls-Royce*, written by Terence Rattigan, produced by Anatole de Grunwald, and directed by Anthony Asquith, the trio who had collaborated on the highly popular *V.I.P.s* the year before. Squeezed in between such glossy competition, *The Yellow Rolls-Royce* had only a rather modest reception by audiences and critics, winning no awards and praised only for its spectacular locales in the English countryside and in Italy and Austria. But over the decades, *The Yellow Rolls-Royce* gained status as a classic, in part thanks to the DVD edition by Warner Bros. in 2009. To her contemporaries who thought Bergman's film career over by the midsixties, Bergman sent a message that when romantic intrigue called she could still deliver the goods.

PLOT

The Yellow Rolls-Royce is an anthology, a grouping of short stories with different plots and characters but bound by a common theme. All three episodes of *TYRR* are about a woman at the cusp of middle age who suffers a romantic heartbreak that leaves her a changed, more mature person. All three women are beautiful and pampered either by wealth or a doting husband or a gentleman friend. There is a connecting link, a visual image that appears in all episodes, establishing a chronological sequence that enables the episodes to flow smoothly from one to the next. In this case, it is a luxury car—a yellow Rolls-Royce, Model Phantom II—owned by the protagonist in each of the episodes, thus serving as the unifying image and framing device for all.

The yellow Rolls-Royce is bought, fresh minted, by Lord Charles Frinton (Rex Harrison) for his beautiful wife, Lady Eloise (Jeanne Moreau). This is a gift on their tenth anniversary, as Lord Frinton is preparing to celebrate his certain victory the following day at the Ascot Gold Cup. Lady Eloise, however, has an assignation with her lover, John Fane (Edmund Purdom), a handsome rake who alternates aristocratic lovers with the adeptness of a jewel thief picking up diamonds. Lord Frinton catches him and his wife in a compromising position inside the Rolls-Royce, parked in a line of luxury cars, while the Gold Cup race is going on. Since divorce is out of the question, they agree to remain status quo. Lord Frinton, on their way back to their palatial residence, asks her if she loves Fane. "I am mad about him," she responds. "Does he love you?" he wants to know. "I don't think so," she says. "Then why, in heaven's name?" he asks again. "That question is unanswerable," she concludes. They are greeted by a crowd of guests, all congratulating the lord on his victory. He hands the cup to a butler, and then he turns to the chauffeur and tells him to take the Rolls-Royce back to the dealer. "Why?" the man asks, puzzled. "It displeases me," he answers with a frown. Lord Frinton had won his game, but lost the love of his wife. The Rolls-Royce did not meet expectations. End of round one.

More than twenty thousand miles and several years later, the Rolls-Royce is found in Genoa, Italy. Its latest owner, a maharaja, had lost his fortune at a casino and with it his expensive car. As it sits in an Italian dealership, Paolo Maltese (George C. Scott), with his fiancée, Mae Jenkins (Shirley MacLaine), and his chauffeur/bodyguard, Joey Friedlander (Art Carney), buys the car on an impulse to please his *fidanzata*. Maltese, a notorious gangster and friend of Al Capone, has taken this trip to introduce his American girlfriend to his family (we never see them) and to impress her with the architectural marvels of his country at the most famous tourist hot spots in Italy. He is frustrated that she can't appreciate the importance of "Sole Mio" (the equivalent of "The Star-Spangled Banner" in the States, he explains to her), but she is so bored with the idea that he starts braying "Sole Mio" himself, and the cacophony provokes jeering ladies from an upstairs window to toss coins at him. They are standing in front of a car dealership, and the owner, Bomba (Riccardo Garrone), enraged with the ugly singing of Maltese, reprimands him severely but freezes with terror when he realizes this is the notorious gangster, feared everywhere. When Mae admires the Rolls-Royce, Maltese asks the price for "this old heap," and Bomba, still shaking, mutters an improbable figure, $15,235.57. "Pay the full price," Maltese orders Friedlander, too proud to negotiate. Enter Stefano (Alain Delon), a street photographer who lures vain ladies—English, German, American—into posing for him, and soon Mae becomes his target. The difference this time is that he has a real attraction for her, and she for him. An easygoing Italian (although Delon is French), he doesn't understand that toying with Maltese's affianced is a dangerous game. At first, he is paid and rudely dismissed, but when Maltese is called back to the States for some "business" (he shoots a rival gangster, Bugs O'Leary),

Mae, who can't resist going to Soriano to find him, is seen dancing with him to the tune of "Forget Domani"—"Forget Tomorrow." Mae and Stefano are next seen bathing in the waters of Caligula Pond, surrounded by sharp-pointed rocks where Caligula, the Roman emperor, flung those he didn't like from his palace above (we see the ruins in a long shot). There is kissing, followed by lovemaking in the Rolls, the window shades again providing privacy for the culprits. A troubled Friedlander, who has guessed what happened, tells Mae to cool it if she wants to save her life, his for knowing and not telling, and Stefano's. Maltese will hunt Stefano down if he knows that she loves him, Friedlander tells her. "Survival" is the name of the game, he tells Mae. In tears, she turns Stefano away, moments before Paolo arrives. He is hiding in a corner, as if he has smelled something. But when he sees her crying—she is crying for Stefano—he gets curious. "I was worried about you, you idiot!" she tells him, and he remarks that she is "already behaving like a wife." She wants to get out of this place, go back to Miami, and get married. She has understood Friedlander's motto of "survival." As for the Rolls-Royce, it is passed on to the next owner.

A few years later, the yellow Rolls-Royce is sitting at an Italian repair shop in Trieste, a sign, "OCCASIONE" (Discount), appearing on its windshield. Trieste is on the border of what then, in 1941, was Yugoslavia, a country about to be invaded by Germany. A rich American woman, Gerda Millett (Bergman), offers to buy the car, shrewdly bargaining the asking price from six to five thousand, and is getting ready to travel to Yugoslavia to meet the Queen Mother. An assistant from the vice-consul, Ferguson (Wally Cox), approaches her as she is sitting in the lounge of a luxury hotel to warn her that her trip must be canceled. "Why?" she asks imperially. There has been a coup d'état, the Queen Mother has been deposed, and in her place eighteen-year-old King Peter has been established on the throne, he explains. Annoyed, Mrs. Millett inquires why an assistant from the vice-consul has been sent to warn her instead of the consul himself. She is a rich American widow who despises President Roosevelt for taking her money (in heavy taxation of the rich) and declares the president should stay away from "these futile European wars."

Overhearing this conversation, a dark-haired man approaches her and asks her to take him along with her. Astonished, she finds him and his idea preposterous, but in the end she accepts, possibly won over by his pleading but more so by his nice curly hair and burning black eyes. (At this juncture, Omar Sharif had not yet adopted his absurdly straightened hair and pulled-back eyebrows of *Doctor Zhivago* a year later, thus looking more natural as a Yugoslavian.)

The improbable romance adventure begins. After they are past Trieste and just before they reach the border, Davich (Sharif) asks her Italian chauffeur, Michele (Carlo Croccolo), to pull over on the side of the road and, holding a pistol, demands that he transfer Mrs. Millett's luggage to the front seats. When she, astounded, asks him what all this means and why he is threatening Duchess (her dog) with his pistol, he explains that he has to hide in the trunk of her car in order to cross the border. He is a "proscribed" person. And how can she manage that, she asks? "Use the magic of your charm," he responds, "Drop a few names." "And what does that mean?" "Say you are personal friend of President Roosevelt," he responds, before he huddles into the trunk. She shivers just hearing the name Roosevelt but complies.

She manages the ensuing skirmish with the border guards adroitly. Pretending that she admires the magnificent view, she lets her chauffeur hand them her passport, receiving knee-buckling compliments from the guard, but when Duchess begins to sniff and bark at the trunk, the guards demand that she open the trunk. "I've lost the key!" she says and threatens to call her "friend" President Roosevelt if they dare break the lock. She tosses Duchess into the backseat with an unladylike "Bitch!" and demands her passport. They comply, saluting and wishing President Roosevelt to win a fourth term. "What a very encouraging thought," she responds sourly, ordering Michele to drive off.

From now on, everything that is improbable happens. She demands that Davich leave the car—which he does—and then drives to the luxury hotel, where, dressed in magnificent white, she orders a martini, ready for a relaxing dinner. As an obsequious violinist approaches bowing, with gypsy tunes, the roar of planes is heard and soon bombs begin to fall. As the waiters disappear into the shelter, Michele invokes the "Madonna" and mutters, "Father, Son . . . and Holy Ghost," and vanishes. Undaunted, she continues her dinner when an alarmed Davich reappears. "Oh, it's you again," she comments, irritated that he has interrupted her dinner. But the sight of flames of a burning city convinces her that there is trouble. Trouble? No problem. Mrs. Millett pulls off the tablecloths, which later she shreds, showing a local woman of a bombed house how to shred them and use them for bandages.

Even Davich begins to be intimidated by this formidable woman who refuses to be daunted by anything in her way, including the Nazi tanks rolling into town. When he says he will "requisition" her car and her chauffeur, as he can't drive, she offers to drive for him: "Everybody in America can drive a car," she assures him—although apparently she has never been behind a wheel. Boldly, she drives around steep ravines—"nothing to it"—with the

Davich (Omar Sharif) and Gerda Millett (Bergman) after their brief love adventure. MGM / Photofest © MGM

scared Davich grabbing the wheel on occasion, until they get to the camp where he is expected. (The scene evokes Hitchcock's *To Catch a Thief*, where Grace Kelly drives dizzily around chasms, while Cary Grant is grasping his knees nervously.)

From now on he is in charge, but that does not mean she is giving up being bossy—and magnanimous. She has been smitten by this dark-eyed, magnetic foreigner, who has also been touched by this cantankerous yet big-souled woman. He discovers in her a generosity of spirit when he sees her helping the victims of bombing and carrying a child out of the ruins. To his amazement, she finds a way for him to transport his men from their current position to a location where they can fight. The Rolls-Royce, she tells him can carry sixteen men at a time—that means four trips for his fifty-seven men. "Who gave you this information?" he tells her, amazed. "I counted them!" she responds nonchalantly. She also refuses to take up space from the rooms his men sleep in. She will sleep in the Rolls-Royce. He declares with strong emotion how great she is, but she dismisses his words as "sentimental gush." Yet, when she has lain down and he leans forward and kisses her, she accepts his kiss, despite her comment that all this is so foolish. "Is that so bad?" he comments in response. Thusly, the Rolls-Royce scores its third love scene—all of them ill-fated, it seems, as they cannot last. She returns to the hotel, orders the Rolls-Royce to be sent to America, and when an amazed Hortense, her "confidential," asks her what happened, she says, "Absolutely nothing happened!" The viewer knows otherwise.

THEMES

Romantic love assails middle-aged women, compelling them to give up tempting liaisons for the sake of survival. Lady Frinton certainly does that as does Mae Jenkins, both realizing that life must go on without the luxury of romance. Gerda Millett wants to stay in the mountains in Yugoslavia and fight in the war against the Germans, but Davich reminds her she would be more useful sending help from America. All these "accommodations" make sense, and all three women comply willingly, perhaps realizing that peace with the male in charge is better than war and rejection. Strong women in subordinate situations accept the cards dealt to them.

A theme song in the second segment is "Forget Domani." Translation: forget tomorrow, and live today—the equivalent of Rome-spawned dictum of carpe diem, first attributed to the Roman poet Horace and then used in various forms by Western literature poets (an example is Robert Herrick's [1591–1674] poem "To the Virgins, to Make Much of Time"). "Forget Domani" is a lilting melody, composed by Riz Ortolani and sung by Katyna Ranieri, heard when Mae dances with Stefano as their romance flourishes momentarily. The song continues in the soundtrack as they are driving through southern Italy. Friedlander then issues a warning: Tough men in power—the modern equivalent of Caligula—sprung from the same peninsula that invented la dolce vita and carpe diem, hunt down those opposing their wishes. Forgetting tomorrow comes with a price.

Woman wins. Start with Eloise—she has the last word: "I suppose we have to go on living," she says, self-consoling. She takes the cup at the end of the ride and enjoys the cheers of the crowd. She had her fling and still maintains marital security. The uxorious Lord Frinton had placed all his bets for his happiness on pleasing his beautiful, elegant, and aristocratic wife, Eloise. When one of his female guests remarks that she is "extraordinary," he assures her that Eloise is "ideal." But then he adds: "I guess to be ideal is to be extraordinary." Ironically, it takes him only twenty-four hours to discover that his wife may still be extraordinary but is by no means ideal. His pride is ravaged beyond repair, and neither a golden car nor a Gold Cup can restore it. Eloise, on the other hand, still has the glitter associated with aristocracy and the admiration due a beautiful woman—even one of mature years who stepped just a bit out of bounds.

Mae Jenkins shows she has learned the lesson from Friedlander: let the Rolls go, along with the flirtatious Stefano. She strokes the Rolls's headlights with her fur affectionately, saying good-bye to the car that sheltered her lovemaking, bidding adieu to her momentary dolce vita, aware that she will be safely sheltered under Paolo's powerful wing. She, like the other two women, has it both ways, getting their moment of rapture with the lover of their choice, reassured of their female allure, thus entering maturity with an assured step. Who knows what will follow. She actually has the last word: back to Miami, certain marriage—for a hat girl, not so bad. In the end, it was Paolo Maltese who weighs flattery over his strong suspicions.

Gerda Millett sleeps in the Rolls to avoid inconveniencing Davich's men. She and Davich are seen kissing after she has lain down to sleep in the car backseat. In the morning the first thing the viewer sees is Duchess sleeping in the fender, and the curtain drawn. No doubt, it was a *carpe noctem* affair—she had "seized the night" (which is actually a more convenient way for lovemaking). It was a win-win proposition: She had her adventure and her lover in the space of no less than forty-eight hours. "Hearts are never broken," Gerda Millett tells Davich as she departs, "just bruised. They always mend." (Gerda has done better than her "confidential," Hortense, who always moaned about her adventure with the Moroccan soldiers during the Spanish Civil War. She sighs at the thought she has never been raped—a point Gerda keeps emphasizing!)

CONCLUSION

In all this, the Rolls-Royce is the protagonist. Even Bergman says so in her memoirs.[2] The car has all the devices needed for an object that is glorious and convenient for a lovers' nest. It has shades that can be drawn over both side windows and the backseat, thus being good for lover hideouts. It has a rather spacious trunk, used to carrying both cargo and human beings (or a dog). It has a telephone, from where orders can be transmitted to the driver, as Mae does, thanking Friedlander for his foresight and advice. It is a large and quite sturdy vehicle, so much so as to survive rugged mountain roads being driven by a nondriver and transporting bunches of humans outweighing its capacity—all this without as much as a scratch (though with a few repairable dents). Shipped back to the States, it may yet have a future, as Rolls-Royces come with a lifetime warranty. Phaeton driving his chariot through the skies could not have had a more magical flight.

What is remarkable in this movie, in which Bergman appears only in the last part, is that she is something her admirers have never seen: intractable, iron willed, aloof, brazenly aristocratic. Gerda Millett (obviously of European extraction as one can tell from her accent and manners) travels through Europe in a notorious Rolls-Royce (for the viewers of this film), visiting capitals, especially those that have kings. She is also at her most regal in stature and elegant shape—even more so than in the ephemeral position she gains in *Anastasia*. Still astonishingly beautiful, though nearing fifty, her blue eyes sparkle, an advantage accentuated by Panavision and Metrocolor. Her initial contempt for the war zone turns into shock when she witnesses a bombed burning city, only to take a decisive turn to help the war efforts. Love interferes as Omar Sharif comes along, and finally with a nostalgic wistfulness she resigns herself to the fact that she had loved, and that "it is better to have loved and lost than to not have loved at all," as she says in her autobiography, quoting Tennyson.[3] Incidentally, the Rolls-Royce survived several ownerships after the movie was completed in 1964, and was picked up at an auction in 1987, in poor condition, by Neal Kirkham, a restoration specialist, who at considerable expense restored it to the condition it was while filming the movie. The Rolls, in its sparkling glory, won an award at Pebble Beach, California, in 2004.

MURDER ON THE ORIENT EXPRESS

(1974)

★ ★ ★ ★

Director: Sidney Lumet
Screenplay: Paul Dehn, based on the novel by Agatha Christie
Producers: Richard Goodwin and John Brabourne. *Cinematography:* Geoffrey
    Unsworth. *Music Score:* Richard Rodney Bennett
Cast: Albert Finney (Hercule Poirot), Sean Connery (Colonel Arbuthnot),
    John Gielgud (Edward Beddoes), Ingrid Bergman (Greta Ohlsson),
    Lauren Bacall (Harriet Belinda Hubbard), Michael York (Count
    Rudolph Andrenyi), Jacqueline Bisset (Countess Helena Andrenyi),
    Wendy Hiller (Princess Natalia Dragomiroff), Rachel Roberts
    (Hildegarde Schmidt), Vanessa Redgrave (Mary Debenham), Richard
    Widmark (Samuel Ratchett/Cassetti), George Coulouris (Dr.
    Constantine), Anthony Perkins (Hector McQueen), Martin Balsam
    (Signor Bianchi), Colin Blakely (Cyrus B. Hardman), Denis Quilley
    (Antonio Foscarelli), Jean-Pierre Cassel (Pierre Paul Michel)
Studio: EMI Films, Limited
Released: November 24, 1974
Specs: 131 minutes; color
Availability: DVD (Paramount)

In the decade after *Anastasia* (1956), Bergman had made few films that matched her Oscar-winning performance, having spent a great deal of her time in stage and TV productions. When offered a part by Sidney Lumet in the Agatha Christie classic *Murder on the Orient Express*, she was doing

The Constant Wife, a 1927 Somerset Maugham play at the Albery Theatre (now the Noel Coward Theatre) in London, which had a seven-month run. Produced by John Gielgud, the play was a huge success, earning Bergman a great deal of money.[1] When Lumet approached her, asking her to take a part in an all-star cast of *Murder on the Orient Express*, he intended her to play Princess Natalia Dragomiroff, a part that eventually went to Wendy Hiller, as Bergman preferred to play Greta Ohlsson, a timorous Swedish missionary who had been on a fund-raising trip to the Orient. It was a tiny part in a lengthy movie, but, under skillful direction by Lumet, Bergman gave a performance unlike any other of hers in her past, shedding every bit of the glamour she had always projected, and being plain, awkward, and mentally off-key, "a dopey missionary," as she herself called her character.[2] The result was a Supporting Actress Oscar, her third, which put her in a special category of multi-Oscar winners in Hollywood.

Lumet decided that the film would be more successful with an all-star cast, so he secured first the services of the actor best known at the time for his roles as James Bond, Sean Connery, thinking that if Connery said yes, others would follow. Connery gladly accepted, and soon more luminaries of stage and screen followed. Lauren Bacall played Mrs. Harriet Hubbard, a twice-widowed, chatty American woman who prizes vulgarity as a privilege of upper class. A splendidly attired couple, the Hungarian diplomat Count Rudolph Andrenyi (Michael York) is there with his wife Elena (Jacqueline Bisset), and Mary Debenham (Vanessa Redgrave) is a blue-eyed English beauty, whom Poirot spots talking intimately with Colonel Arbuthnot at the Istanbul ferryboat. There is an Italian American car salesman, Antonio Foscarelli (Denis Quilley), and Cyrus B. Hardman (Colin Blakely), a theatrical agent. An American tycoon is also there, Samuel Ratchett (Richard Widmark), accompanied by his secretary-translator, Hector McQueen (Anthony Perkins) and his valet, Mr. Beddoes (John Gielgud). The others include Signor Bianchi, the Italian owner of the line, played by Martin Balsam, who speaks ostentatious Italian. There is also a Greek doctor on the train, Dr. Constantine (George Coulouris), and Pierre Paul Michel (Jean-Pierre Cassel), playing the French conductor of the Calais wagon-lit. Three others are Vernon Dobtcheff as Concierge, Jeremy Lloyd as A.D.C., and John Moffat as Chief Attendant.

Richard Goodwin and John Brabourne, the producers, had difficulty obtaining the rights from Agatha Christie, who was mistrustful of adapters of her works in the 1960s and refused to cooperate, but the producers had connections: John Brabourne was son-in-law of Lord Mountbatten, former viceroy of India and Earl of Burma, who had to exert his influence to convince Dame Agatha to yield. The choice of Albert Finney to play Poirot also presented certain problems. Finney was too young—still in his thirties, while Poirot was middle-aged, closer to his midfifties. Finney was also taller and larger than the small-sized Belgian sleuth of 5'4", so he had to be squeezed into clothes that looked too small for him, thus appearing lumpy and hunchbacked. His voice sounded too high pitched, with an unnatural French accent. Still, Finney managed brilliantly, easily dominating a cast of superstars and winning an Oscar nomination for his role. On the whole, the film won five Oscar nominations and one win (Bergman) along with ten BAFTA nominations and other awards. It brought in a lot of cash at the box office, grossing $36 million in America alone, and all that from the miniscule budget of $1.4 million. It proved one of the most entertaining films of all time, still looking fresh after forty-three years. A new version of *Murder on the Orient Express* was released in 2017, helmed by Kenneth Branagh, who also plays Poirot.

Agatha Christie's famous detective, Hercule Poirot, is a small man of Belgian extraction who has moved to England for reasons that remain vague. It is assumed that he migrated to England along with many other Belgians after the brutal occupation by Germany during the First World War. England provided refuge and sympathy to the Belgian refugees, as Belgium had been an ally during the war. Poirot has been impersonated by several actors on stage and screen and TV, the most successful by measure of appearances being David Suchet in the long-running TV series in 1989–2013, *Agatha Christie's Poirot*. Peter Ustinov played him in *Death on the Nile* (1978) and *Evil under the Sun* (1982), also produced by Richard Goodwin and John Brabourne. Poirot is the only fictional character to receive an obituary, in the *New York Times*, after Dame Agatha decided to give him one more case to solve in *Curtain: Poirot's Last Case* (1975) in which he suffered from arthritis and a bad heart, dying after his case was solved. His last words were *"Cher ami."*[3]

Poirot is a clever, methodical, and fastidious dandy who pays as much attention to his waxed, upward-turned mustache as to the case he is occupied with. His hair is in a net so it will not be disheveled at night, and his attire, shoes, and so forth suggest that one will have to approach him with the utmost courtesy and sufficient awe of his reputation if one expects to engage him in a case. The usual method of Poirot is to gather as many clues as he can in a case, set his "little gray cells" (read: his genius) in motion, deducing from given facts, eliminating targets, often beating his chest for being "fooled" by this or that little blunder of his. This is part of his act, for he is quite conscious of the theatricality of his movements, thus cultivating an aura of self-worship. He is there to reenact and display his mental powers—or to capture an audience's or reader's attention. His finale is to assemble a group of people, "the usual suspects," as one might say, and stage a theatrical summation of the story during which he provides a full range of options before he gives the solution. His roundabout method is designed to increase suspense by his throwing hints at the most obvious suspects, switching his attention to others; then, as if in a quick afterthought, he nails the person least suspected. This is Agatha Christie's method, actually; she makes it hard for the reader of her tightly knit narratives to guess the murderer (or murderers, since there might be more than one). She throws red herrings, cleverly booby-trapping the reader's path, satisfied that the unraveling of her mysteries are hard-won prizes for human acumen. After all, Poirot, the little egotistical popinjay, is Agatha Christie's means of human provocation: Poirot must deceive to a greater extent than he is deceived.

PLOT

The film begins with a silent montage of images and newspaper clippings highlighting a notorious case of the abduction and murder of a young heiress, Daisy Armstrong, in 1930, and the subsequent death of her mother and father, as well as a servant of the Armstrong family and the man who was executed for the abduction and murder—the wrong man it seems. Thus, the viewer is alerted as to the subject matter of the story about to unfold. The connection works, for just as soon as Poirot shows up with a large group of people boarding the Orient Express, one knows that there will be murder most foul ahead. Poirot does not have a reservation, but he is accommodated by his friend Signor Bianchi, the Italian director of the line, and he is offered a berth, shared with another passenger in the wagon-lit. The Express is departing from the European side of Istanbul, to traverse Bulgaria, Yugoslavia, and France, and from Calais wagon-lit passengers are to continue on to England. Among them is the American tycoon Samuel Ratchett, who tells Poirot that his life has been threatened and asks him to protect him for a price of $15,000. He shows him a small pistol he carries with him. Poirot turns him down, saying he has made enough money to satisfy both his needs and his caprices.

During the second night Ratchett is found stabbed to death, and Poirot, invited by Signor Bianchi, proceeds to interrogate, in turn, all twelve passengers on the Calais wagon-lit, doing so while a snowplow is slowly edging nearer to free the train, stuck in a snowdrift. Poirot seems intent to finish the investigation before it is turned over to the Yugoslavian police. Ratchett had also an impeccably mannered valet, Mr. Beddoes, who actually discovers that something is amiss when he knocks on his boss's door with his "pick-me-up" in the morning. As there is no answer, they use the conductor's passkey to open the door and find Ratchett dead on his bed, his eyes open. Dr. Constantine, the Greek doctor, is summoned to verify the cause and time of death. He determines that Ratchett had been stabbed twelve times, and while some wounds were superficial, a few were deep enough to cause death. A smashed watch shows 1:15 a.m., so it is assumed that that was the time of the murder. Ratchett was unable to resist, having been sedated before he was killed. As a proof, Poirot shows them the small pistol Ratchett had under his pillow; he had made no effort to reach it. Soon he unveils Ratchett's true identity by reading a half-burned note he finds in the ashtray next to him. He places it on top of a hatbox frame, then uses a flame from molten wax he used to wax his mustache, and in the momentary flare, he reads part of the name "Daisy" and some letters from her surname, Armstrong. He deduces right away that Ratchett's real name is Cassetti, the Mafia mobster who had abducted and killed Daisy Armstrong, a notorious case having its origin in the Lindbergh baby's abduction. Quickly, Poirot points out that the man had been responsible for five deaths. Aside from the child Daisy, her mother, Mrs. Sonia Armstrong, had died of grief during the birth of a stillborn baby. A maidservant named Paulette killed herself after being implicated in Daisy's murder, and British army colonel Hamish Armstrong, Daisy's father, committed suicide out of despair. Cassetti betrayed his partner in crime, accusing him of the murder, and after his execution escaped with the ransom money. The name "Cassetti" brings back the memory of those deaths, and Poirot picks up the clues from that point on. He surmises immediately that the murder is connected to the Armstrong case.

Aside from the half-burned note, Poirot finds some other clues: a handkerchief with the initial *H* and a used pipe cleaner next to the murdered man's side table. Later more clues are revealed: a button from a missing wagon-lit conductor's uniform found a bit later in a suitcase; a passkey in the pocket of the uniform; and a bloodstained knife, which soon proves to be the murder weapon.

With such clues in hand, Poirot proceeds to interrogate each of the twelve people on the Calais wagon-lit. The interrogations seem to come in random order, but Poirot has already concluded that the murder was not committed by an outsider who invaded the train at night and then quickly exited, leaving the uniform behind. He says so to his sidekick, Signor Bianchi, who naively and loudly concludes that "he [or she] did it!" after each interrogation. Poirot patiently waits, noting each person's behavior, tone of voice, and even accent. His true aim is to determine, judging from the answers he gets, why and to what extent the answers he gets are, as he calls them, "evasions." He intuits that each of the suspects is hiding something, but he waits patiently until all of them are given a chance to tell their story. These are memorable little scenes, each with a color of personality or ethnicity, provoked by Poirot's relentless, if polite, interrogation. One of the most interesting is Wendy Hiller's crusty rendition of Princess Natalia Dragomiroff, who never smiles on principle (doctor's orders) and who deflects each probing of Poirot's with sangfroid, pretending they give her a migraine. "Two aspirin," she commands imperially to her attendant, Hildegarde Schmidt (Rachel Roberts), who scurries away to comply with her mistress's order. Another interesting confrontation is that with Colonel Arbuthnot (Connery), who seems sensitive about Poirot's rather forceful

Timorous missionary Greta Ohlsson (Bergman) chats with scheming Harriet Hubbard (Bacall).
Paramount Pictures / Photofest © Paramount Pictures

interrogation of his inamorata, Mary Debenham, rushing into the compartment she is being interrogated in and with a Bond-like punch knocks Pierre Paul Michel, the conductor, out of his way. "Sorry if I hurt the lad," he says in his familiar Scottish brogue. "Provocation."

So it goes with the rest of the passengers, until Ms. Ohlsson's turn comes. A cinematic trick is used in the scene that features Bergman. Lumet decided, since the scene was so brief, to film the entire 4.5-minute sequence in one take. Bergman was already familiar with long shots (a process difficult for both actor and cameraman), since Hitchcock's *Under Capricorn*, during which she had to undergo a ten-minute take. Poirot moves to her other side, leaving her face covered for a second or two, but listens, as she continues with her mangled English; adept in Swedish and several other languages, Bergman does not have trouble imitating bad English. She draws out her vowels: "Boorn baackwards," meaning that she was born mentally disabled, thence her mission in life is to help "baackward children," and goes to "Aafrica" to accomplish that. Jesus appeared to her one day, urging her to help "little brown babies." She has seen children that are "forward" (lucky or rich); she believes in God (with a frown)—but her parents didn't (nod of disapproval). She looks offended by the inquiry and provides not the slightest clue during her interrogation with Poirot. She shakes her head disapprovingly when her parents are mentioned ("They did not believe in God!"), tightens her lips, sobs. Shifting emotions, she says she is proud of her work; humiliated by the inquiry, she cries; she does her best to fool Poirot that she had nothing to do with the murder.

Poirot's Summation

After examining each one of the suspects, Poirot gathers all twelve wagon-lit passengers, as he suspects all of them—except himself and Signor Bianchi—in the dining compartment and announces his conclusions. He states that there is the "simple" solution, which is that an unknown person invaded the stopped train at night, murdered Ratchett, and exited, after discarding the uniform with the missing button. As Dr. Constantine gasps in disbelief with a "But . . . ," Poirot hurries to explain that there is also the "complex" solution. Harriet Belinda Hubbard uses her second husband's name; her first husband was Greenwood (Grunwald in German), and her maiden name is Linda Arden, an actress, whom Greenwood/Grunwald had married. Linda Arden is supposed to be bedridden at this time. Mrs. Sonia Armstrong was her daughter, and Daisy her granddaughter; Jacqueline Bisset as Countess Helena Andrenyi is also her daughter and Mrs. Armstrong's sister. Though a sensitive soul, Countess Helena too sought revenge with the assistance and understanding of her husband, Hungarian diplomat Count Andrenyi. Colonel Arbuthnot had known Col. Hamish Armstrong in India and is intent upon revenge for his death. He is in the middle of divorce proceedings, suing his cheating wife in London; therefore he does not want to reveal his liaison with Mary Debenham, a teacher of shorthand in Baghdad, but one who had been in America as Mrs. Armstrong's secretary. Greta Ohlsson had been a nursemaid to young Daisy Armstrong, present during the kidnapping, therefore also bent on revenge. Princess Natalia Dragomiroff proves the most evasive of them all; she turns out to be the godmother of Sonia Armstrong, who had married the much-decorated Col. Hamish Armstrong. The princess was also an intimate friend of the supposedly bedridden Linda Arden, none other than Mrs. Hubbard now on the train. The princess's maid, Hildegarde Schmidt (Rachel Roberts), had been a cook at the Armstrong house, a fact elicited by Poirot when he flatters her for her good cooking.

Other suspects include Edward Beddoes, Colonel Armstrong's batman, and Cyrus B. Hardman, who pretended he was a "cop" sent from the Istanbul Pinkerton Agency to protect Ratchett, but in reality he had fallen in love with Paulette, Armstrong's maid, who committed suicide when she was implicated in the murder. Paulette's father, conductor Pierre Paul Michel, had lied that she had died of scarlet fever when young, and he breaks down when Poirot reveals the truth about her suicide. Poirot's first suspect investigated is Hector McQueen, Ratchett's secretary and interpreter. He had met his boss in the Orient, and, since he had lost his money, he had accepted the position. He was the son of an attorney who prosecuted the case, and he was very fond of Mrs. Armstrong, who had tried to advance his budding acting career. He had joined Ratchett in the East, aiming to help the conspirators to murder him. He is seen (during the reconstruction of the murder) dropping a powder into Ratchett's drink, sedating him, thus paving the way for the others to slip in under the supervision of Harriet Hubbard, who stated that the missing button Poirot found in the uniform had belonged to the Mafioso who supposedly used the uniform to enter the train to kill Ratchett. There was also a passkey found in the uniform, supposedly used by the phantom suspect to enter the wagon-lit. Poirot established that these "clues" were red herrings to misdirect the inquiring body—Bianchi, Dr. Constantine, and Poirot. Mrs. Hubbard's / Linda Arden's considerable acting skills were used to maximum effect, and she appears to her audience as a flippant, spoiled rich woman whose husbands had been mere stooges to entertain her. When asked whether she could know there was a man in her compartment in the dark, she answered she could tell anyway. "With your eyes closed?" asked Poirot. "That helped," she responded sneeringly. The ever-smiling and idiotic-looking Antonio Foscarelli, the Italian American car salesman, had been a chauffeur in the Armstrong household. He is savaged by Mr. Beddoes who, when asked if Foscarelli spoke English, says, "A kind of English, sir. He learned it in a place called Chicago."

Poirot leaves it up to Bianchi to decide which solution he will announce to the Yugoslavian police at Brod, just as the train has been freed by the plow and is about to move again. . . . Or will he accept the "simple" solution and tell the Yugoslavian police that a man had entered the train, murdered Cassetti, and escaped unobserved? After all, they had the uniform and the missing button as evidence. Bianchi selects the simple explanation, and Poirot, with some misgivings, goes along.

THEMES

One can draw two thematic lines in *Murder on the Orient Express*: one ethical, the other cinematic. The ethical theme arises when one ponders how Agatha Christie treats murder—her constant topic. Christie's moral stance on murder is stern. She almost never allowed a murderer or a person who committed a crime to escape.[4] In his earliest cases, Poirot had a sidekick, Captain Hastings, and a plodding Scotland Yard inspector, James Japp, who made certain the law was enforced. Poirot himself would allow no less. One could say that he went into the detective business not merely to enrich himself (he always was affluent), though we rarely see him getting paid for his services, and on a few occasions see him bail his assistant Hastings out of financial trouble. When Ratchett approaches him with his offer of $15,000, Poirot is neither impressed by Ratchett's crude manner nor tempted by the significant offer. He undertakes the investigation, however, once the villainous Ratchett/Cassetti is dead, as a matter of course, perhaps provoked by his vanity but most certainly by Signor Bianchi's pleading. His ego is stroked, but that is not the only reason why he goes into an investigation involving so many dissimilar individuals. He is morally outraged by the enormity of Ratchett's crimes and, as it turns out, by the actions of the perpetrators of the Express crime. During his summation, he makes several references to *Macbeth*, Shakespeare's darkest tragedy. "The light thickens," he says, misquoting on purpose ("the plot thickens" is the right quotation): He actually means the light of truth, which had evaded him up to this point (he beats his chest in mock self-condemnation). Later, he quotes, "The iron tongue of midnight . . . strikes twelve!" Here the point is more direct; twelve is a significant number—there are twelve members in a jury, "twelve men good and true," as Colonel Arbuthnot had told him during the interrogation. There are twelve passengers in the wagon-lit, excepting Signor Bianchi, Dr. Constantine (sharing the same cabin), and himself. When his speculation proves a certainty, Poirot leaves the decision-making to Signor Bianchi, who does not hesitate to choose the simple solution for reasons of his own. The scandal of arresting twelve passengers, most of them of high social position, would have destroyed the reputation of his line, for one thing; he also did not want to leave matters to the Yugoslavian police, who possibly would not have gone through the interrogation of the crime in as clearheaded a way as Poirot had. Poirot withdraws, accepting Bianchi's decision, saying he would be left to do "battle with his conscience."

The moviemakers also had a say in this decision. As Lumet says in his DVD commentary, this was entertainment of high order, and he would like his audiences to have a "feel-good" impression, so the movie ends on a note of gaiety: The participants in the murder, free from blame—or blemish, as it were—clink glasses of champagne, cheering their "victory." Agatha Christie has shown Poirot celebrating his victory on occasion, after a murder has been neatly uncovered. Once, in the TV movie *Peril at End House*, Poirot (David Suchet here) is offered an ice cream by his colleague Hastings, as he sits on a beach enjoying his triumph. His lifts his mustache with two fingers of his left hand, so the cone could go into his mouth without staining it. In the case of *Murder*, though, some shade of guilt stains Poirot's conscience.

Cinematically, the movie acquires a huge advantage by assembling a group of proven superstars (not all were, of course) who accepted bit roles, something attesting to the acuity of the producers Goodwin and Brabourne and director Lumet. Albert Finney of course takes on the big role, the leading part. As Poirot, Finney shows that his eccentric detective has a fiery imagination—yes, he had one!—and is provoked by the rich tapestry of human types, as he understands the task of spotting a killer among them is huge. While Finney takes on the plum role, several other deserve plaudits. A few deserve mentioning here. John Gielgud's Mr. Beddoes is a smug, servile pawn, an ex-batman born only to serve the superior (military) class. After all, the phrase "The butler did it!" elevates butlers to the rank of archvillains, and that in itself is a distinction. A butler is trained to conceal and control his emotions while he is exposed more than any other to human vagary. Gielgud, who could play Romeo, Hamlet, or Caliban, could also serve valerian to a crook whom he was about to stab with the same starched apathy he would serve tea to a toothless and deaf patroness. Here aristocracy is paired with commonness: Count Rudolph Andrenyi and his plushly attired wife Elena (or Helena, as Poirot points out) stand out as the gamma and epsilon of bred elegance, while Helena's mother, Mrs. Hubbard (Harriet Belinda, or Linda Arden), as played by Lauren Bacall, could not have been more vulgar. She is praised as the greatest tragic actress of her day in America (she is supposed to have been bedridden at the time), yet her manner, dress, and her disdain for those around her, including Poirot, suggest that she is either putting on an act or is really common. It takes great skill, even for an actress of Lauren Bacall's caliber, to cultivate such an impression. Introduced to the audience as a grand dame, wearing the widest hat ever invented, slanted as to almost conceal one of her eyes and half her face, as Linda Arden she justifies her reputation as the greatest tragic actress of her day. She conceals her righteous indignation by appearing sassy and vulgar during the interrogation, but embraces her daughter Helena affectionately after the mystery is solved. After multiple appearances as James Bond, Sean Connery leaves no doubt that his simmering Scottish blood could come to a boil at a moment's provocation. "You speak warmly," Poirot points out to him when Arbuthnot rises after one of Poirot's insinuations, but he sits down again, showing an officer and gentleman's self-control.

CONCLUSION

At the time, 1974, Bergman had the first signs of breast cancer, which eventually killed her. Unwisely (she says so herself in *My Story*), she ignored a doctor's advice to have a biopsy, busy as she was with a play and a movie. She had been a committed artist for decades, known for her promptness, conscientiousness, and obligations to her costars and the expectations of her audiences. She was now fifty-eight, her face was lined, and the lack of makeup, designed to deglamorize her, helped make her be more convincing as the naively conniving Greta Ohlsson. Amid formidable competition (who would not admire Wendy Hiller's deconstruction of Princess Dragomiroff?), with a bit role, she showed why she had mastered the art of acting as much as anyone could. Lord John Brabourne, one of the producers of the film, said he had hurried to see *Casablanca* as soon as Bergman accepted to take the part. Bergman was now nearing her long trajectory of triumphs in the art of acting, as well as experiencing personal triumphs and tragedies. It is said that Humphrey Bogart said during the making of *The African Queen* to the makeup man, "It took me a long time to develop these lines.

Just keep them as they are." Bergman almost did the same: deglamorizing herself, showing that beauty glows in a face by an inner force, something the makeup artists have to adjust to if they wish to preserve it in our idols.

AUTUMN SONATA

(1978)

★ ★ ★ ★

Director: Ingmar Bergman
Screenplay: Ingmar Bergman
Producers: Katinka Farago, Lew Grade, Martin Starger, Richard Brick (English language version). *Cinematography:* Sven Nykvist
Cast: Ingrid Bergman (Charlotte Andergast), Liv Ullmann (Eva), Lena Nyman (Helena), Halvar Björk (Viktor)
Studio: PersonaFilm
Released: October 8, 1978
Specs: 93 minutes; color; in Swedish (with English subtitles) and English
Availability: DVD and Blu-ray (Criterion Collection)

A long time passed between films that Bergman made in Scandinavia; forty years passed between *A Woman's Face* and *Autumn Sonata*. In the meantime she made films in Germany, the US, Italy, and France. *Autumn Sonata* was not a homecoming to Sweden for Ingrid, as it was filmed in Norway during Ingmar's self-imposed exile to that nation because of tax problems in his own country. However, it was the first time she worked with her namesake, the famous director of *The Seventh Seal* and *Wild Strawberries*. The year before filming, Ingrid slipped Ingmar a note at Cannes reminding him of his promise to give her a role in one of his films. Bergman's costar Liv Ullmann was, at the time of filming, about Bergman's age in the original *Intermezzo*. This was Ingmar Bergman's last film made for the theater;

his later films were made for television. This was also Ingrid's last film for cinema.

The director's original script seemed to follow Ingrid's biography, and certainly the film teases the relationship between the artwork and Bergman's life because her character is a famous artist who had not spent enough time with her children. More likely is that the director explored relationships of parents and children through other angles, including his own, as he and Liv Ullmann had a child out of wedlock together. Their daughter Linn Ullmann, born in 1966, plays a young Eva in the film. The film earned Ingrid a nomination for an Oscar as Best Actress and Ingmar as Best Screenwriter. However, the filming was stressful for all involved. Ingmar Bergman said that after read-throughs and the first days of shooting:

> I remember I got this headache. . . . It must have been a headache from sheer fear. What do you do with this incredibly strong and solid human being? How can I get her to dismantle this interpretation of the role that she has already decided on? . . . The first few days of shooting were a nightmare. Ingrid simply wouldn't take direction. She did it her own way and it was terrible.[1]

Liv Ullmann said Bergman had a unique acting process: "Ingrid's way of working is questions first and then I will do it according to the answer I get."[2] Ingrid's main goal in these arguments was to soften Charlotte, but Ingmar refused. Bergman thought Charlotte "intolerable" and she "tried to

Eva (Liv Ullmann) plays the piano, as her mother, Charlotte (Bergman), listens disapprovingly.
New World Pictures / Photofest © New World Pictures

persuade Ingmar to make her less beastly."[3] Many of the film's reviewers called Charlotte a monster, but Bergman gives her director the performance he expected, and, in the end, she is more sympathetic than the other characters who, perhaps, deserve more sympathy.

PLOT

In the film, Charlotte's elder of two children, Eva, is resentful of a famous pianist mother who rarely was home during her childhood. Her husband, Viktor, a minister, introduces her to the audience directly, breaking the fourth wall, and says how much her feelings toward her mother have affected her life and their marriage. He reads from the first of her two books: "One must learn to live. I practice every day. My biggest obstacle is I don't know who I am. I grope blindly. If anyone loves me as I am I may dare at last to look at myself. For me, that possibility is fairly remote." They are both anxious as Eva has invited her mother to visit the parsonage where they live, and she hopes Charlotte will move in with them. Hidden from the audience, and perhaps herself, is her desire to release her pent-up anger with her mother.

Her mother arrives in a Mercedes, complaining of her back pain. Eva carries her suitcase to the room. Charlotte has lost her lover of many years, Leonardo, and, as soon as she sits on the bed, she tells Eva about Leonardo's death at the hospital. The details she gives are quite vivid, especially when contrasted with her memories of her daughters' childhoods, and even her own. Done with the story, she hopes to quit "fretting" about his death. The other daughter, Helena, whom they call "Lena," has been living with Viktor and Eva for two years. She has an unspecified, degenerative disease. This news is a bombshell of pain for Charlotte, who has assiduously avoided Lena for seven years. Helena's joy of seeing her mother is overwhelming for her and heartbreaking for the audience. Charlotte, the exquisite artist, masks her horror and pain of seeing Helena, the daughter she has so long avoided. She is motherly and charming and promises everything she will never fulfill. At first it seems that Eva's motive is to reunite her sister with their mother; later it seems as if it is possible she is using Helena as a weapon against her. She states that she blames Helena's illness on Charlotte. That night Charlotte dreams someone is trying to smother her with hands that look like Helena's.

Several minutes of screen time are taken in preparation for dinner, but the dinner itself is not shown. Paul, Charlotte's manager, calls her after dinner about an opportunity for a well-paying concert date. Excitedly,

Charlotte sits at the piano. Eva replaces her at the piano to give her mother a replay of a small concert she did for children. She plays Chopin's Prelude no. 2 in A Minor while the camera is focused on Charlotte's face, which moves from attempting to find something good to think about her daughter's playing and something good to say about her daughter. Concert over, Eva asks, "Did you like it?" Charlotte answers, "I liked you." Eva moves over on the piano bench, and Charlotte sits by her. Charlotte explains that Chopin's piece is "pain, harsh." Eva stares at her through the song while Charlotte plays, attempting to find love for her. Charlotte is too intent on the music to notice. Her turn playing over, Eva says, "When I was little, I admired you so much. Then I got tired of you and your pianos. Now I admire you again, but in a different way."

Charlotte wants to take a walk, but Eva insists she sit with her in Erik's bedroom, which is unchanged since his accidental drowning. Later, they watch a slideshow of photos of Erik. Both Viktor and Charlotte are horrified by Eva's unrelenting grief and refusal to let Erik go. In the following scene Eva unleashes her years of pain and neglect caused by her mother. No pain is left unspoken. Charlotte was a poor mother even when she was home one summer: "There wasn't one detail that escaped your loving energy," Eva says in frustration. Charlotte lies on the floor to relieve her back pain. Facing her daughter, at one point she resembles Christina in *Christina's World* by Andrew Wyeth. After the storm passes, Charlotte realizes Eva's "hatred is terrible."

The film ends with Eva visiting Erik's grave and a flirty Charlotte on a train with her agent. In parallel edits, the last shots are spliced with Viktor reading a letter Eva writes to Charlotte asking her to return and that she cannot forgive herself for her treatment of her mother. One wonders if these words have meaning. The director gives the audience an extreme close-up of Eva's face. In the letter, she begs, "It can't be too late." Then an extreme close-up of Charlotte's face. The audience would not blame Charlotte for not returning to such verbal abuse again. However, perhaps Eva is still a doll to her or now a beast as well, and as Charlotte says about Chopin's Prelude that could be applied to their relationship, "You have to battle your way through it and emerge triumphant."

THEMES

Death is an important theme in the movie. The Chopin piece was nicknamed "presentiment of death." Many critics consider it dark, even macabre. Eva's difficulty with the piece is that she attempts to make it less dark, and fails. When Charlotte plays it, it becomes technically brilliant but no less difficult to listen to because of its jarring dissonance. Charlotte says, "It is never ingratiating. It should sound wrong." Charlotte faces the pain of the piece and does not reflect on the meaning. Eva attempts to avoid the pain, and, as Charlotte says, the Chopin piece slips into sentimentality. Her obsession with Erik's death and her belief that he is close to her makes her life a death in life. Supporting the theme, the film features an autumn palette throughout the house, the costuming, and even lighting, especially during the scenes of Leonardo's death. In short flashbacks, his white hospital room changes from being washed in white to gold to red and then, after his death, to white again with an open window, symbolizing his final release.

Another theme explores the artist's relationship with her family, what is gained and lost to be an artist. Charlotte pays a high cost for being a world-famous, successful artist. She says, "Only through music I have a chance to show my feelings." Charlotte does not know what it is to be a mother. Moments in her family's history are remembered by her concert or recording schedules. Where nonartists see artists as hardheaded, ignoring the past, and pursuing their artistic agendas without regard to family feelings, artists believe they live in the moment and see nonartists as sentimentalists who refuse to acknowledge pain and, worse, refuse to convert the pain to something useful, like art. Eva says that Charlotte is not just an artist, but "a goddamn escape artist." Eva does not know the life of an artist, but sees that Charlotte was "an expert at love's intonations and gestures." Recent films like *La La Land* (2017), which prominently features a poster of Bergman in an actress's bedroom, have similar themes; however, they spend less time on the process of grieving than what was lost or the process of transforming that grief.

Another theme is human frailty and guilt. After seeing Helena, Charlotte says, "This hurts, Charlotte, hurts, hurts, hurts." In her most revealing moments, she admits that she wanted her daughter to mother her, to teach her how to be a mother. Eva reveals that she never feels like an adult even after effectively humbling her mother near the end of film. Charlotte calls her a "crybaby," and in a long scene of verbal abuse, Eva says, "You managed to injure me for life just as you are injured." She sums it up as "a mother and a daughter—what a terrible combination of feelings and confusion and destruction. Everything is done in the name of love and solicitude." Family miseries, frailty, and guilt are themes explored in earlier Ingmar Bergman films. The intensity of *Autumn Sonata* is achieved by unrelenting verbal abuse squeezed into just a day or two at the mild-mannered parsonage.

Many revelations are made through their painful arguments: Eva didn't love Viktor when she decided to marry him. It is not made clear if she does yet. Eva, as a teen, loved a man who Charlotte thought was an idiot and insisted Eva get an abortion. Viktor did not know about this revelation. Possibly, the story about the Eva's tuberculosis was a cover-up for the abortion. Appropriately, at one moment Helena and Charlotte are both on the floor, where perhaps there could be a moment of epiphany for Charlotte, but there is a closed door between them and they do not see each other. Eva blames Helena's illness on her, because Helena was in love with Charlotte's lover. Viktor seems unable to assist or manage the growing hostilities between the mother and daughter and seems to suggest that all men, even those with ministerial experiences, are unable to enjoin these battles. He says that, unlike Charlotte and Eva, he's "confused and uncertain." Often claustrophobic, the scenes are often played out in small rooms of the house. Ingmar's shots emphasize the physical closeness of the characters by using zoom lenses for close-ups, but the dialogue and the characters' facial movements reveal their emotional distance.

CONCLUSION

Filming at this time was acutely painful to Bergman as she had recently had a mastectomy and was still in bandages, although no one on set knew. The scene requiring her to crawl around the floor was especially excruciating for her. Perhaps her surgery offers an explanation for why her reputation for being easy to get along with on set was put to the test.

Bergman's surgery caused her to be more reflective of her entire career as she thought she was facing its end. Speaking to one interviewer at the time, she said, "If I am to be remembered, well, I hope to be remembered as an actress who was sincere, who gave pleasure to people by her honest work."[4] *Autumn Sonata* brought her seventh Oscar nomination, and her health held just enough for her to play Golda Meir for a television mini-series four years later.

In many of her films, Bergman played the beautiful heroine, the beauty, working opposite a character, a beast, who was as much as a beast as Charlotte; *Gaslight* and *Dr. Jekyll and Mr. Hyde* are the most famous of these. Perhaps this is the first time she plays one herself. In *Murder on the Orient Express*, Bergman's character assists other train passengers in murdering a man. In the American version of *Intermezzo*, Leslie Howard is the musician as beast, and Bergman his student and pianist. Now, forty years later, the tables have turned and the student pianist is now the teacher, and in *Autumn Sonata*, she destroys a family.

For *Autumn Sonata*, Bergman carries the dignity of the golden age of the Hollywood studio system in her portrayal of Charlotte's carriage and demeanor; however, without the honesty in acting that Ingmar required and Bergman reveled in while working with Roberto Rossellini, especially in *Europe '51* and *Journey to Italy*, it is doubtful Ingmar would have asked her to be his Charlotte. One critic points out that "gone was the beauty that disguised her ability."[5] It is her honesty that gives her the gravitas in this role. Ingmar said that "[Ingrid] is not afraid to show herself. She is not like stars, she is an artist."[6]

21

A WOMAN CALLED GOLDA

(1982)

★ ★ ★ ★

Director: Alan Gibson
Teleplay: Harold Gast and Steven Gethers
Producer: Gene Corman. *Cinematography:* Adam Greenberg. *Music Score:*
    Michel Legrand
Cast: Ingrid Bergman (Golda Meir), Ned Beatty (Senator Durward), Franklin
    Cover (Hubert Humphrey), Judy Davis (Young Golda), Anne Jackson
    (Lou Kaddar / Narrator), Robert Loggia (Anwar Sadat), Leonard
    Nimoy (Morris Meyerson), Jack Thompson (Ariel), Anthony Bate (Sir
    Stuart Ross), Ron Berglas (Stampler), Bruce Boa (Mr. Macy), David
    de Keyser (David Ben-Gurion), Barry Foster (Major Orde Wingate),
    Nigel Hawthorne (King Abdullah), Louis Mahoney (Journalist), Yossi
    Graber (Moshe Dayan)
Studio: Paramount
First Aired: April 26, 1982
Specs: 240 minutes; color
Availability: DVD (Paramount)

A Woman Called Golda is a television miniseries that Alan Gibson, the director, had to urge Bergman out of retirement to take the role. She resisted taking on the role of Golda Meir because she had not played historical characters who were so well known. She especially relished roles that allowed her to have a bit of humor, even for a character that it didn't seem to fit, such as in *Autumn Sonata*. Also, Meir was famously staid, as shown in a recent *unbendable* Golda Meir three-inch-high doll manufactured in Israel. According to the manufacturer, Israelis see her "like this, with a pearl necklace and one long dress with dark shoes."[1]

In the film Bergman is regal and commanding. She studied Golda's speech and mannerisms by watching newsreels and even interviewed people who knew her. Bergman's portrayal reveals Meir as human with moments of pathos, dancing with joy at the creation of the new Jewish state, crying with deep sadness after an emotional encounter with a small girl, and easy humor during her speech in front of an assembly of children. Bergman may have taken the role because of the many commonalities between their lives, the most important of which, to Bergman at the time, was that Golda died at the age of eighty from cancer. Bergman herself had been battling cancer for many years. The *Washington Post* at the time said her acting "represents a rejuvenating triumph for Ingrid Bergman, who obliterates all skepticism about her suitability for the role of Golda Meir with what is not so much a performance as a stunning transformation."[2]

The miniseries won Emmy Awards for Outstanding Lead Actress in a Limited Series or Special (Ingrid Bergman), Outstanding Drama Special (Harve Bennett, executive producer, and Gene Corman, producer), and Outstanding Film Editing for a Limited Series or Special (Robert F. Shu-

Judy Davis, who plays the younger Golda, face-to-face with Ingrid Bergman, Golda in her later years. *Paramount Television / Photofest © Paramount Television*

grue). Leonard Nimoy and Judy Davis were nominated for their supporting roles. Ingrid's Emmy was accepted for her posthumously by her daughter Pia Lindstrom.

Another reason she may have taken the role was her work in Germany where she saw the rise of the Nazi Party there during a visit with her aunt and when she worked on the film *The Four Companions* (German: *Die vier Gesellen*) (1938). Bergman had little interest in politics at the time. "I took the German offer because I spoke the language—but not with the intention of staying in Germany at all. I had my eyes set on Hollywood, of course, but it was a question of waiting for the right opportunity. . . . If I knew anything about politics, I would have had more sense than to go to Germany to make a picture in 1938."[3]

The film opens with cuts between shots of a woman at a piano and caravan of government vehicles. Her assistant Lou Kaddar (Anne Jackson) reminds Golda Meir (Ingrid Bergman) to put out her cigarette before she leaves the car. They arrive at the Fourth Street Elementary School Assembly in Milwaukee. Golda is welcomed as their most distinguished graduate. In her address to the children, she uses a quote from Hillel that was important in her life: "If I am not for myself, who will be for me? But if I am only for myself, who am I? If not now, when?" The narrative is driven by questions from the children attending the assembly, interspersed with historical newsreels and occasional commentary from Lou.

The film flashes backs to Golda's family's life in Russia, where anti-Semitics terrorized Jewish citizens. Their father moves the family to Milwaukee where she attends the elementary school she visits in 1969. As a young adult, the first man in her life is Morris Meyerson (Leonard Nimoy). He talks to her about marriage, but Golda (Judy Davis in the role of the younger Golda) is resistant because, as Meyerson says, "she is hypnotized by romantic Zionist business"—Palestine. She wants to be part of the aliyah, immigration to Palestine, and live in a kibbutz. Even her father calls her intransigent on the idea.

Davis is best known for her acting in *My Brilliant Career* (1979), as Adela Quested in *A Passage to India* (1984), and in Woody Allen's film *Husbands and Wives* (1992). The last two roles earned her Oscar nominations. Especially in the Woody Allen movies, she is known for playing neurotic and intelligent women, but as Golda Meyerson, she exudes strength and single-ness of mind and seems to channel Ingrid Bergman's sincerity and drive in her acting. Leonard Nimoy famously drew on his Jewish religion when he adapted a Jewish hand sign to his character of Mr. Spock in *Star Trek*. As a child in temple, he saw it used as a blessing to the congregation and learned "that this is the shape of the letter *shin* in the Hebrew alphabet." Nimoy later acted in his own project about his faith, *Never Forget*, a fact-based drama about a survivor of a concentration camp, Mel Mermelstein, who fought the spread of disinformation by revisionist groups who argued the Holocaust never occurred.

Arriving at Kibbutz Merhavyah as Morris Meyerson and Golda Meyerson, they find that their application to join the community has been denied. Because their taxi had already dropped them off, the leaders agree to let them stay the night; however, the people of the community are immediately taken by Morris's portable phonograph and his record collection. Later the committee votes to keep them both. As she settles into the community life, Golda decides she wants children, but Morris is concerned about the way the kibbutz overplans their lives. He wants to be a "parent, not a visitor." As time passes, the committee asks her to take on more and more responsibility in the administration of the community.

In a symbolic moment showing the choices Golda has to make, she sees Morris falling because of his weakness from malaria. She looks concerned, but instead of helping him she speaks to her boss Ariel (Jack Thompson) about being a delegate to a labor union. Later, when sirens blare because of a raiding party, Morris has problems handling and loading a rifle. Golda takes it and runs toward the action but is stopped by the raiders, who reveal that it is a "totally unauthorized training" exercise. Although she doesn't speak Hebrew well, she is placed on the executive committee of Histadrut, the organized Jewish labor movement in Palestine.

They leave the kibbutz to live in Jerusalem. As the mother of two, she says it is the worst time of her life. Ariel offers her a job in Tel Aviv. With a marriage failing and an unwillingness to let her husband and children "narrow her horizon," she leaves her children with a stranger.

When Hitler is in power, Golda (now played by Ingrid Bergman) works with David Ben-Gurion (David de Keyser) in the Jewish Agency. Reacting to the British white paper that stated a Jewish state should not be created, they decide to fight Hitler as if there were no white paper. They also intend to use the British to train as many Jewish soldiers as they would permit. Two of their most valuable military leaders are Moshe Dayan (Yossi Graber) and Major Orde Wingate (Barry Foster). Wingate, a British soldier who became a Zionist, says, "The Lord is fighting for the children of Israel." Frustrated that the government has allowed him to train only five hundred Israeli soldiers, Golda suggests he train the five hundred, then train another five hundred.

In 1945, the Allied forces liberated German concentration camps; however, the survivors going to Palestine were captured by the British and placed into camps in Cyprus because of a British quota of the number allowed to immigrate to Palestine. Golda is assigned to free them. She begins by attempting to have the British let small children free and then their parents. The British are willing, but the children would be counted toward the quota. While she waits for word from immigrant committees about her proposal, children bring her paper flowers. One girl states she never saw a real flower. In a moment alone, Golda cries for children who never saw real flowers. The people in the camp vote to let the children go first.

On November 29, 1947, Golda announces, on behalf of the Jewish Agency, that Palestine is to be partitioned and Jerusalem is to be international. At a joyous party that night where Golda dances with enthusiasm, her husband Morris arrives and wants to see her. She believes he is drunk, but "the country is drunk," he says. He tells her that she made the right decision to pursue a political life, leaving him and the children behind.

The planned pullout of British troops would leave the new Jewish state open to invasion from Arab countries. One of the advisors gives a fifty-fifty chance of winning, to which Ben-Gurion responds, "As much a chance to win as to lose. Fifty-fifty. Could be worse." Only ten thousand are trained fighters, although the odds should still be in favor of the Israelis. To move the odds more in their favor, Golda meets King Abdullah of Jordan to convince him to stay out of the coming war. To cross into Jordan in secret, she must wear a traditional *abaya* and pretend to be married to her assistant. In one word she tells King Abdullah (Nigel Hawthorne) what she wants: "shalom." She reminds him of his past promises not to attack and asks if that has changed. After several direct questions, he explodes and complains to her male assistant that they shouldn't send him women. She pushes back hard: "If we are attacked we will take whatever territory we want. You don't know how our strength has increased."

She returns believing she has failed to prevent war. Unfortunately, the country has no funds to purchase weapons. Ben-Gurion says it would cost $25 million to buy materiel they need and plans to go to the US to raise it. Golda suggests she go instead because the pending war makes it too important for him to leave. She does go and raises $50 million. While she is away, Israel is invaded by Arab countries in the 1948 Arab-Israeli War. Israel successfully fends off the attacks. Arriving back in Israel, she is called the "woman who made it possible for the Jewish state to be born." As the new minister of labor, she must face a tidal wave of immigrants who need jobs. During this time her husband Morris dies. After being labor minister for seven years, she becomes a doting grandmother, and attempts to make up for not being a mother. She says they are the best years of her life.

Gamal Abdel Nasser of Egypt sends groups to attack Israel, including a grenade attack in the Knesset. Golda saves Ben-Gurion's life, but she is wounded and carries shrapnel in her leg the rest of her life. While she convalesces, Ben-Gurion, whom she calls B.G., reminds her that she has not taken a Hebrew name, which is a requirement for Israeli officials. He suggests a name close to Meyerson: "Meir," meaning "illuminate." Her name would mean "Golden Light." He offers the position of foreign minister to her. The position makes her uncomfortable because of her lack of diplomatic training, "How will I fit in with them?" B.G. says, "You'll make them fit in with you."

During Meir's tenure as Israel's second foreign minister, Egyptian president Nasser nationalizes the Suez Canal and accepts weapons from the USSR. After he closes the canal to Israeli shipping, the Israeli air force attacks Egypt. Because they are so successful in taking land from the Egyptians during the war, the UN pressures them to withdraw. Golda decides to withdraw. At the UN, she appeals to Arab countries to act as their brothers and sisters, but when there is only polite applause she realizes it was a mistake to withdraw. In the 1960s Meir was the only female foreign minister in the world and felt she had accomplished the most in Africa.

At dinner with Ariel, he surprises her that his wife wants a divorce, and once free he would like to marry her. As with any big decision she makes, she says she "must wash my hair and think." The next morning Ariel does not arrive at the street café for breakfast as planned. His apartment manager reports to her that he died once he went into the apartment. Shortly after, she finds lumps that a biopsy reveals are malignant. She keeps the cancer a secret; however, the double blow becomes too much for her. She considers retirement, and two years later she resigns as foreign minister.

In the spring of 1967, she is asked to become secretary general, the leader of the Mapai, the Workers' Party of the Land of Israel. The Six-Day War begins, and Israel retakes Sinai. Jews are now able to visit the Western Wall, and Israel now has defensible borders. Two years later, Meir is a private citizen; the press gives her news that the prime minister has died from a heart attack. Although she is concerned that she is too old, she is elected unanimously to serve as prime minister. When she visits her doctor, he insists she finally has to go through therapy. Although she is not allowed to know the truth, Lou discovers Golda is going into radiology. They both take out cigarettes in symbolic resistance to cancer.

An American senator (Ned Beatty) visits Golda at her home to discuss armaments. He is the key vote on a Senate committee, and she needs the military hardware she can provide. He offers her Lockheed F-104

Starfighters; instead she wants the McDonnell Douglas F-4 Phantom II and M16 tanks. He negotiates for her honey cake recipe. When Egypt mobilizes troops along the Suez Canal, Israeli intelligence reports that it is only training maneuvers. She realizes that it is more than maneuvers when the Soviets transfer their people out of Syria. She mobilizes her troops but avoids a preemptive strike. Doing so, Israel loses half of its planes to Russian missiles. Born with a distrust for Russia and a trust of the USA, she contacts President Nixon who responds with a massive airlift; it is so successful that the USSR presses for a cease-fire. At the end of the Yom Kippur War, the mood in Israel is bleak, and people are openly hostile to Meir and her decisions during the war.

At a dinner in honor of Egyptian president Anwar Sadat (Robert Loggia), she says, "As an old lady I always hoped that we'd have peace" and offers Sadat a gift for his granddaughter. Privately, she says she would have stayed in the kibbutz as she would be more at peace with herself and her whole life. The film ends with a close-up of Golda's unhappy face in the twilight.

CONCLUSION

The film shows a difference between the woman from Milwaukee who interacts so well with children, smiles, laughs, and occasionally hides her smile, and an Israeli politician who led wars and lived with shrapnel in her leg. Bergman's portrayal was of a power leader who was not arrogant or power hungry. Unlike many of her other films, there are few scenes with children, and only glancing acknowledgment of love stories. There are precious few scenes of joy, laughter, or humor. Like many of her films, however, it begins as a "fish out of water" story, a displaced person who works herself up to a position of power, such as in *The Inn of the Sixth Happiness*.

Bergman drove herself to take on challenges. Doing this biographical piece of a well-known and beloved political leader was an artistic challenge for her because it had to be a deeply respectful portrayal. Bergman's oeuvre has many examples of her portraying complicated women with great power and responsibilities, such as *Joan of Arc*. Her love of work rose to the challenge of an extended miniseries with location shoots in the Middle East and must have been physically challenging at her age considering the growing cancer. Just after filming for *A Woman Called Golda* finished, Bergman asked her former husband, Swedish theater producer Lars Schmidt, to take her to the Swedish island that had been their home. There she died, in August 29, 1982, on her sixty-seventh birthday.

NOTES

CHAPTER 1

1. Ingrid Bergman and Alan Burgess, *Ingrid Bergman: My Story* (New York: Dell, 1980), 45.
2. Bergman and Burgess, *My Story*, 45.

CHAPTER 2

1. Ingrid Bergman and Alan Burgess, *My Story* (New York: Dell, 1980), 39.
2. Bergman and Burgess, *My Story*, 58.
3. Donald Spoto, *Notorious: The Life of Ingrid Bergman* (New York: HarperCollins, 1997), 58.
4. Bergman and Burgess, *My Story*, 61.
5. Bergman and Burgess, *My Story*, 99.
6. David W. Smit, "Marketing Ingrid Bergman," *Quarterly Review of Film and Video* 22, no. 3 (2005): 237–50.
7. Smit, "Marketing Ingrid Bergman," 237–50.

CHAPTER 3

1. Robert Louis Stevenson, *The Strange Case of Dr. Jekyll and Mr. Hyde* (New York: Dover Thrift Editions, 2015), 55.

CHAPTER 4

1. Donald Spoto, *Notorious: The Life of Ingrid Bergman* (New York: HarperCollins, 1997), 122.

2. A. M. Sperber and Eric Lax, *Bogart* (New York: Morrow, 1997), 192.

3. Ibid.

4. Charlotte Chandler, *Ingrid Bergman: A Personal Biography* (New York: Simon & Schuster, 2007), 19–21.

CHAPTER 5

1. Donald Spoto, *Notorious: The Life of Ingrid Bergman* (New York: HarperCollins, 1997), 130.

2. The Oscar nominations of *For Whom the Bell Tolls* were Best Picture, Best Actor (Gary Cooper), Best Actress (Ingrid Bergman), Best Supporting Actor (Akim Tamiroff), Best Supporting Actress (Katina Paxinou, won), Best Cinematography (Ray Rennahan), Best Art Director (Hans Dreier), Best Editing (Sherman Todd), and Best Music Score (Victor Young).

3. Ingrid Bergman and Alan Burgess, *My Story* (New York: Dell, 1980), 153.

4. Bergman and Burgess, *My Story*, 153.

5. Bergman and Burgess, *My Story*, 152.

6. The restored version of the DVD was in photochemical, not in digital process.

CHAPTER 6

1. Patrick McGilligan, *George Cukor: A Double Life* (Minneapolis: University of Minnesota Press, 2013), ProQuest ebrary, retrieved June 8, 2016.

2. S. L. Kotar and J. E. Gessler, *Ballooning: A History, 1782–1900* (Jefferson, NC: McFarland, 2011), 226.

3. McGilligan, *George Cukor*.

4. McGilligan, *George Cukor*.

5. Donald Spoto, *Notorious: The Life of Ingrid Bergman* (New York: Harper Collins, 1997), 147.

CHAPTER 7

1. Premiere Collection DVD, 2008, Commentary, "Special Features."

2. Peter Ackroyd, *Alfred Hitchcock: A Brief Life* (New York: Doubleday, 2015), 212.

3. Ackroyd, *Alfred Hitchcock*, 211.
4. Ackroyd, *Alfred Hitchcock*, 211.
5. Donald Spoto, *Notorious: The Life of Ingrid Bergman* (New York: HarperCollins, 1997), 165.

CHAPTER 8

1. Donald Spoto, *Notorious: The Life of Ingrid Bergman* (New York: HarperCollins, 1997), 178.
2. Spoto, *Notorious*, 178. The reference is to Christopher Marlowe's poem about Helen of Troy, who was able—through her beauty—to "launch a thousand ships."

CHAPTER 9

1. Rudy Behlmer, film historian, was an editor of *Memo from David O. Selznick*. Another commentator on the track of Criterion Collection edition is Marian Keane, film historian.
2. Donald Spoto, *Notorious: The Life of Ingrid Bergman* (New York: HarperCollins, 1997), 197.
3. A Freudian interpretation of a son's unhealthy attachment to a domineering mother.

CHAPTER 10

1. Ingrid Bergman and Alan Burgess, *My Story* (New York: Dell, 1980), 202.
2. After the failure of *Arch of Triumph* and the consequent losses, Enterprise Films closed down ingloriously.

CHAPTER 11

1. Ingrid Bergman and Alan Burgess, *My Story* (New York: Dell, 1980), 210.
2. Bergman and Burgess, *My Story*, 213.
3. Carl Theodor Dreyer's distinguished *The Passion of Joan of Arc* (1928), with Renee Falconetti, and *Saint Joan* by Otto Preminger, with Jean Seberg (1957), are some examples. In literature, Mark Twain's *Personal Recollections of Joan of Arc* (1896) keeps up with the legend of Joan of Arc.
4. Another is *The Bells of Saint Mary's* (1945), Bing Crosby being disqualified as a priest.

5. Bergman and Burgess, *My Story*, 223.

6. Bergman and Burgess, *My Story*, 230.

7. George Bernard Shaw, *Saint Joan* (London: Penguin, 1946), 8.

8. Donald Spoto, *Notorious: The Life of Ingrid Bergman* (New York: HarperCollins, 1997), 231–32.

9. Bergman and Burgess, *My Story*, 225.

CHAPTER 12

1. Donald Spoto, *Notorious: The Life of Ingrid Bergman* (New York: HarperCollins, 1997), 296.

2. *Stromboli, Europe '51, Journey to Italy*: Criterion Collection, 2013.

3. Spoto, *Notorious*, 294.

4. Ingrid Bergman and Alan Burgess, *My Story* (New York: Dell, 1980), 281.

5. Elena Degrada, booklet in Criterion Collection, 2013, 24–25.

6. Isaiah 65:1 (New International Version).

7. Roberto Rossellini, "'Ti Amo': An Exchange of Letters," booklet, Criterion Collection, 2013, 46.

8. Rossellini, "'Ti Amo.'"

CHAPTER 13

1. Elena Degrada, professor of cinema studies at the University of Milan, Criterion Collection, "Special Features," Disc 2.

2. Supplements in Disc 2 Blu-Ray, Criterion Collection, "Special Features."

CHAPTER 14

1. Ingrid Bergman and Alan Burgess, *My Story* (New York: Dell, 1980), 394.

2. "Anna Koreff" was used in the film to replace the name "Anna Anderson," the real person who claimed to be Anastasia, then living in Germany. Audio commentary by John Burlingame and James MacArthur, "Anastasia: Her True Story," as seen on *Biography* on the A&E Network Movietone newsreels, Twentieth Century Fox DVD, 2003.

3. A distant relative of the Grand Duchess Anastasia was England's Prince Philip, husband of Queen Elizabeth II. DNA evidence proved that they were unrelated. Audio commentary by John Burlingame and James MacArthur, "Anastasia: Her True Story."

4. Audio commentary by John Burlingame and James MacArthur, "Anastasia: Her True Story."

5. Donald Spoto, her biographer, in his commentary on the DVD edition of Bergman's 1958 movie *The Inn of the Sixth Happiness*.

CHAPTER 15

1. Lucy Fisher, *Shot/Countershot: Film Tradition and Women's Cinema* (Princeton, NJ: Princeton University Press, 2014), 66–67.

CHAPTER 16

1. Donald Spoto, DVD commentary on *The Inn of the Sixth Happiness*.

2. For general reference on the epic film, see introduction (ix–xvii) in *The Encyclopedia of Epic Films* by Constantine Santas, James M. Wilson, Djoymi Baker, and Maria Colavito (Lanham, MD: Rowman & Littlefield, 2014).

3. Bosley Crowther, review of *The Inn of the Sixth Happiness*, *New York Times*, December 14, 1958.

4. Ingrid Bergman and Alan Burgess, *My Story* (New York: Dell, 1980), 441.

CHAPTER 17

1. Bosley Crowther, review of *Goodbye Again*, *New York Times*, June 30, 1961.

CHAPTER 18

1. Donald Spoto, *Notorious: The Life of Ingrid Bergman* (New York: HarperCollins, 1997), 357.

2. Ingrid Bergman and Alan Burgess, *My Story* (New York: Dell, 1980), 479.

3. Bergman and Burgess, *My Story,* 479.

CHAPTER 19

1. Ingrid Bergman and Alan Burgess, *My Story* (New York: Dell, 1979), 389–90.

2. Bergman and Burgess, *My Story*, 532.

3. *https://nyti.ms/11L.sqbEN*

4. Her grandson's comment on the DVD's "Special Features."

CHAPTER 20

1. "The Making of *Autumn Sonata*," *Autumn Sonata*, DVD "Bonus Features," 1978.

2. "The Making of *Autumn Sonata*," *Autumn Sonata*, DVD "Bonus Features," 1978.

3. Jay Scott, "Bergman's Beauty Stirred Film Goers: Ingrid Bergman's Roles—and Life—Thrilled," *Toronto Globe and Mail*, August 31, 1982.

4. Scott, "Bergman's Beauty."

5. Scott, "Bergman's Beauty."

6. Michael Blowen, "She Is Not Like Stars; She Is an Artist," *Boston Globe*, August 31, 1982.

CHAPTER 21

1. Erik Piepenburg, "An Unbendable Golda Meir, Onstage and in Vinyl," *New York Times*, December 7, 2016.

2. *Washington Post*, May 3, 1982.

3. Donald Spoto, *Notorious: The Life of Ingrid Bergman* (New York: HarperCollins, 1997), 61.

4. Jay Robin, "Holocaust Project Lured Nimoy; The Importance 'Never Forget' Made Him Eager to Act Again." *St. Louis Dispatch. Tribute Media Services*. April 7, 1991. p. 62.

FILMOGRAPHY

Munkbrogreven [English title: *The Count of the Monk's Bridge*] (1934) ★
Directors: Edvin Adolphson and Sigurd Wallén. *Screenplay:* Gösta Stevens,
   based on the play by Siegfried Fischer and Arthur Fischer
Cast: Valdemar Dalquist, Julia Caesar, Sigurd Wallén, Tollie Zellman,
   Edvin Adolphson, Ingrid Bergman

Bränningar [English titles: *The Surf; Ocean Breakers*] (1935) ★
Director: Ivar Johansson. *Screenplay:* Ivar Johansson and Henning Ohlson,
   based on the novel by Per Vedin
Cast: Ingrid Bergman, Sten Lindgren, Tore Svennberg, Bror Olsson, Carl
   Ström

Swedenhielms [English title: *The Family Swedenhielms*] (1935) ★
Director: Gustaf Molander. *Screenplay:* Stina Bergman, based on the play
   by Hjalmar Bergman
Cast: Gösta Ekman, Björn Berglund, Håkan Westergren, Tutta Rolf, Ingrid
   Bergman

Valborgsmässoafton [English title: *Walpurgis Night*] (1935) ★ ★
Director: Gustaf Edgren. *Screenplay:* Oscar Rydqvist and Gustaf Edgren
Cast: Lars Hanson, Karin Kavli, Victor Sjöström, Ingrid Bergman

På solsidan [English title: *On the Sunny Side*] (1936) ★★
Director: Gustaf Molander. *Screenplay:* Gösta Stevens and Oscar Hemberg, based on the play by Helge Krog
Cast: Lars Hanson, Ingrid Bergman, Karin Swanström, Edvin Adolphson, Marianne Löfgren

Intermezzo (1936) ★★
Director: Gustaf Molander. *Screenplay:* Gösta Stevens and Gustaf Molander
Cast: Gösta Ekman, Inga Tidblad, Ingrid Bergman, Erik "Bullen" Berglund, Hugo Björne

Dollar (1938) ★★
Director: Gustaf Molander. *Screenplay:* Stina Bergman, based on the play by Hjalmar Bergman
Cast: Ingrid Bergman, Georg Rydeberg, Tutta Rolf, Kotti Chave, Birgit Tengroth

En Kvinnas Ansikte [English title: *A Woman's Face*] (1938) ★★★
Director: Gustaf Molander. *Screenplay:* Gösta Stevens, based on a play by Francis de Croisset
Cast: Ingrid Bergman, Tore Svennberg, Anders Henrikson, Georg Rydeberg, Gunnar Sjöberg, Karin Kavli, Erik "Bullen" Berglund

Die vier Gesellen [English title: *The Four Companions*] (1938) ★★
Director: Carl Froelich. *Screenplay:* Jochen Huth
Cast: Ingrid Bergman, Sabine Peters, Carsta Löck, Ursula Herking, Hans Söhnker

En enda natt [English title: *Only One Night*] (1939) ★★★
Director: Gustaf Molander. *Screenplay:* Gösta Stevens, based on a novel by Harald Tandrup
Cast: Ingrid Bergman, Edvin Adolphson, Aino Taube, Olof Sandborg

Intermezzo: A Love Story (1939) ★★★
Director: Gregory Ratoff. *Screenplay:* George O'Neil, based on a story by Gösta Stevens and Gustaf Molander
Cast: Leslie Howard, Ingrid Bergman, Edna Best, John Halliday, Cecil Kellaway

Juninatten [English titles: *June Night*; *A Night in June*] (1940) ★ ★ ★
Director: Per Lindberg. *Screenplay:* Ragnar Hyltén-Cavallius, based on a
novel by Tora Nordström-Bonnier
Cast: Ingrid Bergman, Marianne Löfgren, Lill-Tollie Zellman, Marianne
Aminoff

Adam Had Four Sons (1941) ★ ★
Director: Gregory Ratoff. *Screenplay:* William Hurlbut and Michael Blank-
fort, based on the novel by Charles Bonner
Cast: Ingrid Bergman, Warner Baxter, Susan Hayward, Fay Wray, Richard
Denning

Rage in Heaven (1941) ★ ★
Director: W. S. Van Dyke. *Screenplay:* Christopher Isherwood and Robert
Thoeren, based on the novel by James Hilton
Cast: Robert Montgomery, Ingrid Bergman, George Sanders, Lucile Wat-
son, Oskar Homolka

Dr. Jekyll and Mr. Hyde (1941) ★ ★ ★
Director: Victor Fleming. *Screenplay:* John Lee Mahin, based on the no-
vella *Strange Case of Dr. Jekyll and Mr. Hyde* by Robert Louis Stevenson
Cast: Spencer Tracy, Ingrid Bergman, Lana Turner, Donald Crisp, Ian
Hunter, C. Aubrey Smith

Casablanca (1942) ★ ★ ★ ★ ★
Director: Michael Curtiz. *Screenplay:* Julius J. Epstein, Philip G. Epstein,
and Howard Koch, based on the unproduced play *Everybody Comes to
Rick's* by Murray Burnett and Joan Alison
Cast: Humphrey Bogart, Ingrid Bergman, Paul Henreid, Claude Rains,
Conrad Veidt, Peter Lorre, Sydney Greenstreet, S. Z. "Cuddles" Sakall,
Dooley Wilson

For Whom the Bell Tolls (1943) ★ ★ ★
Director: Sam Wood. *Screenplay:* Dudley Nichols, based on the novel by
Ernest Hemingway
Cast: Gary Cooper, Ingrid Bergman, Akim Tamiroff, Katina Paxinou, Jo-
seph Calleia, Vladimir Sokoloff, Arturo de Cordova

Gaslight (1944) ★ ★ ★ ★ ★

Director: George Cukor. *Screenplay:* John Van Druten, Walter Reisch, and John Balderston, based on the play *Angel Street* by Patrick Hamilton

Cast: Ingrid Bergman, Charles Boyer, Joseph Cotten, Dame May Whitty, Angela Lansbury

Saratoga Trunk (1945) ★ ★

Director: Sam Wood. *Screenplay:* Casey Robinson, based on the novel by Edna Ferber

Cast: Gary Cooper, Ingrid Bergman, Flora Robson, Jerry Austin, Florence Bates

Spellbound (1945) ★ ★ ★ ★

Director: Alfred Hitchcock. *Screenplay:* Ben Hecht; adaptation by Angus MacPhail, based on the novel *The House of Dr. Edwardes* by Francis Beeding (pseudonym of Hilary Saint George Saunders and John Leslie Palmer)

Cast: Ingrid Bergman, Gregory Peck, Leo G. Carroll, Michael Chekhov, Rhonda Fleming, Norman Lloyd

The Bells of St. Mary's (1945) ★ ★ ★

Director: Leo McCarey. *Screenplay:* Dudley Nichols, based on a story by Leo McCarey

Cast: Bing Crosby, Ingrid Bergman, Henry Travers, Una O'Connor, William Gargan, Ruth Donnelly

Notorious (1946) ★ ★ ★ ★ ★

Director: Alfred Hitchcock. *Screenplay:* Ben Hecht

Cast: Cary Grant, Ingrid Bergman, Claude Rains, Leopoldine Konstantin, Louis Calhern

Arch of Triumph (1948) ★ ★ ★

Director: Lewis Milestone. *Screenplay:* Lewis Milestone and Harry Brown, based on the novel by Erich Maria Remarque

Cast: Charles Boyer, Ingrid Bergman, Louis Calhern, Charles Laughton, Ruth Warrick

Joan of Arc (1948) ★ ★ ★

Director: Victor Fleming. *Screenplay:* Maxwell Anderson and Andrew Solt, based on the play *Joan of Lorraine* by Maxwell Anderson

Cast: Ingrid Bergman, José Ferrer, John Emery, Francis L. Sullivan, J. Carrol Naish, Ward Bond

Stromboli [aka *Stromboli, Terra di Dio*] (1950) ★ ★ ★ ★
Director: Roberto Rossellini. *Screenplay:* Sergio Amidei, Gian Paolo Callegari, Art Cohn, Renzo Cesana, and Roberto Rossellini
Cast: Ingrid Bergman, Mario Vitale, Renzo Cesana, Mario Sponza

Europe '51 [aka *The Greatest Love*] (1954) ★ ★ ★
Director: Roberto Rossellini. *Screenplay:* Roberto Rossellini, Sandro De Feo, Mario Pannunzio, Ivo Perilli, and Brunello Rondi
Cast: Ingrid Bergman, Alexander Knox, Ettore Giannini, Giulietta Masina, Sandro Franchina

Giovanna d'Arco al rogo [English title: *Joan of Arc at the Stake*] (1954) ★ ★
Director: Roberto Rossellini. *Screenplay:* Paul Claudel and Roberto Rossellini
Cast: Ingrid Bergman, Tullio Carminati, Giacinto Prandelli, Augusto Romani

Journey to Italy (1954) ★ ★
Director: Roberto Rossellini. *Screenplay:* Vitaliano Brancati and Roberto Rossellini
Cast: Ingrid Bergman, George Sanders, Maria Mauban, Anna Proclemer, Paul Muller

Non credo più all'amore [English titles: *Fear La paura*; *Angst*] (1955) ★ ★
Director: Roberto Rossellini. *Screenplay:* Sergio Amidei and Franz von Treuberg, based on the novel *Angst* by Stefan Zweig
Cast: Ingrid Bergman, Mathias Wieman, Renate Mannhardt, Kurt Kreuger, Elise Aulinger

Anastasia (1956) ★ ★ ★ ★ ★
Director: Anatole Litvak. *Screenplay:* Guy Bolton and Arthur Laurents, based on the play by Marcelle Maurette
Cast: Ingrid Bergman, Yul Brynner, Helen Hayes, Akim Tamiroff, Martita Hunt

Elena et les hommes [English title: *Paris Does Strange Things*] (1957) ★ ★
Director: Jean Renoir. *Screenplay:* Jean Serge and Jean Renoir

Cast: Ingrid Bergman, Jean Marais, Mel Ferrer, Jean Richard, Juliette Gréco

Indiscreet (1958) ★ ★ ★
Director: Stanley Donen. *Screenplay:* Norman Krasna, based on his play *Kind Sir*
Cast: Cary Grant, Ingrid Bergman, Cecil Parker, Phyllis Calvert, David Kossoff, Megs Jenkins

The Inn of the Sixth Happiness (1958) ★ ★ ★ ★
Director: Mark Robson. *Screenplay:* Isobel Lennart, based on the novel by Alan Burgess
Cast: Ingrid Bergman, Curt Jurgens, Robert Donat, Athene Seyler, Burt Kwouk, Ronald Squire, Peter Chong

Goodbye Again (1961) ★ ★ ★
Director: Anatole Litvak. *Screenplay:* Samuel Taylor, based on the novel *Aimez-vous Brahms?* by Françoise Sagan
Cast: Ingrid Bergman, Yves Montand, Anthony Perkins, Jessie Royce Landis

The Visit (1964) ★ ★ ★
Director: Bernhard Wicki. *Screenplay:* Ben Barzman and Maurice Valency, based on the play by Friedrich Dürrenmatt
Cast: Ingrid Bergman, Anthony Quinn, Irina Demick, Paolo Stoppa, Valentina Cortese

The Yellow Rolls-Royce (1965) ★ ★ ★
Director: Anthony Asquith. *Screenplay:* Terence Rattigan
Cast: Ingrid Bergman, Rex Harrison, Shirley MacLaine, Jeanne Moreau, George C. Scott, Omar Sharif, Alain Delon, Art Carney

Cactus Flower (1969) ★
Director: Gene Saks. *Screenplay:* I. A. L. Diamond, based on the play by Abe Burrows, which was adapted from the play *Fleur de cactus* by Pierre Barillet and Jean-Pierre Grédy
Cast: Walter Matthau, Ingrid Bergman, Goldie Hawn, Jack Weston, Rick Lenz, Vito Scotti

A Walk in the Spring Rain (1970) ★★
Director: Guy Green. *Screenplay:* Stirling Silliphant, based on the novel by Rachel Maddux
Cast: Anthony Quinn, Ingrid Bergman, Fritz Weaver, Katherine Crawford, Tom Holland

Murder on the Orient Express (1974) ★★★★
Director: Sidney Lumet. *Screenplay:* Paul Dehn, based on the novel by Agatha Christie
Cast: Albert Finney, Sean Connery, John Gielgud, Ingrid Bergman, Lauren Bacall, Michael York, Jacqueline Bisset, Wendy Hiller, Rachel Roberts, Vanessa Redgrave, Richard Widmark

A Matter of Time (1976) ★
Director: Vincente Minnelli. *Screenplay:* John Gay, based on the novel by Maurice Druon
Cast: Liza Minnelli, Ingrid Bergman, Charles Boyer, Spiros Andros, Tina Aumont, Fernando Rey

Autumn Sonata (1978) ★★★★
Director: Ingmar Bergman. *Screenplay:* Ingmar Bergman
Cast: Ingrid Bergman, Liv Ullmann, Lena Nyman, Halvar Björk

A Woman Called Golda (1982) ★★★★
Director: Alan Gibson. *Teleplay:* Harold Gast and Steven Gethers
Cast: Ingrid Bergman, Ned Beatty, Franklin Cover, Judy Davis, Anne Jackson, Robert Loggia, Leonard Nimoy

SELECTED BIBLIOGRAPHY

Ackroyd, Peter. *Alfred Hitchcock: A Brief Life*. New York, Doubleday, 2015.

Bergman, Ingrid, and Alan Burgess. *Ingrid Bergman: My Story*. New York: Dell, 1980.

Brunette, Peter. *Roberto Rossellini*. New York: Oxford University Press, 1987.

Ebert, Roger. *The Great Movies*. New York: Broadway Books, 2002.

Harmetz, Aljean. *The Making of* Casablanca: *Bogart, Bergman, and World War II*. New York: Hyperion, 2002. Previously published as *Round Up the Usual Suspects*.

Hecht, Ben. *A Child of the Century*. New York: Simon & Schuster, 1954.

Kobal, John, ed. *Ingrid Bergman: Photographs from the Kobal Collection*. New York: Little, Brown, 1985.

Miller, Frank. Casablanca, *as Time Goes By: 50th Anniversary Commemorative*. Atlanta: Turner Publishing, 1992.

Santas, Constantine. *The Essential Humphrey Bogart*. Lanham, MD: Rowman & Littlefield, 2016.

Shaw, George Bernard. *Saint Joan*. New York: Penguin, 2003. Play premiered 1923.

Sperber, A. M., and Eric Lax. *Bogart*. New York: Morrow, 1997.

Spoto, Donald. *Notorious: The Life of Ingrid Bergman*. New York: HarperCollins, 1997.

Steele, Joseph Henry. *Ingrid Bergman: An Intimate Portrait*. New York: David McKay, 1959.

Young, Cathleen. *Isabella Rossellini: Quiet Renegade*. New York: St. Martin's, 1989.

INDEX

ABOUT THE AUTHORS

Constantine Santas received his PhD at Northwestern University and taught at Milwaukee Downer College (1962–1964) and the University of Illinois at Chicago (1964–1971). He served as chairman of the English Department at Flagler College in St. Augustine, Florida, from 1971 to 2002, when he retired as professor emeritus. At Flagler College, Santas initiated a program of film studies, which continues today. Santas has published literary and film articles and authored translations of three ancient Greek plays, performed at the Flagler College Auditorium. He was a recipient of a Danforth Foundation Teacher Grant (1967–1969) and has been included in *Choice* as an Outstanding National Teacher in 1983, in *Hellenic Who's Who* in 1990, and *Who's Who among American Teachers* in 2002. His publications include *Aristotelis Valaoritis* (1976), *Responding to Film* (2002), *The Epic in Film: From Myth to Blockbuster* (2007), *The Epics of David Lean* (2011), *The Encyclopedia of Epic Films* (2014), and *The Essential Humphrey Bogart* (2016).

James M. Wilson received his PhD at the University of Louisiana, Lafayette. He teaches film, American literature, and creative writing at Flagler College in St. Augustine, Florida. He has written and presented on films by the Coen brothers, cinematographer Roger Deakins, and screenwriter Joss Whedon, among others. Wilson has given presentations about writing at the Association of Writers and Writing Programs, the Florida Institute of Technology, and the University of North Florida (UNF), and he has held workshops at the Deep South Writers Conference and the UNF Writers Conference. He is president of the Florida Literary Arts Coalition. Wilson is also coauthor of *The Encyclopedia of Epic Films* (2014).

9 781442 212145